Building School and Community Partnerships Through Parent Involvement

Kay Wright Springate
Eastern Kentucky University

Dolores A. Stegelin
North Georgia College and State University

VRJC LIBRARY

Merrill,
an imprint of Prentice Hall
Upper Saddle River, New Jersey   *Columbus, Ohio*

Library of Congress Cataloging-in-Publication Data

Springate, Kay Wright.
    Building school and community partnerships through parent involvement /
Kay W. Springate, Dolores A. Stegelin.
        p.   cm.
    Includes bibliographical references and index.
    ISBN 0-13-520545-X (pbk.)
    1. Home and school—United States. 2. Parent-teacher relationships—United
States. 3. Community and school—United States. 4. Education—Parent participation—United States.   I. Stegelin, Dolores. II. Title.
    LC225.3.S68   1999
371.19´2—dc21   98-29488
                                                                                                              CIP

Cover photo: © SuperStock
Editor: Ann Castel Davis
Production Editor: Sheryl Glicker Langner
Design Coordinator: Diane C. Lorenzo
Text Designer: Pagination
Cover Designer: Tanya Burgess
Production Manager: Laura Messerly
Electronic Text Management: Marilyn Wilson Phelps, Karen L. Bretz, Tracey B. Ward
Director of Marketing: Kevin Flanagan
Marketing Manager: Suzanne Stanton
Marketing Coordinator: Krista Groshong

This book was set in Bookman ITC by Prentice Hall and was printed and bound by
R. R. Donnelley & Sons Company. The cover was printed by Phoenix Color Corp.

 © 1999 by Prentice-Hall, Inc.
Simon & Schuster/A Viacom Company
Upper Saddle River, New Jersey 07458

Photo credits: Photos in Chapters 1, 5, 6, 9, and 10 provided by Dolores Stegelin;
Chapters 2, 3, 4, and 7 provided by Kay Wright Springate; p. 199 by Hilda Moore
Wright; pp. 208, 209 by R. K. and Anne Brautigam.

Printed in the United States of America

10 9 8 7 6 5 4 3 2 1

ISBN: 0-13-520545-X

Prentice-Hall International (UK) Limited, *London*
Prentice-Hall of Australia Pty. Limited, *Sydney*
Prentice-Hall of Canada, Inc., *Toronto*
Prentice-Hall Hispanoamericana, S. A., *Mexico*
Prentice-Hall of India Private Limited, *New Delhi*
Prentice-Hall of Japan, Inc., *Tokyo*
Simon & Schuster Asia Pte. Ltd., *Singapore*
Editora Prentice-Hall do Brasil, Ltda., *Rio de Janeiro*

This book is affectionately dedicated to Matthew and Michael Springate and Forrest, Amber, Steve, Heather, and Cory Stegelin.

◇ ◇

Preface

Building School and Community Partnerships Through Parent Involvement is designed as a text for university courses preparing teachers and other professionals to work with young children and their families in a variety of settings, including public and private schools, care facilities, and family service agencies. It can also serve as a resource for practicing early childhood teachers, caregivers, administrators, family service providers, public policy advocates, and government agency officials. The text focuses on the common goal of teachers, caregivers, and families: nurturing the growth of young children. In doing so, in-depth information relative to the diversity of families and the challenges and concerns of families is shared, along with many strategies for building partnerships with families. The role of the family as the first and most important teachers of young children is highlighted throughout the chapters.

◇◇ Content and Format of This Book

The need for parent involvement in schools has never been greater. Although parents are often "included" in the school setting, we, the authors, believe emphatically that parents should be *partners* in the classroom. Parents possess valuable knowledge about their children, are emotionally vested in their children's entire lives, and want desperately to succeed in the parenting role. Teachers should open their arms to parents, embrace them with enthusiasm, and welcome them warmly into their classrooms to serve as co-teachers and confidants. Interactions between parents and teachers should be much deeper than at the cognitive level. Both teachers and parents need the emotional and affective support of one another, and young children need the shared guidance and affection of both their parents and their classroom teachers. So, this textbook is not just about parent involvement, but rather is a passionate plea to teachers to cultivate and maintain genuine, mutual, and enduring human relationships with parents.

This textbook is designed to be practical and useful for the many professionals who work with, and are engaged in, professional program development and implementation with children and their families. Thus, we have striven to develop a logical format that is easy to use. The textbook is divided into three parts, which are now described.

Part I provides an overview and contemporary program models for children, as well as specific collaboration strategies that have proved to be successful. Chapter 1 focuses on the importance and rationale for family-school connections and provides an overview of family and child issues in contemporary American families. Chapter 2 describes the evolution and history of programs and models that serve young children, including the most contemporary examples being used. Chapter 3 describes myriad effective and tried partnership and collaborative strategies for engaging in parent involvement activities with today's hurried and complex American families.

Part II consists of chapters that focus on specific family configurations and individual child needs. For example, Chapter 4 addresses the cross-cultural makeup of the U.S. child population and suggests strategies that increase professionals' sensitivity to the specific needs of these unique families. Chapter 5 focuses on children with disabilities and special needs, the special adaptations required by their families, and the emerging inclusion movement in educational and child care settings in the United States. Chapter 6 provides the professional with a greater understanding of the incidence, complexity, and outcomes for families experiencing separation, divorce, and remarriage, and the special needs of these children in the educational setting. The major research on divorce was conducted in the 1980s, and an effort to provide the reader with significant findings on divorce is made. More recent research on the outcomes of postdivorce for children and families is also included.

In Chapter 7, attention is focused on the adoptive family and the stages of adjustment and special needs that evolve for this family. Chapter 8 addresses emerging and projected family forms for the future, as well as alternative lifestyles that are reflected in today's families and children. The goal of Part II is to provide the professional with an in-depth understanding of today's American family and the idiosyncratic needs and issues that are a part of their daily lives.

In Part III, the final part of our book, Chapter 9 provides the professional with a comprehensive overview of issues with an evaluation of families and family-school processes, including specific assessment and evaluation instruments and tools that can be used by the early childhood professional. Chapter 10, the final chapter, is devoted to the important topic of advocacy for young children and families and is designed to provide the school, child care, or community-based professional with concrete and effective strategies for advocating for parents and the children in their classrooms.

It is an important time for professionals who possess both knowledge and firsthand experience working with young children to become involved in advocacy efforts. As the Children's Defense Fund documents so eloquently each year in its annual report, children in contemporary America experience unusually high rates of poverty, social distress, and involvement with violent crimes. Teachers and caregivers are in prime positions to testify about the needs of children and to influence legislators and other decision makers about the importance of keeping children first in the policy process.

◊◊ **Acknowledgments**

We gratefully acknowledge the contributions of our reviewers for their valuable input and suggestions: Jerold P. Bauch, Vanderbilt University; Marcia L. Broughton, University of Northern Colorado; R. Eleanor Duff, Southeast Missouri State University; Holly Gerkin, Central Michigan University; Carol Gestwicki, Central Piedmont Community College; Diane E. Karther, The University of Akron; Norma Meyerholz, Diablo Valley College; and Linda H. Ruhman, San Antonio College.

◇ ◇

Contents

◊ **Chapter 3**
Building Partnerships with Families   51

PART II
Profiles of Individual Families in America   81

◊ **Chapter 4**
Cross-Cultural Issues Involving Families and the Community   83

◊ **Chapter 5**
Creating Community and School Linkages for Children with Special Needs   123

◊ **Chapter 6**
Children of Divorced and Blended Families   161

◇ Chapter 7
"Chosen" Children   195

◇ Chapter 8
Alternative and Future Family Forms   223

PART III
Evaluating Family-School Processes and Speaking Up for Children   247

◊ **Chapter 9**
Assessing and Evaluating Parent-School Involvement   249

◊ **Chapter 10**
Parent and Child Advocacy   297

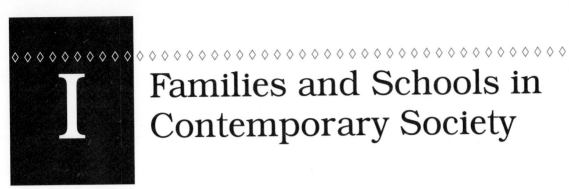

I

Families and Schools in Contemporary Society

1 The Parent-School Connection

Serving Families in a Contemporary Context

Lesson 6: Take parenting and family life seriously and insist that those you work for and who represent you do.

Edelman, 1992, p. 43

Key Terms

Bronfenbrenner
child poverty rates
Children's Defense Fund
domestic violence
economic uncertainty
ecosystem model
exosystem
macrosystem
maternal employment rates

mesosystem
microsystem
NAEYC
NASBE
rates of violence
Reggio Emilia programs
resilient families
single-headed households
welfare reform

Marian Wright Edelman, founder and president of the **Children's Defense Fund (CDF)** and one of America's greatest child advocates, is the author of a most inspirational book that provides readers with 25 lessons for life. Entitled *The Measure of Our Success: A Letter to My Children and Yours* (1992), these 25 lessons include suggestions and admonitions for working hard, setting goals, taking risks, valuing family relationships, being honest, persevering, being confident, always learning, remembering your roots, taking charge of your attitude, and being faithful.

Referred to as a silent legislator, Edelman implores us to hold family life and the role of parent in the highest possible regard. Her impact on work-family-child care legislation is evidence of the effectiveness of her message. In a firm, consistent way, Edelman calls on each one of us—professionals, parents, employers, legislators, decision makers—to make good decisions on behalf of children and families.

Many books have been written about families and schools. Indeed, the importance of parent involvement in children's schools has been a persistent theme in the research and school reform efforts of the last three decades (Bronfenbrenner, 1979; Comer, 1990; Epstein, 1988). Why is it important to look once again at the parent-school-community connection? What new variables affect today's families? Why are schools struggling to understand their child populations better? What makes some teachers excited and inspired by today's children and families but other teachers seemingly overwhelmed and discouraged? What do parents really want from schools and community agencies, and how do they prefer to interface with teachers, administrators, and other school professionals?

Family forms are constantly changing in our contemporary society.

The need for the parent-school connection has never been greater. Home, family, school, neighborhood, and society shape the contours of childhood and adolescence (Edwards & Young, 1992; Goffin & Stegelin, 1992). This chapter provides the reader with (a) a description and profile of contemporary American families and children; (b) the rationale for continuing to build these vital home-school linkages; (c) an overview of communication avenues for parents, teachers, administrators, counselors and psychologists, special education teachers, and other service-related personnel; and (d) an overview of the content of this textbook.

Chapter 1 addresses the following topics:

- The current status and profile of American families
- Current demographics on the contemporary American child
- The importance of forming collaborative partnerships in fostering the growth and development of the child
- Issues that affect families and schools in their efforts to nurture young children
- The interrelatedness of individual children, their families, and institutions in serving the needs of students
- The individual roles of the school, the family, and the community in engaging in partnerships
- The emerging needs of the family
- Strategies for involving families in decision making, classroom activities, parent-oriented activities, and parent-child activities in the home

Let's now begin this journey to rediscover the significance and energy of the American family and the important issues and avenues that professionals must master to meet the needs of young children and their families. In this chapter, *schools* is used to denote early childhood programs and child care arrangements, both public and private, providing care and education for children from birth through age 8. It also denotes the individuals within the schools and centers who provide care and education—administrators, teachers, caregivers, and support personnel.

> Teachers and administrators are not adequately prepared to address the range of children's social and psychological needs. They know what ought to be done, but not how to do it. (Edwards & Young, 1992, p. 85)

◊◊ **Status and Profile of American Families**

Understanding the American family and its pressing issues is crucial to understanding the possible avenues of interfacing with a child, the parents, and the family as a whole. Strategies that worked 10 to 15 years ago do not work today (Wallach, 1993). Why? What is different about today's family?

How do these changes affect the communication patterns and interaction strategies that are successful or unsuccessful?

To understand better the complex needs of the individual child within the school, child care, and community context, we must first understand the child's family of origin. This section provides information on the American family, how it is changing, and how these changes affect the quality and quantity of interactions among the child, the family, the school, and the community.

Violence and the American Family

> Children who grow up in violent communities are at risk for pathological development because growing up in a constant state of apprehension makes it difficult to establish trust, autonomy, and social competence. (Wallach, 1993, p. 4)

Teachers in school settings for young children frequently speak of their concern for the children they teach and the emerging patterns of violence and transitions that children experience within the home and community. According to the CDF (1996), more than 50,000 children have been killed in the United States since 1979 by guns in homes, schools, and neighborhoods. For many inner-city children, violence has become a way of life. A study of more than 1,000 children in Chicago found that 74% of them had witnessed a murder, shooting, stabbing, or robbery (Kotulak, 1990). Violence is witnessed through child abuse, domestic abuse, gangs, drug dealers, drive-by shootings, and other criminal activity in the neighborhoods

To understand the young child, we must first understand the family of origin.

(Wallach, 1993). Concern about the rising **rates of violence** resulted in the National Association for the Education of Young Children (**NAEYC**) establishing a special panel to provide recommendations on how to respond to the manifestations of violence in the lives of children and to develop position statements that identify appropriate guidelines (Slaby, Roedell, Arezzo, & Hendrix, 1995).

Researchers and practitioners alike are acknowledging a growing awareness of the repeated eyewitnessing by young children of violent assaults against others (Slaby et al., 1995). These events are as diverse as preschoolers observing shootings firsthand (Dubrow & Garbarino, 1989) and witnessing stabbings in their immediate neighborhoods (Bell & Jenkins, 1993). In addition, parents often underestimate the amount of violence their children are experiencing, as well as the amount of potentially damaging emotional distress that can result (Richters & Martinez, 1993).

The immediate and long-term effects of violence on the development of the child are still being determined. For infants and toddlers, exposure to violence threatens the development of trust—trust in the caregiving environment and eventually in the children themselves (Wallach, 1993). When families live in a constant state of anxiety or fear, it is difficult for them to provide a safe, consistent, and trusting environment in which their young children can grow and develop. Infants and toddlers, who are in the preoperational stage of cognitive development, must explore their environment and learn about relationships between objects and people in order to grow cognitively and emotionally. When parents cannot allow their children to explore the immediate and surrounding environments, opportunities for this development are hampered.

Preschoolers, who are also in the preoperational stage of cognitive development, need safe spaces and environments to explore. If preschoolers live in dangerous neighborhoods where home and child care environments and economic resources are very limited, then their cognitive and emotional growth is stymied. Drive-by shootings, gang violence, and other random criminal acts have created unsafe neighborhoods in both low- and middle-income areas. Children today are more likely to live a passive, less physically active existence simply because parents are more fearful of the immediate neighborhood than in the past; they don't let their children stray very far from home, if the children play outdoors at all.

Domestic abuse is another form of violence that negatively affects young children. This type of abuse can take several forms but usually involves some kind of child abuse (emotional, verbal, physical, or sexual) or abuse between parents. When children are subjected to both **domestic violence** and neighborhood violence, the overall negative effects are much greater (Wallach, 1993). When children must defend themselves both within the home and within the immediate neighborhood, basic developmental tasks, such as developing a sense of trust and feelings of self-worth, are affected. Preoperational children are especially vulnerable to blaming themselves for the pain they see and experience in their families. In turn, children who have feelings of low self-esteem are not as confident in their own abilities at school. Teachers receive these children into classrooms on a daily basis, and they are complex to understand and teach. Teachers must understand the ramifications of violence in the lives of young children if they are to intervene effectively on the children's behalf in the classroom. The trauma of violence leaves a long-lasting effect on children, and the major effect during childhood is usually regression (Wallach, 1993).

Teachers in schools and child care arrangements can have a positive impact on the lives of children who experience violence. Among the appropriate interventions they can provide are these:

- Help children identify violence and its consequences.
- Recognize and talk with children about real-world violence.
- Recognize and respond to children's traumatic reactions to violence.
- Train children in basic violence-related safety and self-protection.
- Help reduce "disciplinary" violence toward children.
- Support families in their helping children to cope with violence. (Slaby et al., 1995, pp. 8–9)

Early childhood teachers also play a crucial role in helping identify children who may be the target of such violence as child abuse or neglect. By documenting their observations, early childhood teachers can play a pivotal role in confronting the issue of violence in the personal lives of the children they teach. Through modeling of appropriate child management and discipline methods, teachers demonstrate to parents more effective ways of communicating with and managing their children. Finally, violence is of such concern to most parents today that teachers will find a ready audience for parent education meetings and may have a relatively easy time finding resource people in the community and targeting violence as a major issue or theme in their parent education programs. Key points for teachers to remember are listed in Figure 1.1.

Female Employment

Perhaps the most important factor in the changing face of the American family is the rate of female employment. This variable alone accounts for many stressors encountered by, and adaptations required by, children, their parents, and subsequently the schools and child care centers that serve them. Whether the family is a dual-earner or **single-headed household,** employment of the mother affects the dynamics of the family system dramatically. Since 1987, over 50% of mothers of infants have been in the labor force (U.S. Department of Commerce, 1989), and an even higher percentage of mothers of preschool and school-age children have been employed. Accord-

- Model disciplinary methods to children that discourage violence.
- Analyze your own feelings, attitudes, and experiences about violence.
- Assist children in identifying kinds of violence and sources of violence in their lives.
- Be alert to signs of children's trauma related to violence.
- Be familiar with and follow appropriate guidelines for reporting suspected abuse and neglect to authorities.
- Support families in their efforts to cope with fears and concerns about violence in their neighborhoods.

Figure 1.1   Key points for teachers to remember
Source: Slaby, Roedell, Arezzo, and Hendrix (1995).

ing to Olmstead (1992), over 66% of children under age 6 have mothers in the labor force. Although a substantial number are not working full time, it is clear that many more mothers than ever before are leaving their infants and toddlers in out-of-home care by nonfamily members. The need for after-school care and transitional child care options has also increased dramatically. Whether this employment situation and subsequent child care need is through choice or necessity, it contributes to family stress.

In addition, **welfare reform** programs are designed to help mothers participate in the workforce in new and creative ways. Welfare reform accounts for the addition of some low-income women to the already growing list of employed mothers. Although requiring parents on welfare to work and to be gainfully employed does make sense from an economic and political perspective, it has added another dimension of stress for these families. Child care is now necessary for families who are working to get off the welfare roles; these families are seeking many diverse avenues of before- and after-school care, as well as care for their infants, toddlers, and preschoolers. Financial restraints prevent them from securing quality, consistent child care in homes or centers; often, children are left to fend for themselves or with unwilling neighbors or relatives.

The need for quality child care to accommodate this societal trend of maternal employment continues to challenge early childhood professionals and policymakers. At least 40% of all care and 75% of family child care in the United States is entirely unregulated and thus does not meet even minimal standards of health and safety; Ryan (1992) reports that 80% to 90% of day care settings are unlicensed. More than 10 million children under the age of 6 have mothers in the workforce; 35.6% are in family day care or are cared for in a relative's or sitter's home; 24.3% are in organized child care programs; and the remaining 10.2% are in either kindergarten or other forms of child care (Hoyt & Schoonmaker, 1991). As **maternal employ-**

*Over 50% of mothers of
infants are in the labor
force.*

ment rates continue to escalate, the challenge of providing quality, safe, and
developmentally appropriate child care remains one of the greatest issues
for America's early childhood teachers and administrators, as well as for
legislators and other decision makers.

Divorce, Separation, and Remarriage

Another important family variable is the experience of divorce, separation, or
remarriage. During the past two decades, substantial changes have occurred
in the marital status and living arrangements of Americans (Saluter, 1989).
One of the most noted changes in American families is the increase in the single population, reflected in the delaying of marriage and in the dissolution of
marriages. More than half of all first marriages result in divorce, and the rate
is even higher for subsequent marriages (Darden & Zimmerman, 1992;
Walsh, 1992). Divorce rates are associated with such demographics as age at
marriage, and teenagers who marry face the highest divorce rate. Schools
deal with this phenomenon as they enroll more and more young children who
are the product of teenage marriages or teenage pregnancies. The crisis of the
absent father is being addressed by child advocacy groups, as approximately
25% of U.S. children have little or no contact with their dads (Louv, 1993).

Early childhood teachers and caregivers interact daily with children who have little contact with a father figure in their lives.

Divorce may often be the best option for some couples, and the emotional reprieve it provides the family may be in the best interests of all, including the children. Divorce places an inordinate amount of stress on the family financially and emotionally, however. Children of all stages of development, from preschool through the adolescent years, must somehow negotiate the difficult and emotional terrain of their parents' separation and divorce (Wallerstein & Blakeslee, 1995). Often overcome with their own emotional needs and issues, parents frequently do not have the emotional resources to address their children's anxieties. Children frequently blame themselves for the divorce, unable to understand the complexity of adult relationships. Thus, children find themselves in a maze of home-school-community existence, greatly in need of emotional support from adults. The issues around divorce, remarriage, and stepfamilies are discussed more fully in Chapter 6.

Economic Uncertainty

The U.S. economy is strong, and many new employment opportunities exist, particularly in the areas of technology and service. At the same time, transformations in urban economies have limited the kinds of jobs available to high school graduates and dropouts (Edwards & Young, 1992). The workplace and the demands of jobs contribute considerable anxiety to American families. Work sites are usually separate from the other areas of people's lives: shopping, child care, extended families, and supportive neighbors. Thus, for most American families, fragmentation occurs because of the emphasis on the importance of work and careers but without sufficient support for the general fabric of the family.

Gone are the days when mother or father could make a long-term, 20- or 30-year commitment to a place of employment and count on its security until retirement. Although many new occupations have emerged in the areas of service and technology, U.S. workers of all educational and income levels face much less job security. Corporations are downsizing, moving to managed health care programs, and looking for comprehensive ways to cut costs. Workers who have been loyal to the same employer for many years are finding themselves unemployed and needing to retool. Even higher education, a traditional bastion for job security, is scrutinizing tenure and questioning the long-term employment commitment to its highly educated workforce. Children whose parents are experiencing workplace stress are also anxious and uncertain. "If Daddy's job ends, what will that mean?" "If Mommy's company relocates to Atlanta, will I have to move and give up all my friends?" These are typical concerns and anxieties of children today.

In addition to increasing job insecurity, American parents work in settings that frequently are not "family friendly." Some successful efforts have been made to identify and publicly reward those corporations that provide benefits and support mechanisms for employees and their families. Such benefits as child care on-site or through vouchers, parental leave for child-birth and neonatal care, sick leave for parents with children who are ill, and tax-deferred benefits related to parent and child care needs all contribute to a sense of well-being for American parents who work. Unfortunately, changes in this progressive direction are slow and frustrating.

Child Poverty

One out of every four children in the United States lives in a family whose income is below—often far below—the poverty level, and that **child poverty rate** doubles among Blacks and Latinos (CDF, 1991). Although poverty rates seem to rise and fall for the overall American population, children remain the most impoverished age-group, and obstacles to their well-being continue to mount. Child poverty brings with it a host of other related family issues, such as inadequate health care and insurance, immunization needs, poor nutrition, inadequate housing, HIV/AIDS, substance abuse, and chronic violence (Edwards & Young, 1992). The poverty issue is reflected in the escalating rates of crack (cocaine) use. The crack epidemic is touching every corner of low-income African American communities (Drug Enforcement Agency, 1996; Edwards & Young, 1992), as well as rural and suburban areas. Effects of crack are reflected in the school-age population in the United States, and American teachers in early childhood settings must deal not only with the care and education of these children but also with the needs of parents.

In addition to crack and cocaine, the use of heroin has escalated significantly during the past decade. The availability of higher purity heroin has meant that users now can snort or smoke the narcotic. Evidence suggests that heroin snorting is widespread or increasing in areas where high-purity heroin is available, generally in the northeastern United States (Drug Enforcement Agency, 1996).

In short, the child who functions within the school- or community-based educational setting is a product of his or her immediate environment. As **Bronfenbrenner**'s (1979) ecological model suggests, no one is an island. Issues that affect parents also affect children; the parent who is stressed has children who are also stressed. Teachers, administrators, counselors, and other professionals in school, child care, and community settings must be able to observe, record, and evaluate child behavior that reflects stress or developmental concerns or both. As classrooms become more diverse in terms of ethnicity, socioeconomic levels, and developmental ranges, the professional must be prepared and trained to deal with the subsequent complexity of the classroom.

American families reflect fast-paced, hectic, fragmented lifestyles that are focused on economic and emotional survival. These variables seem to apply to all children regardless of socioeconomic level. Emotional stressors may not originate in financial problems for many middle- and upper-income families, but these families are just as vulnerable to the emotional effects of divorce, drug use, unemployment, neighborhood violence, and family-related issues. Perhaps the best way to describe the American family in the 1990s is weary yet resilient. With violence increasing in all neighborhoods, the American family seems to seek a return to basic feelings and needs for survival. This very basic need and instinct must be recognized, acknowledged, and addressed by the school- and community-based professional.

Resilient Children and Families

With all the complexity in the lives of American families, children and parents are amazingly resilient. Case studies document children who have survived very difficult and challenging odds. Children who grow up in violence-infested neighborhoods; who are exposed at early ages to drug abuse; who experience the emotional turmoil of families in transition because of divorce, remarriage, mobility, and other reasons; and who otherwise have had to overcome seemingly insurmountable odds can, in fact, develop into productive, hopeful young adults.

This resilience of children and families is impressive. Each family has its own goals and paints its own portrait as it interfaces with society and the schools. Teachers who view families from the strength and resilience perspective are most likely to succeed in their interactions with children and parents. This individuality is what each family brings to the parent involvement component of any early childhood setting (Edwards & Young, 1992). It is important for teachers to keep these family variations in mind as they assess, plan, implement, and evaluate parent and family involvement initiatives and programs. "Until schools acknowledge the range in dispositions, backgrounds, experiences, and strengths among families, efforts to establish sound home/school communication and partnerships will falter" (Edwards & Young, 1992, p. 86).

◊◊ Status of Children in the United States

The Children's Defense Fund (CDF) is one of the most visible advocates for the rights and well-being of children in the United States. Its recent yearbook, *The State of America's Children* (1996), depicts America's young and school-age children as being in peril. For nearly a decade, children have experienced the highest rate of poverty of any segment of the U.S. population. Along with the issue of poverty, violence in the lives of young children has increased dramatically, creating concern for the long-term well-being of America's young children. The policy agenda for the CDF focuses on issues (listed in Figure 1.2) that reflect the daily lives and needs of children.

Figure 1.2   Moments in America for children

Adapted from Children's Defense Fund (1996).

• Every 9 seconds	a child drops out of school.
• Every 10 seconds	a child is reported abused or neglected.
• Every 14 seconds	a child is arrested.
• Every 25 seconds	a baby is born to an unmarried mother.
• Every 32 seconds	a baby is born into poverty.
• Every 34 seconds	a baby is born to a mother who did not graduate from high school.
• Every 1 minute	a baby is born to a teenage mother.
• Every 2 minutes	a baby is born at low birthweight.
• Every 3 minutes	a baby is born to a mother who received late or no prenatal care.
• Every 4 minutes	a child is arrested for an alcohol-related offense.
• Every 10 minutes	a child is born at very low birthweight.
• Every 15 minutes	a baby dies.
• Every 2 hours	a child is killed by a firearm.
• Every 4 hours	a child commits suicide.
• Every 7 hours	a child dies from abuse or neglect.

◊◊ Legislative Efforts on Behalf of Families

Among the most pressing issues for children in America today are those related to quality health care, access to quality child care and early education, economic support for low-income families, and safe communities in which to live. To address these issues, pending legislation includes bills for expanded Head Start programming, increased child care assistance, access to comprehensive health insurance coverage at birth, reduced poverty, and provision of safe after-school care for nearly half of all poor 6- to 12-year-olds throughout the United States for the next 5 years (CDF, 1996). As these new initiatives are legislated, schools, child care centers, and community-based programs will become the major avenues for program implementation. For example, expanded Head Start means the creation of new collaboration between Head Start and state-funded preschool programs, usually based in schools, child care centers, or community-based sites.

With the national effort to balance the budget being a high priority, the needs of children over the next 10 years are of concern to advocates for child well-being. In the rush to welfare reform, which certainly can be understood and justified from an economic standpoint, the immediate needs of children may not be adequately assessed and anticipated. With welfare time limits being implemented in many states, women with young children are now pursuing career options, vocational training, or other self-support avenues but without sufficient support for their children's day care or after-school care needs.

The long-term benefits of welfare reform may be worthwhile, but the short-term outcomes for young children whose welfare-dependent parents are riding the turbulent waters of reform and change at both the state and federal levels may make the children the ultimate victims. When financial support systems are withdrawn, reduced, or dramatically altered within a short period of time, teachers, administrators, and other professionals committed to the education and care of children must be aware of these changes and the subsequent behavioral and emotional changes in the children in their classrooms.

Recent Data on Child Care and Early Education

- About seven million children of working parents are cared for each month by someone other than a parent.
- The challenge of finding decent and affordable child care is a dominant feature of most working parents' lives.
- The supply of child care is most inadequate in low-income neighborhoods, which tend to lack the necessary economic base to support good child care programs.
- The average cost of serving one child in a child care center is $4,940 per year.
- Only 1 out of 7 child care centers and 1 out of 10 family child care homes are of high enough quality to enhance children's development.
- In 1995, Head Start served 752,000 children—about 36% of those eligible.
- Some employers are designing child care programs to fit the company's work schedules—for example, Toyota Motor Manufacturing in Georgetown, Kentucky.
- Some employers are pooling resources to conduct joint child care projects, as a consortium of employers in Phoenix and a group of employers in the hotel industry in Atlanta did. (CDF, 1996)

The status of America's children continues to be a concern for early childhood teachers, advocates, and policymakers, and the voices of school and child care teachers and administrators will continue to need to be heard (Stegelin, 1992). Professionals who work with children on a daily basis are in the best position to observe, assess, and document the needs of these children. As welfare reform unfolds, economic characteristics will change as reflected in the changing employment arena and escalating rates of divorce and remarriage. As the world continues to move to a multicultural perspective, the young children in America will continue to need support from parents, teachers, and the community.

◊◊ Interrelationships Among Families, Schools, and Communities

Given the complexity of parenting in the 1990s, some may take comfort in viewing families as those presented in the popular television programs of the postwar 1950s. In *Leave It to Beaver,* Beaver's mother was always available to provide his lunch and a well-balanced dinner and to listen to after-school conversations and needs. Children left home in the morning to play safely in their own neighborhoods, unsupervised until lunch or dinner. "Father," the kind and gentle Jim Anderson on *Father Knows Best,* was always available to give sound advice and good guidance to his children—Bud, Betty, and Kathy—and was never without a "white-collar" job. We saw families presented as existing perfectly and with little need for community support.

Not unlike those families popularized four decades ago, families today hold the same common desire to raise healthy and happy children in a safe and comfortable environment. A variety of factors affect families as they work to reach this goal. One is the economic struggle that many families experience as mothers and fathers leave the home each day to go to one or more jobs.

In a 1996 Family Re-Union V Conference co-chaired by President Bill Clinton and Vice President Al Gore, parent panelists indicated a desire (a) to have more time with their children, (b) to be able to provide their children a decent standard of living without sacrificing quality parenting, (c) to know that their children were in nurturing, safe, and healthy environments while the parents were at work or training, and (d) to have employers who understand, value, and respond appropriately to family issues (Daniel, 1996, p. 2).

As we study how families use existing resources to meet the economic, educational, and caring needs of individuals within the family, including both the adults and the children, it is important to remember that each individual within the family, regardless of age, is engaged in ongoing development in relation to his or her sociocultural world (Erikson, 1950).

Ecosystems, the School, and the Family

Bronfenbrenner's (1979) *ecological systems theory* continues to serve as an appropriate model to justify and support the home-school connection. The interrelationship of the developmental process and the environment can be seen clearly in the **ecosystem model.** In this approach, Bronfenbrenner sees each person's development as being embedded in a series of environmental systems that are all interrelated.

The **microsystem** consists of those individuals and events closest in one's life; the primary example is the nuclear family, with each person influencing and being influenced by other members. Other microsystems are the child care setting, the school, the church, and the home of an extended family member. Thus, the school and the child care setting are immediate resources for the family and fall within the most intimate of connections for families.

Relationships that develop and exist between and among these microsystems are labeled **mesosystems.** Each individual's environment also includes **exosystems,** examples of which are school boards, governmental agencies, the workplace, and other community agencies and institutions. The microsystem, mesosystem, and exosystem all exist within the context of the larger culture, known as the **macrosystem** (see Figure 1.3).

◊◊ Parents, Schools, and Communities

A Case for Parent Involvement

The family serves as the "cradle" in caring for and nurturing children. The family serves to wrap the child in the kind of security from which the child emerges comfortably to interact with peers and adults in a variety of settings and to take a place in the world. The family knows and loves the child. In the title of her much-debated book, Hillary Rodham Clinton (1996) borrowed the African proverb *It takes a village to raise a child.* Mothers and fathers, brothers and sisters, grandparents, stepparents, foster parents, early childhood teachers, child care providers, school administrators, neighbors, and other individuals within the community are all a part of this village. As these lives intertwine, each person contributes something of his or her own culture to the growing child.

Figure 1.3
Bronfenbrenner's ecological
model of the environment

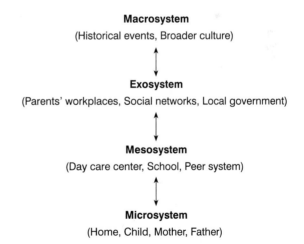

Macrosystem
(Historical events, Broader culture)

Exosystem
(Parents' workplaces, Social networks, Local government)

Mesosystem
(Day care center, School, Peer system)

Microsystem
(Home, Child, Mother, Father)

Bronfenbrenner's ecological model of the environment views the child's world as a series of nested structures. The *microsystem* refers to relationships between the child and the immediate environment, the *mesosystem* to connections among the child's immediate settings, the *exosystem* to settings that affect but do not contain the child, and the *macrosystem* to the broader cultural context in which development takes place.

***Grandmothers, grandfathers, aunts, and uncles all form the village of people
who help raise a child.***

As stated by Lyon (1995),

> Culture rules how we position our bodies, how we touch each other, what we
> regard as mannerly, how we look at the world, how we think, what we see as
> art, how we sense time and perceive space, what we think is important, and
> how we set immediate and lifelong goals. (p. 21)

This text is focused on the role that teachers and caregivers can play in
empowering families in the care and education of their children; the strategies
presented in this chapter (and elaborated throughout the book) are for teachers in enhancement of their communication and collaboration with families.
This process, however, as noted by Bronfenbrenner in his discussion of
mesosystem, is an interaction between and among schools, families, and the
community, with all parties responsible for the success of the interaction.

Collaborative Role of the School

What is the appropriate role of the school in the lives of children and families? How involved should the school and the child care or classroom
teacher become in the personal lives of the children they teach and care

for? How far into the home and the neighborhood should the school's responsibility extend? What forms should these partnerships take?

Because of the complexity of families today, school professionals need to think and behave in terms of interactions with parents and families (Edwards & Young, 1992). Boundaries that separate home, school, and neighborhoods are blurring and so provide a rich opportunity for teachers to connect with parents and families in new and creative ways. Parents still seek a safe place to go to talk about their children, and families still search for places where they can interact with other families. Schools and teachers must dance on the fine line between providing plenty of support for children and families and intrusion. Schools must do more than just encourage parent involvement that is isolated from the larger social and educational context of the classroom. In short, teachers have become a sort of service broker for children and their families (Edwards & Young, 1992).

Families, schools, and communities have a common goal: to nurture and guide children to adulthood. "Although the process of cultural transmission takes place as the child interacts with the total social environment, in contemporary American society we regard families and schools as being primarily responsible for seeing that preparation for adulthood takes place" (Phillips, 1994, p. 137). Teachers and caregivers, in their actions and in their words, certainly impart values and ideas about how people should treat each other. They set models for children to follow in terms of the importance of education and the value of the family and impart ideas about the children's self-worth. Such enculturation by schools is called "education" (Phillips, 1994, p. 138).

Working with parents has been a critical component of early childhood education (Powell, 1991). More than three decades ago, the United States addressed the crucial issues in building partnerships with families to meet the needs of their children. As part of a concerted effort to provide equal opportunities for citizens (Economic Opportunity Act of 1964), Project Head Start was conceived. The focus of this program, piloted as a summer project in 1965, was to intervene in the lives of young children in the areas of health and nutritional services, social services, and education. The creators of this program and of subsequent early childhood intervention programs since the 1960s believed that, by providing economically deprived children and families these services, young children would not enter first grade at a disadvantage, compared with their more affluent peers, and remain at that disadvantage throughout the school experience. The creators also recognized that a child is an integral part of a family and that "schooling" does not take place simply within the school. Therefore, the focus became empowering families by involving parents in decision making, in the classroom, in parent-oriented activities, and in home activities with their children (U.S. Department of Health and Human Services [DHHS], 1990, p. 4).

Throughout the years, various organizations representing professionals in the field have continued in this support of the inclusion of families in the care and education of young children by schools. Partnerships are empha-

sized by NAEYC in the document *Developmentally Appropriate Practice in Early Childhood Programs Serving Children From Birth Through Age Eight* (Bredekamp, 1987). This work represents the early childhood profession's consensus of developmentally appropriate practice and serves as a guide for the standards used in accrediting early childhood programs. The standards include, but are not limited, to, the following:

- Informing parents of the program's philosophy
- Informing parents of operating policies
- Providing an orientation for new children and families
- Communicating about child-rearing practices with parents
- Making parents welcome visitors in the classroom at all times
- Encouraging family member involvement in the program in various ways: implementing a system to communicate daily happenings to parents; reporting changes in the child's physical or emotional state to parents; conducting conferences to discuss children's needs, progress, and accomplishments
- Informing parents of activities through notes, telephone calls, bulletin boards, newsletters, and so forth

Partnerships among teachers, parents, and children are encouraged by NAEYC.

The National Association of State Boards of Education (**NASBE**) also reported on the critical role of parent involvement and the principle that only through sincere respect for the parents' role can teachers begin to see parents as a source of support for their work. The NASBE report *Right From the Start* (1988) indicates that programs serving children preschool through Grade 3 should do the following:

- Promote an environment in which parents are valued as the primary influences in their children's lives and are essential partners in the education of their children
- Recognize that the self-esteem of parents is integral to the development of their child and should be enhanced by the parents' positive interaction with the school
- Include parents in decision making about their own child and on the overall early childhood program
- Ensure opportunities and access for parents to observe and volunteer in the classroom
- Promote exchange of information and ideas between parents and teacher that will benefit the child
- Provide a gradual and supportive transition process from home to school for those young children entering school for the first time (p. 19)

Collaborative Role of Families

Although family members typically view themselves as deeply involved in the day-to-day care and nurturing of their young child, they are less comfortable with the role of teacher of the young child. In fact, the family serves as the child's first and most important educator. In addition to the physical and emotional care and nurturing the family provide for the young child, the adults within the family model their own commitment to education and learning and the value they place on themselves and on other individuals.

Robert Glaser (1985), in the foreword of *Becoming a Nation of Readers: The Report of the Commission on Reading*, states: "The parent and the home environment teach the child his or her first lessons and they are the first teachers of writing, too" (p. vi). According to Powell (1989), it is the parent's responsibility to determine what is in the best interests of the child. Powell outlines three major premises about families and society that constitute the foundation of most arguments for families and early childhood programs to establish and maintain partnerships: (a) doctrine of parents' rights, (b) family influences on the child, and (c) democratic processes. The *doctrine of parents' rights* reflects the American belief that parents have the right and responsibility to determine what is in the best interests of their child. These premises are also reflected in the earlier work of Head Start policies.

In its first manual of policies and instructions, issued in 1967, four areas of parent participation were outlined for the Head Start program. These areas have been used for the past 30 years and are still being used:

1. Parents as decision makers
2. Parents as paid staff, volunteers, or observers in the classroom
3. Parents involved in activities that they themselves have helped develop
4. Parents working at home with their own children in cooperation with Head Start staff to support the child's Head Start experiences (DHHS, 1990, p. 4)

The premises described by Powell are also reflected in current legislation. For example, P.L. 99–457, the Education of the Handicapped Act Amendments of 1986, reinforces this premise by including parent involvement as a significant component of the education process.

Collaborative Role of Communities

Communities have always served a crucial role in the support of child and family development in the United States. Much research has been conducted on the role of the community in the lessening of stressors and the provision of support services for children, parents, and families. As the United States has grown and evolved from an agricultural society to a densely populated, industrial culture, the feeling among many families is that the nurturing, supportive, and connecting role of the community has somehow been diminished. Much can be learned about the role of the immediate community in the lives of developing young children from models used in other countries.

One of the most interesting, contemporary models of community involvement in early childhood programs is found in the schools of Reggio Emilia, in northern Italy. In this community, children engage in ongoing project work that involves the collaborative efforts of both adults and children. For example, Edwards, Gandini, and Forman (1993), in their noted book on Reggio Emilia, *The Hundred Languages of Children*, describe successful projects undertaken and completed jointly by young children and their adult teachers, parents, and other community members. One such project, "An Amusement Park for Birds," focused on children working with adults to decide what type of park to build for birds. The project flowed over a period of months as the children's observations and investigations of the lives of birds were facilitated and documented by adults. The "finale" of the project was a wonderful park for birds, complete with feeders and waterwheels and even a sunbathing beach (Forman et al., 1993)! Adults from the community contributed both time and materials to this effort.

Another project, wonderfully documented in the traveling Reggio exhibit, brings a farm family into the school prior to the annual harvest of grapes.

The children learn from the farmer what will happen when they visit the farm to assist with the harvest. The children and teachers travel to the farm, where they pick grapes, sort grapes, wash grapes, and mash grapes. These new "farmers" return to the school, where the children and the adults celebrate the harvest with food and grape juice.

Reggio Emilia has made a profound impact on American early childhood programs, in part, because of its tremendous valuing and inclusion of the community in the early childhood learning environment. Reggio Emilia has expanded on the Italian principle of community involvement—*gestione sociale*—in early child care and education by engaging parents and other adults in the community in the actual educational "happenings" of the school. Adults attend evening meetings that are open to discussions and that are designed to involve the community in the work of the school. One such experience focuses on "meetings around a theme," wherein parents, teachers, and all others connected with the school are invited to discuss and debate a topic, such as the role of the father or children's fears (Edwards et al., 1993, p. 98).

Perhaps the **Reggio Emilia programs** for early childhood have had such appeal to Americans because they cause Americans to reflect on their own past. Rural, agrarian America resembled Reggio Emilia because of its close connection between the immediate community and the school. Parents knew and cared about other children and served as important role models for them. There was a sense of "shared parenting" and "shared responsibility" not only for one's own child but for the neighbors' children as well. Such is the case in Reggio Emilia: The community embraces warmly the young children and their families, seemingly to invest all the more in the rich culture of northern Italy and to preserve its sense of connectedness over the decades. We were both reared in rural settings (one author in Kansas, the other author in Kentucky), and we both believe that the connection of the school or child care center to family and community, as reflected in Reggio Emilia, is a vital and essential component that is either missing or greatly diminished in the lives of contemporary young children.

These examples depict the inclusion of families and community members in more than just the fund-raising and carpooling events that sometimes characterize American communities. They exemplify the sense of commitment that adults can demonstrate when the school values their expertise and assistance in the education of their children. According to Loris Malaguzzi, founder of the Reggio early childhood programs, "We must forge strong alliances with the families of our children" (Phillips, 1994, p. 61).

◇◇ An Overview of Collaboration Strategies

Parents, teachers, and caregivers can employ numerous strategies to ensure that communication between home and school remains strong and healthy.

These strategies can be classified into two main categories: (a) one-way strategies and (b) two-way strategies. Chapter 3 elaborates on these avenues of communication and provides suggestions for their effective use.

In selecting and implementing communication strategies, schools must be sensitive to parents' work schedules, families with single parents, families who may be homeless, transportation constraints, need for child care, language barriers, families caring for intergenerational members, and other sensitive issues. Schools must also listen to the families as they share their strengths and concerns. This can be done formally and informally. Successful home-school communication is based foremost on the unique needs and characteristics of each family involved. The professional who is able to assess informally and formally each family that is represented in his or her classroom will ultimately be successful in communication efforts.

Each individual within a family has his or her own learning style. Just as the professional makes routine judgments about how to interact effectively with individual children in the classroom, the same must be done with respective families. Adults are usually rushed and sensitive to time constraints. If a professional can remember that a parent's schedule may be a confounding factor in successful communication, he or she can work to develop individual family strategies. For example, a family with a newborn will not appreciate telephone calls early in the morning or late at night. The parent in a single-parent-household will not appreciate having all parent meetings at night. A family with a child with disabilities or special needs may also have medical issues that complicate their lives. Remembering that individual families have unique profiles will assure the professional of continuous and successful communication.

As teachers, administrators, caregivers, and other professionals who work with children select and implement strategies for engaging families in work and play with their children at home and at school, it is important to remember that the children are the focus of all communication. If all participants in the communication exchange can remember to stay child-focused, then issues will be addressed in an objective, forthright, and efficient way. This means that professionals must gain the trust and respect of the parents of his or her class. Parents will then be comfortable and willing to share necessary information with the professional. Likewise, the professional will be able to share all types of information with the parents because of the mutual trust.

Parent involvement activities should include the range of specific learning styles and talents represented by adults and the general ways that people learn. Most professionals who work with young children are knowledgeable about child development and child learning styles and needs. They need to engage in ongoing efforts to understand adult education and learning styles, and this is the challenge to each professional who desires to establish and maintain a successful parent involvement program.

◊◊ **Summary**

This chapter presents the rationale for the continued importance of establishing effective home-school connections. Such national advocates for children as Marian Wright Edelman of the Children's Defense Fund implore us as professionals to put children first always, citing convincing data about the vulnerability of America's youngest citizens today. The teacher, caregiver, or program administrator is in a unique position to both observe and document the need for parent involvement and strong school-home-community ties.

Summary Statements ◊

- Marian Wright Edelman is the Executive Director of the Children's Defense Fund and one of America's most visible child advocates; her publications provide current data on the status of young children in the United States.

- Although parent involvement and education have been a traditional part of American education over the years, the needs and complexities of today's families and classrooms have never been greater.

- Strategies used in parent-school interactions and program development 10 to 15 years ago are not effective with today's complex family makeup and lifestyles.

- Violence may be the most changing variable in the lives of young children and their families; violence is redefining the way families, schools, and communities are able to interact with one another.

- Maternal employment is a way of life in the United States, as over 60% of mothers are employed. To provide effective parent involvement strategies, schools must be able to recognize child and family needs related to maternal employment.

- Divorce, separation, and remarriage occur in more than 50% of today's American families, and research reflects that emotional repercussions can be expected for young children through adolescence and even adulthood.

- Economic uncertainty contributes to child and family stress and is created through job mobility, downsizing of companies, and changing job needs.

- Technology and a fast-changing economy in the United States have changed the employment options and security for most Americans. Teachers need to be aware of the effects of mobility, job transitions, and income-related stressors on the children in their classrooms.

- Ethnic and developmental diversity is projected to increase dramatically as the new century arrives; parent involvement strategies continue to be shaped by these forces.

- The child poverty rate is 25%, the highest proportion of poverty in the U.S. population. America's children are the victims of increasing rates of violence, abuse, neglect, teenage pregnancy, AIDS, and poverty, as documented by data from the Children's Defense Fund.

- America's families and children are amazingly resilient; teachers should determine the strengths of each child and family and shape programs and interactions around these strengths and assets.

- Today's families hold the same desire to raise healthy and happy children in a safe environment as families in the "Leave It to Beaver" era. But the interrelationships among families, schools, and communities are much more complex now and must be negotiated first.

- Bronfenbrenner's ecosystem model provides an accurate portrayal of the interrelationships that exist among the child, the family, the school, the community, and the society at large. This model helps the professional see his or her role within the whole spectrum of system dynamics for the young child and the family.

- The collaborative role of the school is important because of the positive modeling that can occur within the school setting and by the teachers, administrators, and support personnel in these settings.

- The role of the family in educating the child and in serving as the child's first teacher is crucial, and schools must work to encourage and validate that role for the family.

- The collaborative role of the community and the many agencies within the community is essential if children and families are to identify and meet the necessary resources for their lives.

- The Reggio Emilia early childhood programs of northern Italy are representative of a strong parent involvement model for Americans because of the close and intricate relationships among child, parent, school, and community at large.

- Appropriate collaborative strategies for teachers and schools will depend on the individual families in their educational setting. Successful parent involvement strategies depend greatly on the teacher's ability to observe, assess both formally and informally, and then implement and evaluate specific, individualized, and measurable strategies for communication with parents and families.

- Parent education and involvement may have been an important part of American education over the years, but contemporary American families seek the traditional goals of security and happiness within much more complex lifestyles. The challenge of today's teachers and schools is to continue to strive for these basic, traditional goals that preserve families while taking into consideration the many forces that affect the child and his or her family.

Activities ◇◇

1. "It takes a village to raise a child" is an African culture's reflection on how best to bring up a young child. What forces in America today encourage and discourage this concept? List examples and discuss as a class.

2. American television is thought to have a considerable impact on the modeling of values and lifestyles for America's young children. Identify five current programs that model constructive family values and five that do not. Why did you choose these? Provide a rationale for each selection.

3. Children's and families' well-being in the United States is closely tied to legislation at both federal and state levels. List five pieces of legislation enacted

since 1990 that have affected American families; discuss that impact for each piece of legislation selected.

4. The movie *Terms of Endearment* portrays a family over time. View this movie in class and write an essay that includes (a) a comparison of this plot with the happenings in a typical American family today; (b) a discussion of what has held this family together; and (c) the role a school could play in easing the issues for the children in the movie.

5. Read at least two recent articles on the Reggio Emilia early childhood programs of northern Italy. As a class, compare and contrast this approach with traditional early childhood approaches in the United States; identify those elements of Reggio Emilia that you believe might be most helpful in enhancing programs for children in the United States.

6. Invite a family counselor to class to discuss the following: (a) What are the most common issues that families present today to family counselors? (b) How has the typical family changed during the past 10 years in the United States? (c) What forces seem to be most difficult for the family unit? (d) What strategies for communicating with parents and families have worked best for the therapist?

7. Role-play a meeting between a teacher in a kindergarten classroom and two parents who are currently separated. Identify issues that seem to be most toxic and difficult for this family and the child. List issues that are creating the greatest impact on the child.

8. Write an essay that contrasts today's American family with the family form of one of your grandparents. Identify such factors as (a) length of marriage, (b) number and spacing of children, (c) schooling and child care experiences, (d) parenting styles, (e) economic and financial constraints, (f) experiences with the extended family, (g) job and employment experiences, and (h) role of the church and other community agencies and institutions in their daily lives.

References ◊

Bell, C. C., & Jenkins, E. J. (1993). Community violence and children on Chicago's South Side. *Psychiatry, 56,* 46–54.

Bredekamp, S. (1987). *Developmentally appropriate practice in early childhood programs serving children from birth through age eight.* Washington, DC: National Association for the Education of Young Children.

Bronfenbrenner, U. (1979). *The ecology of human development.* Cambridge, MA: Harvard University Press.

Children's Defense Fund (CDF). (1991). *The state of America's children.* Washington, DC: Author.

Children's Defense Fund (CDF). (1996). *The state of America's children.* Washington, DC: Author.

Clinton, H. (1996). *It takes a village to raise a child.* New York: Touchstone.

Comer, J. P. (1990). Home, school, and academic learning. In J. I. Goodlad & P. Keating (Eds.), *Access to knowledge: An agenda for our nation's schools.* New York: College Entrance Examination Board.

Daniel, J. (1996). Family-centered work and child care. *Young Children, 51,* 2.

Darden, E., & Zimmerman, T. (1992) Blended families: A decade review, 1979–1990. *Family Therapy, 19,* 25–31.

Drug Enforcement Agency. (1996). *Drugs of abuse.* Arlington, VA: U.S. Department of Justice.

Dubrow, N. F., & Garbarino, J. (1989). Living in the war zone: Mothers and young children in a public housing development. *Journal of Child Welfare, 68*, 3-20.

Edelman, J. (1992). *The measure of our success: A letter to my children and yours.* Boston: Beacon Press.

Edwards, C. P., Gandini, L., & Forman, G. (1993). *The hundred languages of children.* Norwood, NJ: Ablex.

Edwards, P. A., & Young, L. S. (1992, September). Beyond parents: Family, community, and school involvement. *Phi Delta Kappan, 74*(1), 74, 76, 78, 80.

Epstein, J. A. (1988, January). How do we improve programs for parent involvement? *Educational Horizons*, pp. 58–59.

Erikson, E. H. (1950). *Childhood and society.* New York: Norton.

Forman, G., Gandini, L., Malaguzzi, L., Rinaldi, C., Piazza, G., & Gambetti, A. (1993). *An amusement park for birds.* Available from Performanetics Press, 19 The Hollow, Amherst, MA 01002.

Glaser, R. (1985). Foreword. In R. C. Anderson, E. H. Hiebert, & I. A. G. Wilkinson (Eds.), *Becoming a nation of readers: The report of the Commission on Reading.* Washington, DC: National Institute of Education.

Goffin, S., & Stegelin, D. (1992). *Changing kindergartens: Four success stories.* Washington, DC: N.A.E.Y.C.

Hoyt, M., & Schoonmaker, M. E. (1991, October 15). When parents accept the unacceptable. *Family Circle*, pp. 81–87.

Kotulak, R. (1990, September 28). Study finds inner-city kids live with violence. *Chicago Tribune*, pp. 1, 16.

Louv, R. (1993, July). The crisis of the absent father. *Parents*, pp. 54–56.

Lyon, S. (1995). What is my culture? *Child Care Information Exchange, 8*, 1.

National Association of State Boards of Education (NASBE), Task Force on Early Childhood Education. (1988). *Right from the start.* Alexandria, VA: National Association of State Boards of Education.

Olmstead, P. (1992). Where did our diversity come from? *High/Scope ReSource, 11*, 4–9.

Phillips, C. B. (1994). The movement of African American children through sociocultural contexts: A case of conflict resolution. In B. L. Mallory & R. S. New (Eds.), *Diversity and developmentally appropriate practices: Challenges for early childhood education* (pp. 166–182). New York: Teachers College Press.

Powell, D. R. (1989). *Families and early childhood programs.* Washington, DC: National Association for the Education of Young Children.

Powell, D. R. (1991). Parents and programs: Early childhood as a pioneer in parent involvement and support. In S. L. Kagan (Ed.), *The care and education of America's young children: Obstacles and opportunities.* Ninetieth yearbook of the National Society for the Study of Education (pp. 91–109). Chicago: National Society for the Study of Education.

Richters, J. E., & Martinez, P. (1993). The NIMH Community Violence Project: I. Children as victims of and witness to violence. *Psychiatry, 56*, 7–21.

Ryan, M. (1992, August 30). Who's taking care of the children? *Parade Magazine*, pp. 3–5.

Saluter, A. F. (1989). Singleness in America. In *Studies in marriage and the family.* Washington, DC: U.S. Department of Commerce, Bureau of the Census.

Slaby, R. G., Roedell, W. C., Arezzo, D., & Hendrix, K. (1995) *Early violence prevention: Tools for teachers of young children.* Washington, DC: National Association for the Education of Young Children.

Stegelin, D. A. (1992). *Early childhood education: Policy issues for the 1990s.* Norwood, NJ: Ablex.

U.S. Department of Commerce. (1989, August). Maternal employment and female-headed households. In *Statistical brief: Bureau of the Census.* Washington, DC: Author.

U.S. Department of Health and Human Services (DHHS). (1990). *A handbook for involving parents in Head Start* (DHHS Publication No. 90-31187). Rockville, MD: Author.

Wallach, L. B. (1993). Helping children cope with violence. *Young Children, 48*(4), 4–11.

Wallerstein, J. S., & Blakeslee, S. (1995). *The good marriage: How and why love lasts.* Boston: Houghton Mifflin.

Walsh, W. M. (1992). Twenty major issues in remarriage families. *Journal of Counseling & Development, 70*, 709–715.

2 A Mosaic of Parent Involvement Models
Historical and Current Perspectives

Each child experiences two childhoods—his and that of his parents. Each parent experiences two childhoods—his and that of his child.

Childhood, *Great Expectations,* 1991

Key Terms

baby boom
CEC
child study movement
Comenius
culture
curriculum enrichment model
developmentally appropriate
    practice
exosystem
far environment
Froebel
Goals 2000
Hall
human-built environment
Lanham Act
Locke
macrosystem
mesosystem
microsystem
Middle Ages
miniature adult

Montessori
NAEYC
natural physical-biological
    environment
near environment
parent cooperative
Pestalozzi
Piaget
P.L. 99-457
protective model
Reformation
Renaissance
Rousseau
school to home transmission model
SECA
sociocultural environment
Spock
systems
Vygotsky
Watson
WPA

Across generations, the worlds of our childhoods are intertwined. Our children experience the history of our pasts, one unseen to them. Our parenting reflects and sometimes rejects the attitudes, beliefs, and practices that were characteristic of our own parents. Similarly, our children will take into their lives as parents what we have brought from our parents and what beliefs, attitudes, and practices we have given to them as their parents. In many ways, what we do and share with our children today is taken across time into a world that we may never see but in which we will play a role.

The roles that parents have played in our families have traveled across time and will continue into the centuries beyond. These roles mirror the concerns of societies and communities at large. They will carry the effects of who we are at a given period in time—our genetics, joys and sorrows, economic securities and uncertainties, societal issues, health status, ignorances, and insights. In this chapter, we explore roles of parents and families in the context of the history of "humanness." Some of these issues are revisited in subsequent chapters.

Perhaps of greatest interest to us is what might have occurred during our time—our great-grandparents, grandparents, parents, and ourselves. As we look back and through the 20th century and ahead into the 21st, we will find an interconnectedness between the increasing knowledge we have

Through time and historical events, adults have been involved in the care and education of children.

acquired about the significance of learning, health care, and **developmentally appropriate practice** (DAP) in the early years and the number of programs available for children and their families. Our intent is, in part, to enhance the quality of life for families and children and, in part, to maximize the academic achievement of children so that they can compete in the increasingly technological, global marketplace. The ongoing challenge for the early childhood professional has been and will continue to be the advocacy of those practices that are nurturing and appropriate for the young child and that will provide a solid foundation for the skills needed to compete in one's world.

In our exploration of the journey of parents over time, we consider the following:

- The interrelationships of families to the near and far environments
- Attitudes toward children and families during specific times in history
- The history of families and children, including political, scientific, and historical events that have shaped the role of parents and the view of childhood
- Models for involving parents

◊◊ Interconnectedness of Families to Near and Far Environments

To provide a simplistic example of the interrelatedness of families to their worlds, think about the human body and the way it functions as a set of systems. If one loses use of a limb, the body and the brain adapt by shifting the responsibility to another limb, incorporating new strategies for accomplishing tasks, and/or incorporating an artificial device. Many body systems will be affected and will need to accommodate this change.

When a parent becomes ill in a family, other family members must make changes to accommodate the loss of that person's contributions and to care for that individual. These accommodations may include increased employment, new tasks, a change in residence, and time spent in a hospital. When a school system changes its hours of operation to times later than when parents typically go to work, families must accommodate by seeking additional child care, changing work schedules, giving added responsibility to children, or imploring the schools to consider families. For a time, families work to reestablish equilibrium within their households.

Using these examples, we can consider how the family functions as a system that is affected from within and through entities outside the family. Urie Bronfenbrenner (1979) described this as the *human ecological system.* Bronfenbrenner noted four **systems** that form the context for human growth and development and the functioning of the family. The **microsystem** involves the child's very **near environment**—the family. Other microsystems that will closely affect the child include the school or day care setting. Interrelationships among the microsystems form a child's **mesosystem.** A family depends on a child care provider to furnish quality care for the child. If this care does not occur within the child care microsystem, the family microsystem will be affected. Similarly, a family crisis, such as death of a family member or a divorce, could affect the microsystem of the school, with a child's behaviors and performance affected.

Exosystems also affect families. We may not see or be directly involved in exosystems. Perhaps the school system changes its bus schedule and the family is affected. Perhaps the day care center changes its hours of operation or dramatically increases its fees. Families may have little or no control over these events, but they certainly affect the lives of families.

Finally, the broadest context in which families function is the **macrosystem.** This includes the political and historical events that affect families. The launch of *Sputnik 1* by the Soviets in 1957 thrust Americans into a period of concern for improving the quality of education in the United States. The civil rights movement succeeded in gaining more opportunities for minorities. Recent scientific discoveries in brain research have provided a bounty of public information about the importance of prenatal care and nurturing the young child.

Bronfenbrenner's human ecological system continues to be explored by those who work with families and children. Bubolz and Sontag (1993) view

The lives of children are affected by many systems, including the family and those systems found within the community.

the family as an open system with interconnectedness across (a) the natural physical-biological environment, (b) the human-built environment, and (c) the sociocultural environment. In other words, families have functioned throughout time and continue to function today within the context of the natural physical-biological, human-built, and cultural environments.

The **natural physical-biological environment** includes the natural resources with which we are blessed or that might be threatened. Rain, water sources, land, trees, and climate are among these resources. Although we often take these for granted, we know they are threatened by human consumption and misuse of the environment. In many parts of the world and across time, these elements have served to enhance or threaten a way of life. For example, the community that has a precious mineral as a resource will profit; the community that lies in the shadow of a great volcano is at unrest. Although our view of parenting focuses on the care and nurturing of the child, the ease and comfort and manner of doing so by a parent will vary with the physical and biological resources that are available.

Coupled with the natural physical-biological environment, humans created a **human-built environment,** which includes rural and urban communities. It also includes systems for health care, schooling, manufacturing, business, government, religions, and so forth. Along with the very positive aspects of our civilizations are negative aspects—problems we have created, including toxic wastes that pollute the water and air and destruction of land and life for the purpose of war. Parents' attitudes toward their role in parenting across time will reflect the current availability of human resources and the attitudes of their society toward the role of the family in the functioning of the community.

Cultural practices, languages, laws, and values characterize the **sociocultural environment.** Humans within a society must decide what is important for maintaining not only the quality of life for individuals and families but also the functioning of the community and society. Not all individuals, however, have had the same amount of "voice" or power in making and influencing these decisions. Throughout history, certain groups have been underrepresented, less valued, and even targeted for oppression. The plight of Jewish families during the Holocaust and the children of African American families during and following the period of slavery in the United States are two prominent examples. Values placed on education, freedom of speech, equality of human life, and preservation of human life are all a part of the sociocultural context within which humans live.

Given an understanding of the family living, growing, and functioning in the context of the near environment and the **far environment** (that beyond the family, such as the community and the world), we can begin to look at some events that have affected the role of parents throughout time. We can also look at the role of parents and families as the world experiences the birth and infancy of a new millenium.

◊◊ A History of Families and Childhood

The only way to explore the roles of families in the lives of children across time is to investigate and attempt to understand the context in which children were viewed during different times in history. In his efforts to do this, Trawick-Smith (1997) divided this work into five time periods that reflect the models provided by DeMause (1974) and Pollack (1983). Prior to discussing this framework, which begins after the birth of Christ (A.D.), let's take a brief look at the history of families and the views of children before the birth of Christ (B.C.).

"During prehistoric times, just as today, the first teachers—the socializ-ers—were parents and families" (Berger, 1997, p. 37). According to Berger (1997), members of primitive societies educated their children, not in school, but in the context of families and communities to gather and hunt and pro-duce food in ways that could maintain the group. Values and laws of the group were passed on so that children could function as a part of the **culture** and the culture would continue. In this role, children were highly valued.

Egyptian artwork from the years B.C. depicts children at play and being held and comforted by adults. Written records indicate that schooling out-side the home took place (Osborn, 1991). "Formal systems of education also existed in ancient India, China, and Persia, as well as in the pre-Columbian New World, particularly in the Indian cultures of the Mayas, Aztecs, and Incas" (Berger, 1997, p. 37).

The view of the ancient Greeks and Romans also reflects a concern for family life and the education of children. It should be noted, however, that a primary concern for children and their education was based on the rearing of good citizens who could protect and maintain the culture and civilization. It should also be noted that infanticide was a common practice of both the Romans and the Greeks.

In ancient Greece, Plato (427–347 B.C.) and Aristotle (384–322 B.C.) addressed the rearing of children in such a way that the stability and future of the culture and civilization were continued. Parents could choose to send their children to private schools of their choice. An increasing interest in the education of children for the benefit of the state was expressed by lead-ers of the time, however, including Plato and Aristotle, who stressed that an event of such importance should not be left to chance (Berger, 1997).

In both Rome and Sparta, education remained in the hands of families. Young children had few rights, and laws forbade the rearing of children who were described as "deformed." Those children who were selected to survive were educated by their parents to be good and productive citizens. Children of primary school age were already in training to be soldiers for their country.

Even though the plight of children was difficult during this time, with their primary function as citizens of the state, Berger (1997) notes that fam-ilies were seen as important or first educators of their children. However, "a subsequent decline in the importance of the family occurred during the Middle Ages, and concern for parent involvement did not emerge until many centuries later" (p. 39).

At this point, Trawick-Smith's (1997) model will be employed to guide the discussion of children and families through time. As noted later, the value placed on children has been and continues to be affected by the context of the historical events and cultures within which they are reared.

A.D. 1 to 1600

During the period A.D. 1 to 1600, European history details the period of the **Middle Ages** beginning at about 400 and ending at about 1400. This was a period of the feudal system, with distinct class distinctions among individuals. Children of serfs and peasants worked alongside their parents in maintaining the properties of the feudal estates. Life was poor and harsh, and education was not a consideration for these children. Their noble counterparts, however, began at an early age their education for the life of nobility. Regardless of their preparation for a skill or for assuming positions of leadership, these children were also without childhoods. By age 7, they were sent to apprentice with other families—the jobs in keeping with their position as nobles or as commoners (Berger, 1997).

The expectation that children would behave and think as **miniature adults** is reflected in the depiction in early paintings of children in adult clothing and with, understandably, somber faces. Their roles, poor health care, and high death rate and the continued practice of infanticide were all factors that denied them the joy we see in childhood today. Important events that occurred during this time period include the Renaissance and the Reformation.

The **Renaissance** marks a time across the 14th, 15th, and 16th centuries when Europe experienced the revival of art, literature, and learning. This period also marked the end of the medieval world. The **Reformation** was the 16th-century religious movement that aimed at reforming the Roman Catholic Church and resulted in establishing Protestant churches. In 1439, Johannes Gutenberg invented the printing press. Following this invention, the production of books, once given to reproduction by hand, increased dramatically. The increased availability of books and knowledge played a significant role in improving the quality of life for families.

Changes in the religious aspects of society also affected family life. "The most important aspect of the Protestant reformation was the concept of a priesthood of believers, in which people were expected to learn to read and study the Bible for themselves and thereby find their own salvation" (Berger, 1997, p. 41). The Bible, made available by the printing press and printed in the language of the people, was the subject of study. Martin Luther urged parents to educate their children.

1600 to 1800

The concept of *original sin*, with children born with evil to be expelled by harsh discipline, was prevalent from 1600 to 1800. Events in Europe were mirrored in communities being established in America. In 1642, the Massachusetts Act requiring all families to teach their children to read the Bible and laws of the land was enacted. In 1687, the "old Deluder Satan" Law requiring communities of more than 100 to establish schools was put into place (Barbour & Barbour, 1997). In these colonial schools, "the major component of schooling was discipline and moral education based on the prevailing beliefs that to spare the rod was to spoil the child" (Roopernarine & Johnson, 1993, p. 2).

Important philosophers who emerged during this time made lasting contributions to early childhood education and the accompanying role of families. Among them were Comenius, Locke, Rousseau, Pestalozzi, and Froebel. These social thinkers rejected the notion of original sin and viewed children as born innocent of sin (Berger, 1997).

Comenius (1592–1670), born in Moravia, was a member and bishop of the Moravian Brethren. In *Didactica Magna*, Comenius spoke to the importance of education in the early years. The *School of Infancy* addressed the role of the home in the early education of young children. *Orbis Pictus* was the first picture book for children.

John **Locke** (1632–1704) "challenged the beliefs of the medieval church that children were born with a fully formed nature or soul, and thought that, instead, they, like other natural phenomena in the universe, were subject to the effects of the environment" (Roopernarine & Johnson, 1993, p. 3). Locke, an Englishman, is well known for his notion of *tabula rasa*, in which he described the newborn with a mind as a "blank slate" to be molded and shaped by parents and teachers. Locke also supported the concept of *hardening* that was prevalent at the time: It was thought that children subjected to cold baths and other methods of "hardening" would become more resilient to disease (Berger, 1997).

Jean Jacques **Rousseau** (1712–1778) emerged during this time as another significant philosopher affecting the lives of children and families. His book *Emile* encouraged greater freedoms for children and the nurturing of children in the early years by their mothers. This concern for children was an interesting contrast to his treatment of his own five children, who were placed in foundling homes soon after birth (Berger, 1997).

Locke, Rousseau, and Comenius played significant roles in the philosophies of Johann **Pestalozzi** (1747–1827), who was later hailed as the father of parent education. His book *How Gertrude Teaches Her Children* emphasized the role of the mother and gave parents strategies for teaching their children. These strategies included using objects to learn to count and recreation, games, and nutritious snacks (Berger, 1997). A Swiss educator and social activist, Pestalozzi went beyond the work of his predecessors by actually establishing a school, the Education Institute in Bergdorf, Switzerland (1801), which put philosophy to practice. One of his major contributions was the belief that all children, not just those of the upper class, might benefit from education (Roopernarine & Johnson, 1993). In addition, he rejected the notion that punishment should be linked with learning and originated the idea of group instruction.

Frederick **Froebel** (1782–1852) also advocated for the goodness of children, the concern for the early years, and inclusion of the parents in a child's education. This German educator began a "garden for children," now known as kindergarten, employing many strategies of Pestalozzi. Froebel saw mothers as the first educators of their children and wrote a book, *Mother Play and Nursery Songs With Finger Plays*, for mothers to use with their children at home. Froebel organized his curriculum for kindergarten around the natural unfolding of the child, with the mother as an active participant (Berger, 1997).

1800 to 1900

The lives of Pestalozzi and Froebel extended into the 19th century, as did the work of Locke, Comenius, and Rousseau. In Germany in 1851, the German government banned kindergarten education because the government "was suspicious of what it believed was an atheistic attitude in Froebel's emphasis on play and the transcendental idea of God as incarnate in humankind" (Roopernarine & Johnson, 1993, p. 9). Froebel's work carried into other parts of the world, however. In 1860, Elizabeth Peabody established the first English-speaking private kindergarten in America in Boston. In 1873, Susan Blow, who had worked with Peabody, opened the first public kindergarten in America in St. Louis.

Documents began to appear during this time to assist parents in their roles. These included magazines, such as *Parents' Magazine* (1840–1850), designed to give parents suggestions for breast-feeding, toilet training, and other useful parenting tips in child rearing (Berger, 1997). While strides were made in the education of young children and the provision of support for families in child rearing, life continued to be difficult for children and families. The 19th century not only was marked by the War of 1812, but also was torn apart by the Civil War. Whereas most of written U.S. history depicts the lives of children of European descent, little is written about the lives of children growing up in slavery or of Native American children who witnessed the death of their families and loss of their homes. Ogbu (1988) details the effects on parenting that resulted from the oppression faced by many nondominant cultural groups. The enslaved parent and child's relationship focused on maintaining the family by obeying the parent, being quiet, and listening to instructions. Independent thought and action on the part of the enslaved could result in beatings, death, or being sold away from the family. Parenting, then, was direct and firm.

During this time, children of all backgrounds engaged in hard labor in factories and on frontiers. Their lives were often harsh and brief. Many were born so that parents might have more laborers, and this was their worth. It also reflected a time when being able to work and produce meant a family could survive. Adulthood came early, and many times this, too, was brief.

At the end of the 19th century, pioneers in the field of child study, including Pestalozzi and Charles Darwin (1809–1882), "published biographies of their own children in an attempt to capture milestones of human growth (Trawick-Smith, 1997, p. 29). The role of parents continued to be highlighted, and concern for their role in the education of their children was reflected in the founding of the Parent Teachers Association (PTA) in 1897 (Berger, 1997).

1900 to 1950

At the turn of the 20th century, the foundation had been created for the acknowledgement of the significance of the early years. This, coupled with an increasing interest in scientific research about human development, fed the growing **child study movement.** G. Stanley **Hall** (1844–1924) was an eminent psychologist who is credited as the founder of the field of child study in the United States. One of his greatest contributions was the integration of the fields of child study and education (Trawick-Smith, 1997).

The concern for establishing developmental norms led to the creation of normative charts by researchers, including Arnold Gesell. A problem with these studies, as noted by Trawick-Smith (1997), is the sole focus on White, middle-class children as the subjects of the research.

During this time, the country demonstrated heightened concern for the welfare of children who continued to be exposed to the cruelties of hard labor, dangerously strict parents, and neglect. The first White House Conference on Care of Dependent Children was called in 1909. The Children's Bureau was created in 1912 as a result of this conference and marked the federal government's first display of concern for children (Berger, 1997).

Parents' interest in how best to rear their children was reflected in the onset of women's magazines with articles addressing the care of the home and children. These magazines included *Good Housekeeping, Ladies' Home Journal*, and *Woman's Home Companion* (Berger, 1997). Government also began to disseminate information relative to strategies for child care. The first *Infant Care* book was disseminated by the federal government in 1914. This book and other parenting articles advocated strict schedules for infant feeding and sleeping and forbade such damaging behaviors as thumb sucking (Berger, 1997).

Parents' interest in participating in the education of their young children was demonstrated by the establishment of the first **parent cooperative** in the United States. This school, founded by faculty wives at the University of Chicago, followed the work of English nursery schools established by Margaret McMillan in 1911. McMillan was an advocate of parent involvement and education through play: "Parent cooperatives and the growth of the nursery schools in the United States strengthened and promoted parent education" (Berger, 1997, p. 60).

The 1930s and 1940s brought difficult times for children and families in the United States. Just out of World War I, the country found itself in the Great Depression, which left many families without food or shelter. The United States entered World War II in 1941, and countless women were left to raise families, earn a living, and assist in the war effort. These two historical events had lasting effects on the field of early childhood: The Depression brought Works Project Administration (**WPA**) nurseries, which not only created jobs but also provided women the opportunity to work. World War II brought **Lanham Act** nurseries, which were open 10 to 12 hours per day, 6 days per week, and provided mothers the time to work and participate in the war effort. Following the war, funding for these centers was suspended, and women were encouraged to return to their homes (Roopernarine & Johnson, 1993).

During and following this period, researchers in the child study movement began to focus on the emotional development of children. This would not be surprising, given the grave emotional tasks that had been faced by many families and their children during the years of the Depression and world war. The work of Sigmund Freud (1856–1939) became the subject of discussion. "Childhood fears and behaviors such as shyness or aggressiveness took on new meanings when applied to the child's unconscious and were carefully recorded by teachers" (Roopernarine & Johnson, 1993, p. 19). Play was seen as therapy. Parents had also been exposed to the behaviorist theories of John B. **Watson** during this time and were faced with choices about the best methods for addressing the emotional concerns of their young children. A famous publication that became a much-used and -quoted resource for parents was first published in 1946. In *The Common Sense Book of Baby and Child Care*, Benjamin **Spock,** M.D. (1903–1998), put to rest the concerns and fears of many parents determined to do their best in rearing their children. In contrast with the strict rules applied to child rearing in the early part of the century, Dr. Spock urged parents to enjoy their children and to enjoy being parents. His book addressed a wide range of concerns for parents, including feeding, toileting, sleeping, illnesses, and discipline. This book continued to influence parenting into the 1950s and beyond (Berger, 1997).

1950 to 2000

The period 1950 to 2000 was ushered in by the Korean War. But by 1953, relieved to be at the end of a long period of wars, Americans appeared to relax and enjoy a period of prosperity. Popular television shows depicted the American family as two parents, two or three children, father as a professional, and mother as a loving and ever-tidy housewife. These characteristics prevailed in *Father Knows Best, Leave It to Beaver*, and *The Donna Reed Show*. This was the period of the **baby boom** for the many families who had postponed children until after the war years. The effects of this great increase in babies continues to be seen in both social, political, and economic arenas of our world. In the 1950s, schools in the United States reflected the influences of John Dewey's (1859–1952) progressive movement. Barbour and Barbour (1997) note that these swings from conservative to more progressive philosophies reflect the perceived needs of the American public at the time. "For example, with new immigrants and a growing urban, industrialized society, a movement emerged in the 1920s and 1930s for more openness in education—with schooling tailored to the needs, interests, and abilities of the children" (p. 29).

"Dewey did more than any other person to redirect the course of education in the United States" (Morrison, 1998, p. 75). His child-centered curriculum reflected the interests of children and focused on the child's active participation in learning. He also stressed the usefulness of using daily life experiences as learning opportunities. "Teachers who integrate subjects, use thematic units, and encourage problem-solving activities and critical thinking are philosophically indebted to Dewey" (Morrison, 1998, p. 76).

Early childhood educators began to study more about the work of developmental theorists, including Jean **Piaget** (1896–1980) and Lev **Vygotsky** (1896–1934). These theorists believed that children construct knowledge through their interaction with materials, people, and events. Cognitive development was seen as a continuous process of learning though play. Piaget also stressed the unique ways in which young children approached learning situations, as compared with adults, and he outlined an age/stage model of cognitive development.

The launching of the artificial satellite *Sputnik 1* by the Soviet Union in 1957 brought a new wave of concern to the United States. Why were the Americans not the first to make this journey into space? Was something wrong with the educational system that put us in second place in the "race for space"? A concern for educational systems that were more academic became prevalent. People had even greater interest in not only how children learn but also how children learn best. At the same time that we as Americans were troubled by the prospects of being second in a space race, we were also troubled about the inequality we saw about us in economics, education, living conditions, and services. We were concerned about the inequalities between people of color and people who are White, those who are male and those who are female, those who have disabilities and those who do not. We began to think about our future as being in the hands of our children, and the notion of investing in children as investing in the future emerged.

Educators and policymakers concerned about the quality of education for the nation's children and about meeting the needs of all children seemed to find answers in research addressing the development of intelligence. James McVicker Hunt, in *Intelligence and Experience* (1961), challenged the notion that intelligence was fixed; he said that, rather, intelligence could be enhanced by positive environmental experiences. Jean Piaget's work was cited as a model to be used in the early years, which were emphasized as important years for learning.

Two historical pieces of legislation gave rise to many programs for young children and their families: The *Civil Rights Act* was enacted in 1964 and the *Elementary and Secondary Education Act* in 1965. Project Head Start, Title I, and Chapter I programs were also implemented in 1965 to begin building a system of equal educational opportunity for all children.

Particularly during the 1960s, many federal programs were based on the idea of conserving one of the country's greatest resources—its children. Head Start, Follow Through, and child welfare programs are products of this view, which has resulted in a "human capital" or "investment" rationale for child care and other services. (Morrison, 1998, p. 53)

"Following the civil rights movement, social issues were of great concern and again schools were pressured to change to a curriculum more responsive to all children" (Barbour & Barbour, 1997, p. 29). This concern became realized in a dramatic way with the passing of P.L. 94-142, the *Education of All Handicapped Children Act*, in 1975 (in 1990, renamed the Individuals with Disabilities Education Act [IDEA]).

Doors have been opened several times through history to look at parents and the home as indicators of how a child will fare in education and in life. The work of Hunt (1961), Bloom's (1964) *Stability and Change in Human Characteristics*, and the desire of a nation to learn what is most important in *every* child's education thrust researchers into the world of children at home and the parents' role in their child's education. Researchers with the Dave (1963) study made the following conclusions with respect to the home environment:

Our study has led us to understand the significance of bringing meaningful print to children at an early age.

- Work habits of children and parents
  Children from homes with routines, structure, and shared responsibilities do better in school.

- Academic guidance and support
  Children need someone at home who will offer them encouragement in their schoolwork, understand their strengths and limitations, and be aware of what they are studying.

- Stimulation to explore and discuss ideas and events
  Children need someone who provides them opportunities to know about events in the world through print materials at home, trips to libraries, and participation in family hobbies and activities.

- Language development in the home
  Children need opportunities to see and hear adults use oral and written language in the home.

- Academic aspirations and expectations
  A child needs an adult at home who will set high but realistic standards for the child's school efforts and to aspire to the highest levels of education.

Child study has led us to understand that children learn best through opportunities to engage in "hands-on" experiences.

According to Bloom (1981),

> My own speculation is that parents are still the key in the learning of their children because they are likely to be a constant factor in their children's lives. When parents are very effective (or when they can learn to be more effective) in supporting the child's learning, they remain with the child over his or her years of schooling. (p. 90)

Programs such as Head Start responded to these concerns by including parent involvement as a required component. Parents work in classrooms as volunteers, participate on advisory boards, and receive education with respect to such topics as child guidance, health care, and developmentally appropriate activities. The 1960s and 1970s will be remembered as a time of change. Americans participated in, and recovered from, the deep wounds of an unresolved war in Vietnam. A concern for social issues brought laws and programs that have prevailed. These changes followed, and were accompanied by, a period of unrest on campuses and in cities across the continent. We lost great political leaders and humanitarians, including President John F. Kennedy; his brother, presidential candidate Robert Kennedy; and Reverend Martin Luther King, Jr., perhaps the greatest civil rights leader of all time, to assassins.

This was a time of "free love, flower children, hippies, and love children." The drug culture came into the open. Families were divided by separation and divorce in record numbers. Many mothers began to seek employment outside the home, and the number of child care arrangements broadened. Awareness of the needs of minority groups was demanded. We hailed parents as the first teachers of their children and began to educate government leaders, educators, parents, and business leaders about the importance of the early years in learning. We also saw families struggle with changes in family structures, including changing gender roles, nuclear families isolated from extended families, divorce, remarriage, and single parents. Families struggled with issues of quality, affordable child care and the effects of mothers going to work on the young child. These individuals and families were pioneers of issues that remain concerns in our society today.

The 1980s saw Americans attempt to "make sense" of what we had learned in the 1960s and 1970s. Many programs for children experienced reduced funding or were eliminated. Head Start, however, has stood the test of time and political skirmishes and remains funded. Organizations and individuals advocated for quality in child care and early childhood programs. The National Association for the Education of Young Children (**NAEYC**) published its first edition of *Developmentally Appropriate Practice in Early Childhood Programs Serving Children from Birth Through Age Eight* (Bredekamp, 1987), which has served as a model for developing and implementing quality programs across the country. The Southern Early Childhood Association (**SECA**) and the Division for Early Childhood of the Council for Exceptional Children (**CEC**) are among the professional groups that have advocated for quality services for all young children and for improving the quality of life for all families.

Such advocacy efforts resulted in the passing of **P.L. 99-457,** which addressed the needs of children with disabilities from birth to age 3 and their families at the federal level and in the widespread urging for reform at the local level. One example of this effort was the 1989 ruling by the Kentucky Supreme Court that declared the system of public schools in the state unconstitutional. The massive reform that followed is known as the Kentucky Education Reform Act (KERA, 1990). Among the outcomes of KERA have been public programs for 4-year-olds labeled "at risk" because of income level; Family Resource and Youth Service Centers, which coordinate community services to families; school-based decision-making councils; and revisions in curriculum across all grade levels (Lindle, 1994).

In the 1990s, Americans became increasingly aware of the advanced technological capabilities and marketing strategies of other countries. Japan provides a solid example. While the United States was striving to maintain a strong and effective posture in the global economy and to provide appropriate educations for a tapestry of children and families with a variety of needs, the rigor of its educational system again came under scrutiny.

> An important political and educational event occurred in 1989 when President George Bush and the governors of all fifty states met at the University of Virginia to set national education goals. One result of this meeting was the release in 1991 of *America 2000: An Education Strategy*, which outlined six educational goals or national standards. (Morrison, 1998, p. 41)

These goals became the basis of the ***Goals 2000: Educate America Act of 1994.*** The following goals are to be achieved by the year 2000:

1. All children in America will start school ready to learn.
2. The high school graduation rate will increase to at least 90 percent.
3. All students will leave grades four, eight, and twelve having demonstrated competency over challenging subject matter . . . , and [all students will be] prepared for responsible citizenship, further learning, and productive employment.
4. The nation's teaching force will have access to programs for the continued improvement of their professional skills.
5. The United States students will be first in the world in mathematics and science achievement.
6. Every adult in America will be literate.
7. Every school in America will be free of drugs and violence and will offer a disciplined environment conducive to learning.
8. Every school and home will engage in partnerships that will increase parental involvement and participation in promoting the social, emotional, and academic growth of children. (Morrison, 1998, p. 41)

As reflected in *Goals 2000*, Americans are attempting to meet the needs of every child as she or he comes to this world and to the early childhood program door. Teachers and educators are learning more about planning and implementing curriculum strategies that address the cultural backgrounds and multiple intelligences (Gardner, 1983), or the different ways of knowing of children. These professionals are deep into the practice of mainstreaming children in least restrictive environments and of learning to manage the medications and behaviors of children with attention deficit disorder and those who suffer from the effects of mothers who used illegal drugs or alcohol during pregnancy. They are learning to care for children with AIDS and children left homeless.

Some parents and families, buoyed by the wave of new research on brain development presented in popular magazines (*Newsweek,* 1997) and seeking to do best for their young children, play music to the child *in utero,* search for the best day care situations and schools, and join the endless lines of van pools to various extracurricular activities. Other parents struggle to put food on the table and a roof over the heads of their children and to show the love they have in their hearts to their children.

With these great challenges and needs to be met, how have parents and teachers viewed each other over time to work toward common goals for their children? What models have seemed to stand the test of time and the changing needs of society?

◇◇ Models for Involving Parents

Many times, a discussion of models for involving parents in their children's education actually becomes a discussion of models of early childhood programming (e.g., **Montessori,** child centered). Although each of these models has a definite outlook on the way parents should and should not be involved, they are not models of parent involvement in the strict sense of the term. Susan Swap (1993) addresses the models of home-school relationships in her book *Developing Home-School Partnerships: From Concepts to Practice.* The models are (a) the protective model, (b) the school to home transition model, and (c) the curriculum enrichment model.

Protective Model

The **protective model** is designed to separate the functions of school and home. Assumptions that characterize this model are as follows:

- Parents delegate to the school the responsibility of educating their children.
- Parents hold school personnel accountable for the results.
- Educators accept this delegation of responsibility. (Swap, 1993, p. 28)

Although this model has been characteristic of both public and private school situations, it eliminates the notion that parents are their child's first and most important teachers and that the parents really know their child better than anyone else does. It also represents an example of situations in which parents are very willing to abdicate this aspect of their parenting duties. Some parents will do so because their self-regard in terms of what they think they know about their child is very low, because this was the way of their own parents, or because they are afraid to create or deal with possible conflict. This model would certainly not be advocated for parents seeking care of their young child.

School to Home Transition Model

In the **school to home transition model,** efforts of parents in supporting the objectives of the school are encouraged and sought. Assumptions are as follows:

- Children's achievement is fostered by continuity of expectations and values between home and school.
- School personnel should identify the values and practices outside school that contribute to school success.
- Parents should endorse the importance of schooling, reinforce school expectations at home, provide conditions at home that nurture development and support school success, and ensure that the child meets minimum academic and social requirements. (Swap, 1993, p. 30)

The role of parents in supporting the school through holding bake sales, building playgrounds, providing class materials, and preparing food for school parties typifies this model. Two-way communication is not actively sought or encouraged (Swap, 1993). Many of these tasks are also suited to those parents who are available, possess certain skills, and have the social know-how to fit into particular groups. This model does not reflect parents as being truly equal partners with school personnel in the care and education of children.

Curriculum Enrichment Model

The **curriculum enrichment model** is representative of many early childhood programs and certainly of the advocacy works of such groups as NAEYC and SECA. Programs, such as Head Start, that advocate developmentally appropriate practices for young children and the view of parents as the child's first and most important teachers complete this category. The "logic" that drives this curriculum is that (a) continuity of learning between home and school is of critical importance in encouraging children's learning; (b) the values and cultural histories of many children are omitted from the standard school curriculum, leading to a disruption of this continuity between home and school and often to less motivation, status, and achievement for children in school; and (c) these omissions distort the curriculum, leading to a less accurate and less comprehensive understanding of events and achievements and to a perpetuation of damaging beliefs and attitudes about immigrant and oppressed minorities (Swap, 1993, p. 38).

Assumptions guiding this model are as follows:

- Parents and educators should work together to enrich curriculum objectives and content.
- Relationships between home and school are based on mutual respect, and both parents and teachers are seen as experts and resources in the process of delivery. (Swap, 1993, p. 39)

This model provides many opportunities for schools to function "without walls" as parents and community members share their areas of expertise with children and children "make sense" of what they are learning in school as they see its relationships to the outside world. Parents can serve as volunteers within the classroom, reading to children and assisting children in work with manipulatives and physical activities. Parents can play an active role in decision making with respect to services to children via such tools as site-based decision-making councils and policy councils. The child is seen as a part of a family system, with experiences at school affected by experiences at home and experiences at home affected by experiences at school. Finally, this model, representative of the era of the 1960s from which it flourished, speaks to the interconnectedness of humans across and within frames of time and across and within locations of learning, be it home, school, or community.

Families, teachers, and caregivers must work cooperatively to ensure that children have opportunities to build relationships with peers and to explore their near environments.

The rearing and educating of children is a complex task and takes the work of parents, families, teachers, caregivers, community leaders, policymakers, and more. Throughout history, the role of the family in relation to education has been altered by time and events. Since the beginning, however, the parent has been the child's first teacher, and the parent will see the course of the child's education across the school experience. Throughout this text, we explore ways in which families can share in the care and education of their children at school and at home.

Summary Statements ◇

- A child's experiences with parents reflect the styles of parenting that have come across time and historical events.

- Families operate as systems and are interconnected with other systems, including schools, churches, and other families.

- According to Bronfenbrenner, families function across microsystems, mesosystems, exosystems, and macrosystems.

- Families operate across environments, including the natural physical-biological environment, the human-built environment, and the sociocultural environment.

- Across time, families have played a role in the education of their children. The methods of doing so have differed according to the context of the historical situation.

- During the Middle Ages, children were viewed as miniature adults, and the period of childhood ended by age 7.

- The Reformation and the Renaissance brought change to the role of parents in the family as they were once again valued in the educating of their children.

- During the Reformation, the printing press made books more available, particularly the Bible; during the Reformation, parents were told to use the Bible in instructing their children.

- The work of philosophers including Rousseau, Comenius, Pestalozzi, Locke, and Froebel was helpful in dispelling the religious concept of *original sin*, in which children were born inherently evil. They also played a significant role in promoting the importance of the early years and the critical role that parents, particularly mothers, played in nurturing their young children.

- The field of child study broadened at the turn of the 20th century, with theorists including Pestalozzi and Darwin publishing biographies of their own children.

- Children raised in situations of oppression are likely to be parented in more directive ways to ensure their safety.

- Piaget was a noted theorist during the 20th century who affected work with young children and their families.

- Spock's book on child care was helpful to parents of the 1940s and beyond in developing a more relaxed attitude toward their role.

- *Sputnik 1* was instrumental in moving parents and policymakers in the United States to explore the rigors of its school system.

- The 1960s and 1970s were a period of social unrest and demands of freedoms of individuals regardless of race, gender, disability, religion, or ethnic background. From this period came programs that have affected families in this country. Head Start was among those programs that enlisted families in the care and education of young children in an early childhood setting.

- Several models can describe parent involvement. They include the protective model, the school to home transition model, and the curriculum enrichment model.

Activities ◊◊◊◊◊◊◊◊◊◊◊◊◊◊◊◊◊◊◊◊◊◊◊◊◊◊◊◊◊◊◊◊◊◊◊◊◊◊◊

1. Divide into small groups. Using chart paper and markers, prepare a timeline that reflects the role of families in the lives of children. Each group may select given centuries so that discussion can be more focused on specific time periods. Discuss reasons why parents may have assumed particular roles during this time. Be prepared to share your beliefs with other groups.

2. Review the information about how families function as systems within the context of other systems. Think about your family. List the entities that affect the functioning and well-being of your family. Group those according to whether they are representative of the natural-physical, human-built, or sociocultural environment. Share your findings with other members of your class to note similarities and differences and issues you may have overlooked.

3. Discuss the perceived role of children during the time of the ancient Greeks and Romans. Do any examples in today's world seem to replicate in any

way the use of children for the benefit of a group? Discuss your thoughts with fellow classmates.

4. Describe evidence of children being viewed or expected to act as miniature adults today. Consider their care, the media, fashion, discipline, and so forth.

5. Do library research on the practice of infanticide. Do any countries practice infanticide today? If so, what is the role of the parent/family in this practice?

6. Do library research on world events during the time of World War II. These might include the funding of child care centers in the United States, the Holocaust in Germany, and the "going to war" by fathers across the world. What effects might these events have had on the role of parents at that time, and what possible lasting effects could they have had on parenting today?

7. Visit a local Head Start program. List the ways in which the curriculum enrichment model of parent involvement is implemented.

References ◊◊

Barbour, C., & Barbour, N. H. (1997). *Families, schools, and communities: Building partnerships for educating children.* Upper Saddle River, NJ: Prentice Hall.

Berger, E. H. (1997). *Parents as partners in education.* Upper Saddle River, NJ: Merrill/Prentice Hall.

Bloom, B. S. (1964). *Stability and change in human characteristics.* New York: Wiley.

Bloom, B. S. (1981). *All our children learning: A primer for teachers, parents, and other educators.* New York: McGraw-Hill.

Bredekamp, S. (Ed.). (1987). *Developmentally appropriate practice in early childhood programs serving children from birth through age eight* (Exp. ed.). Washington, DC: National Association for the Education of Young Children.

Bronfenbrenner, U. (1979). *The ecology of human environment.* Cambridge, MA: Harvard University Press.

Bubolz, M. M., & Sontag, S. (1993). Human ecology theory. In P. G. Boss, W. J. Doherty, R. LaRossa, W. R. Schumm, & S. K. Steinmetz (Eds.), *Sourcebook of family theories and methods: A contextual approach* (pp. 419–448). New York: Plenum Press.

Childhood. (1991). In *Great expectations* [Video]. New York: Ambrose Video.

Dave, R. H. (1963). *The identification and measurement of environmental process variables that are related to educational achievement.* Unpublished doctoral dissertation, University of Chicago.

DeMause, L. (1974). The evolution of children. In L. DeMause (Ed.), *The history of childhood.* New York: Psychohistory Press.

Gardner, H. (1983). *Frames of the mind: The theory of multiple intelligences.* New York: Basic Books.

Hunt, J. M. (1961). *Intelligence and experience.* New York: Ronald Press.

Lindle, J. C. (1994). Kentucky's reform opens doors to family involvement. *Dimensions in Early Childhood, 22.*

Morrison, G. S. (1998). *Early childhood education today.* Upper Saddle River, NJ: Merrill/Prentice Hall.

Newsweek. (1997, Spring/Summer). Your child [Special issue].

Ogbu, J. U. (1988). Cultural diversity and human development. In D. Slaughter (Ed.), *Black children and poverty: A developmental perspective* (pp. 11–28) San Francisco: Jossey-Bass.

Osborn, D. K. (1991). *Early childhood education in historical perspective* (3rd ed.). Athens, GA: Education Associates.

Pollack, L. A. (1983). *Forgotten children.* London: Cambridge University Press.

Roopernarine, J. L., & Johnson, J. E. (1993). *Approaches to early childhood education.* New York: Macmillan.

Swap, S. M. (1993). *Developing home-school partnerships: From concepts to practice.* New York: Teachers College Press.

Trawick-Smith, J. W. (1997). *Early childhood development: A multicultural perspective.* Upper Saddle River, NJ: Merrill/Prentice Hall.

3 Building Partnerships with Families

Strategies for Collaboration

If this school was going to change its course and assume more than academic responsibility for its students, it would require a collaboration of minds, hearts, and hands.

Quint, 1994, p. 5

Key Terms

collaboration
common goal
culture
decision-making council
diversity
handbook
learning styles
multiple intelligences

newsletter
one-way communication
parent conference
parent meeting
respect
two-way communication
volunteer

The opening quote is a comment from Carole Williams, a Seattle school principal whose work in coming to terms with the dramatic needs of 350 children has been detailed in *Schooling Homeless Children: A Working Model for America's Public Schools* (Quint, 1994). These children, like many other children in America and across the globe, deal daily with issues of survival, including physical and emotional violence in their homes, schools, and neighborhoods; homelessness; parents emotionally and/or physically unavailable for parenting; and general lack of support systems. Williams' answer was to recognize that professionals within the schools must concern themselves with more than academics, which for many children and families were secondary to issues of survival. In your career, you may serve families headed by one parent responsible for supporting the family, managing the home, and raising the children; families with well-educated parents; families of children with disabilities; families headed by individuals who have been incarcerated; families with hours committed to volunteer time at the local school; families who distrust schools because of past personal experiences; foster families; and families who place their children's education above all else.

Regardless of lifestyle and resources, both human and material, families are the first teachers of young children. Even when those resources are limited, families care deeply about their children. Among the most poignant examples describing the work of families with their children is the ethnographic research of Denny Taylor and Catherine Dorsey-Gaines (1988). In *Growing Up Literate*, the authors document their fieldwork with families living in poverty in the inner city of a major metropolitan area in the Northeast. Irrespective of their financial situation, parents (a) were determined to raise healthy children, (b) provided loving environments, (c) created structured home environments with expectations for cooperation and participation, (d) were concerned about their children's safety and well-being, and (e) valued a growing sense of competence and independence.

Richard Clifford (1997), president of the National Association for the Education of Young Children (NAEYC), affirmed the position of early childhood professionals with respect to the family when he stated:

> We agree that we must recognize the child in the context of the family; appreciate and support the close ties between the child and the family; respect the dignity, worth and uniqueness of each family member; and help both children and adults reach their full potential. (p. 2)

This type of effort takes a partnership created by joining heads, hands, and hearts of loving adults—teachers, parents, grandparents, stepparents, administrators, caregivers, social workers, medical personnel, community members, and others. It also takes economic commitment and a willingness to advocate for resources for families. If partnerships are to be successful, all of those involved must be encouraged to make contributions of their gifts, talents, and resources to the lives of the children and families.

Teachers and administrators must remember that the parent is the child's first and most important teacher.

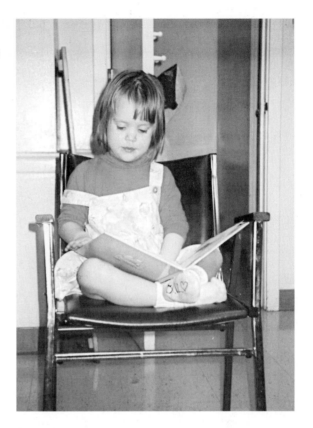

As we as teachers and caregivers work to build partnerships with families, we must do the following:

- *Examine* our own prejudices and preconceived ideas about how interested and capable families are on the basis of such factors as income, education, or ethnic background

- *Ask* parents what they need to assist them in nourishing the growth of their children, rather than make those decisions for them

- *Be creative* in developing strategies for involving families with diverse life situations, including dual-career families, single-parent families, families in need of child care to attend meetings, families with limited transportation, and families who for some reason feel intimidated by the school environment

- *Advocate* for the time and economic and human resources that are needed to implement programs involving families

- *Make declarations* in print, spoken words, and actions that address the school's commitment to involving families in the lives of children at school

The materials in this chapter are designed to address communication strategies that you may choose to employ in working with families. We

All adults working with children must seek ways to collaborate in their efforts to guide the growth of the children.

explore "lessons" from teachers in the field and teachers in preparation. Sample exercises are incorporated for practice. Later chapters provide you with opportunities to apply the strategies to specific situations, including working with families with adopted children, families affected by divorce and remarriage, and families with children with special needs. Techniques include the following:

- One-way communication strategies for involving families, including newsletters, policy manuals, happy grams, and bulletin boards
- Two-way communication strategies, including parent conferences, home visits, family theme bags, parent meetings, volunteer participation, shared videos, shared journals, and decision-making boards
- Selection of strategies based on the characteristics, strengths, and needs of families

◊◊ Collaborative Strategies

Parents and caregivers employ many strategies to ensure continuity between home and school. Some strategies involve **one-way communication** tools, such as policy manuals or handbooks, newsletters, and notes. Printed information involving one-way communication is essential for communicating with other people about the coming curriculum unit, an upcoming parent meeting,

Teachers must be aware of the diversity of families as they seek strategies to build partnerships with families.

"trashables" needed for classroom activities, school enrollment policies, and so on. Many schools employ voice mail, sending the same message from the teacher or administrator to all parents in the school. Such communication seeks to inform and document but does not always require a response. Hence, the communication is one-way. The handbook, used in the following example by Ms. Carole, is one way we use this type of communication.

At the beginning of each school year, Ms. Carole prepares a list of policies that are necessary in the operation of the school. This information is organized into the school handbook, along with the school calendar, daily schedule, and other important information. During the orientation meeting at the beginning of school, Ms. Carole discusses the policies and encourages discussion about their importance and relevance to the operation of the program.

In some situations, adults need more direct contact with all parties giving and receiving information. This requires **two-way communication** strategies. These include conferences, home visits, parent education meetings, parent volunteers, and impromptu conversations. Frequent two-way communication between home and school has long been viewed as an element of good practice toward achieving program-home continuity (Powell, 1994, p. 168). Consider the following example:

> Before the beginning of a new school year, Ms. Donna, head teacher at the Burrier Child Development Center, visited each child at home. She took games and books for the children, her camera to take photographs of the children at home, and any last-minute information for the parents. The children and parents got to know Ms. Donna. The photographs were placed on the bulletin board at school and were there for the children to see on arrival. These visits made the transition from home to school much easier for *both* children and adults.

Obviously, printed material is essential for providing information and documenting policies and procedures. The printed word cannot replace the invaluable information and insights we gain, however, when we look into another person's eyes, watch his or her body language, receive verbal responses, and have opportunities to make immediate responses to the other's comments and questions. This is particularly true in Ms. Kathy's nursery classroom at Ecumenical Preschool, where children come together from many parts of the world.

> When asked which strategy she found most helpful in communicating with parents who speak little or no English, Ms. Kathy indicated that, generally, someone in the community or family would serve as an interpreter. With time and patience and through trial and error, information can be shared.

As a teacher, caregiver, or administrator, you will take part in making decisions about the type of communication (one-way or two-way) that is needed for a particular event. These selections should take into consideration the type or intent of information to be shared, the need for input from family members, the characteristics of the families you are serving, and the viewpoints of the families on this topic.

At this point, you may find it helpful to explore your ideas about families and the types of expectations you may have, knowingly or unknowingly, of families. Many of these expectations and ideas come from your personal experiences with your own family. The first exercise in the set of additional exercises at the end of this chapter may be helpful to you as you examine your perceptions of families. In exploring your ideas, keep in mind the following:

A family is like no other family,
Like some other families and
Like all other families.
Hildebrand, Phenice, Gray, & Hines, 1996, p. 5

Strategies Involving One-Way Communication

Many methods for communicating with families involve print. They inform but do not involve two-way conversation, either oral or written, between individuals. Examples are handbooks, newsletters, bulletin boards, and notes or "happy grams." Teachers should be sensitive to families in which an individual does not read English or in which literacy is an issue. Compiling a list of individuals who are capable of interpreting oral and printed information to non-English-speaking families is helpful. Sensitivity should also be shown to families with joint custody arrangements so that both parents or guardians receive information about their child and school activities.

Handbooks.   A parent **handbook** is extremely helpful in keeping family members informed about the routine practices of the school. Many of these practices will be dictated by state and local licensing requirements, local public school policies, and/or requirements of accrediting agencies such as the National Academy of Early Childhood Programs, a division of NAEYC. Handbooks may be disseminated at the beginning of the school year during a parent orientation meeting so that individual policies can be discussed. They should also be available for distribution as new children enroll in the program. The handbook not only informs families about developmentally appropriate practices but also offers topics for discussion relative to the policies and practices. It serves as a written reminder when administrators, parents, or teachers do not follow stated policies and practices.

The handbook should be neat, organized, and without grammatical errors. The contents may include, but are not limited to, the following:

Name, address, and telephone numbers of the school

Staff names

Statement of philosophy and goals

Description of the school environment

Description of the curriculum

Hours of operation

Daily schedule

School calendar

Attendance policies

Costs of the program and procedures for making payment

Transportation information

Drop-off and pick-up information

Immunization and health requirements

Sick child attendance policies

Emergency procedures including for a sick or injured child

Weather emergencies

School clothing requirements

Articles to bring or not bring to school

Information about snacks and meals

Guidance policies

Field trip policies

Information about celebrations

Parent inclusion activities

Tentative curriculum units or projects

Information about licensing and accreditation agencies

Newsletters.   According to Harms and Cryer (1978), a **newsletter** has four objectives:

1. Keeping parents informed about activities conducted in the classroom each week
2. Giving parents insight into the educational purposes underlying activities
3. Enhancing children's and parents' abilities to communicate with each other
4. Reinforcing and extending school learning into the home, especially in the area of language development (p. 28)

With these objectives in mind, a teacher can prepare a 1- or 2-page weekly newsletter. Many teachers like to give these newsletters to families the week before the activities will occur so that parents can talk with their children about daily activities during the week and so that field trip information can be addressed. A newsletter may include the following:

A brief description of the daily activities for the week, with related concepts or goals

Words and movements to new songs and fingerplays being introduced

Information about field trips or special visitors to the classroom

Requests for parent participation

Requests for recyclables from home

Suggested activities for families to do at home that extend the concepts being introduced at school

Community events, parent-child "field trip" sites, and announcements of parenting workshops and experiences

As with other print materials, a newsletter is a representation of the school and should be neatly presented without grammatical errors. Many teachers draw or use "clip-art," or computer drawings, to emphasize their theme or project work with children and to attract the attention of family members to the newsletter. Children's art is also very useful here.

Activities that can be done at home with children should be kept in the context of daily activities. Families cannot always afford to purchase the materials a teacher may suggest, but they can save both time and money by using daily life experiences as teaching experiences for their children. For example, children in the classroom may be studying different types of homes. A drive or walk around the neighborhood or surrounding community provides great discussion among family members about different types of homes and the common bonds of love that may be found within those homes. Children can do simple rubbings of different construction materials found in homes, such as wood or stone, with the guidance of their families. Similarly, when color is being explored at school, children can be engaged in the sorting of laundry or the cans and boxes of food in a cabinet.

Recently, four students engaged in practice teaching in the Burrier Child Development Center collaborated on a month-long unit titled "Trains." The children explored and investigated types of trains, train personnel, use of trains, and safety with trains. The newsletter in Figure 3.1 is a sample of what may accompany a week of upcoming activities about trains. Work on ways you might enhance this newsletter by adding or deleting information and with illustrations. Brainstorm other ideas for how families can be involved in the children's work on trains.

Bulletin Boards.   In many early childhood programs, families provide their children's transportation to and from school. When adults accompany children into the school, they can see what is happening in the classroom and also view print materials such as those found on the parent or family bulletin board. Attractively arranged and uncluttered, this board should be located in an area easily viewed by parents as they bring children into the classroom. Displays may include schedules, thematic units and other classroom events, menus, celebration experiences, community happenings, field trip information, and relevant brochures and handouts. This is also an excellent space to provide photographic documentation of the children's activities and ongoing project work. Photographs should include written information that describes the event or experience being depicted. (Photographs must not be taken without written consent of parents, as well as consent of the preschool program administrators and teachers.)

Each day, Ms. Donna, head teacher of the Burrier Child Development Center, takes digital camera photographs of the children engaged in project work, playing in centers, or going on field trips. A photograph is selected and posted on the parent bulletin board, with a description of the day's event. Parents can ask their children to tell them more about the experience documented by the photographs.

Happy Grams.   A *happy gram* is a spontaneous form of written communication that shares a happy event or accomplishment with the family. Simply written on a sheet of paper, it states the event, such as "Today, Joshua put on his shoes and tied the laces by himself." Teachers may draw a parent's immediate attention to the message by using a clip art or drawn character and brightly colored paper designated for happy grams. These efforts to keep families aware of developmental accomplishments assist them in

Figure 3.1   A sample newsletter designed to share daily events with families

Dear Families:

   During the next 4 weeks the children and staff of the Burrier Child Development Center will be exploring "Trains." During the first week, we will focus on the many different types of trains and all the parts that make up trains. Isaac's father, Pat, will be visiting on Wednesday to share the model train set that he and Isaac have collected. This will give us a chance to look at the types and parts of trains more closely.
   The children will share in our reading of *The Little Engine that Could* by Watty Piper and *Freight Train* by Donald Crews. These books are available at the local library. We will also be singing a new song about trains. Ask your child to share this song with you!
   Several freight trains pass through town. A schedule is attached. Perhaps with your child you can watch one of these trains pass through town.
   Please help us collect empty cereal boxes, paper tubes, shoe boxes, egg cartons, wire, oatmeal boxes, and other "collectables" so that the children can construct their own trains. At the end of our 4 weeks, we hope to have a complete train set available constructed by the children.
   Please share other ideas you might have about trains. We're looking forward to a fun time!

   Mr. Heather, Ms. Terra, & Ms. Tonya

remaining "rooted" in their children's daily life while they are away at work and also serve to build bonds among caregivers and family members.

Strategies Involving Two-Way Communication

Parent-teacher conferences, home visits, parent meetings, classroom volunteer programs, and parents as members of boards and site-based decision-making councils all provide opportunities for ongoing two-way communication between and among school personnel and family members. Also, less traditional forms of two-way communication strategies are designed to meet the needs of working families and families involved in the care of younger children or other relatives. These strategies include family theme bags, classroom videos, and journal activities.

Family Theme Bags.   Many teachers, including Jeanne Helm (1994), use *theme bags* as a method for involving busy families in the lives of their children at school. For the safety of younger children, these bags should be made of cloth. Helm reports that each of her theme bags has a literacy focus reflecting the child's naturally emerging literacy. She includes an introductory letter, a journal for recording the events of the home experience, a puppet or stuffed animal, a file folder game, "what if" cards, songs and fingerplays, a storybook, and art supplies (p. 48). Such activities help family members (a) succeed in their role as educators of children, (b) feel like a part of the schooling experience, and (c) provide a point of reference for discussions in parent-teacher conferences and conversations.

Classroom Videos.   Many teachers find it increasingly difficult to involve family members in the firsthand experiences of their children at school. As an alternative measure, some teachers (Greenwood, 1995) support the use of videos that, in effect, bring activities of the classroom to the home. This nonprint medium captures the interests of parents and can be viewed at convenient moments during a family's day. Families without videotape players at home may view the tapes at school. Greenwood, a kindergarten teacher, tapes thematic unit activities, celebrations, classroom visitors, and "author's chair" activities. The videos are checked out and accompanied by a comment sheet so that the teacher can reflect on the viewpoints of the families. As with the theme bags, the videos provide a point of interest for discussions among family members and teachers. Written parental permission is required prior to videotaping children; consent must also be obtained from program personnel.

Family Journals.   The use of "journals" that travel back and forth between school and home has been a successful tool for bridging gaps in communication for some teachers. Some journals include written discourse of the teacher and the parent (Harding, 1996); others also include written discourse prepared by the child (Manning, Manning, & Morrison, 1995).

Children engaging in the written aspects of emerging literacy can use "newsbooks" designed to communicate weekly with their families about school events (Manning et al., 1995, p. 34). Each child has a three-ring binder that serves as the journal or newsbook. The teacher prepares a weekly newsletter with the input of the children. The children watch as the teacher engages their input with the draft design of the newsletter on chart paper. A copy of the final newsletter is included in each child's journal. Each child also writes a personal letter to his or her family each week. Both the teacher newsletter and the child's letter are sent home in the newsbook each week, along with paper for a parent's response. The children can share these letters with the teacher and their peers. No child is penalized because a parent has not responded. The letters and newsletters collect in the newsbook during the year as a record of events and the child's progress and interests. Teachers who use journals to communicate with families about their children's interests, fears, and daily activities notice the invaluable insights they gain concerning each family's goals and concerns for their child (Harding, 1996).

Home Visits.   *Home visits* have been a part of early childhood programs for many years. Teachers often arrange a visit to each child's home prior to the beginning of the school year or before the child begins his or her school experience. These visits provide an opportunity for parents and teachers to get to know one another away from groups of other children and for parents and teacher to spend time together in the company of the child. Depending on the goal of the program, home visits have been included as an effective means to teach parents, assist families, bring materials and information to both child and parents, and establish a relationship between home and school (Fox-Barnett & Meyer, 1992, p. 46).

The type of home visit that works best in focusing on the growth and development of the child involves a "child-centered" approach. During this type of visit, parents and teacher may engage in play with the child, discuss what the child will be doing at school and the role the parents may play, and basically get to know one another. The purpose of this visit is not to engage parents in filling out forms or other administrative tasks. Although teachers do become more aware of the strengths of individual family members in parenting, it is also not the purpose of this visit to "judge" the child's home environment.

Teachers should always schedule prearranged home visits and make an attempt to visit the home when each of the adults involved in the child's care is present. Visits will need to accommodate parent work schedules. A 1-hour visit is generally appropriate.

Many teachers find it helpful to organize a home visit kit. Materials are placed into a basket or other container that can be covered. Teachers may want to include the following:

A camera for taking photographs for the children to share once in the classroom (always get permission from the adult)

A favorite book for children

A simple game or puzzle

Markers and paper

Something special to leave with the child as a reminder of the visit

During the visit, the teacher can read the book to the child. If visits are made prior to the beginning of school, the book can serve as a good transition tool for each child visited; it can then be available for reading in the classroom on the first day of school. An adult, either parent or teacher, can encourage the child in working the puzzle, drawing, or engaging in some other favorite activity during the visit. Such activities provide a focus of discussion related to the child and occupy the child. Photographs taken can be displayed on the bulletin board or in a scrapbook at school as documentation of the visit and as another tool for easing the child's transition from home to school.

While a practicum student in the Burrier Child Development Center, Ms. Naomi shared a wonderful idea of taking an album containing photographs of her family, of her home, and of her as a child to her home visit. This assisted the family in getting to know her and more about her native country, Japan.

To make the most of the visit, it is appropriate for the home visitor to request that the television be turned off during the visit, that a space be set aside for using the materials with the child, and that both parents participate. The teacher can model activities with the child, involve the parents as teachers, and encourage both the parents and the child.

As visits are made at the beginning of and throughout the school year, it is important that you consider the following:

- Families are of many kinds. Respect for the child dictates that the teacher remain nonjudgmental with regard to family lifestyle.

- Knowledge of **culture** is important in working with families. However, teachers sometimes stereotype families with knowledge they may obtain about specific cultures. Derman-Sparks (1989) cautions teachers to remember that although cultural patterns are real and affect all members of an ethnic group, families live their cultures in their own individual ways (see Chapter 4).

- Listen to individual members of families for ideas about ways you can assist them in fostering the growth and development of their children. Encourage them to verbalize what they feel comfortable in doing with and for their children.

- Recognize the stresses placed on families, including dual careers, economic uncertainty, care for elderly grandparents, care for younger children, and information that bombards children from various media, including print, television, video games, and computer technology.

- Be prepared to work as a team member with each family.
- Be prepared to admit to family members that you may not have all the answers but that you are willing to assist them in finding appropriate resources.

In addition to the 1-hour home visit described, programs may also be home-based, with the child's school program occurring in the home. Head Start provides a long-term example of such a model that exemplifies the focus on reinforcing the parent's role as the primary educator of the child (U.S. Department of Health and Human Services [DHHS], 1990). Other programs are offered as support for families with young children with disabilities. Activities prepared and implemented by home-based teachers are designed to foster the development of the child, with or without disabilities, and to encourage the parents in their role as their child's first and most important teachers and caregivers.

Some families do not want teachers to visit their homes. Obviously, home visits are an impossibility for families who are homeless and for some families who live in chaos. Teachers can offer alternatives, such as visiting at a library or having a picnic in a local park. These alternatives provide one-on-one attention and an opportunity for enhanced communication and understanding relative to the child. As noted by Fox-Barnett and Meyer (1992), "Children who experience one hour of the teacher's undivided attention feel special and important" (p. 46). Adults may have similar feelings.

Conferences with Families.   Although families should always have opportunities to schedule parent-teacher conferences, schools should schedule set parent-teacher conferences at least twice during the school year. These conferences should be a time for sharing information about the children's interests and emerging styles of learning, interesting anecdotes, and developmental progress over time in each aspect of development. During these conferences, it is important to remember that parents know their children best and that conferences are indeed for sharing. Preparing for and implementing the **parent conference** include the following steps: (a) compiling documentation of the child's progress that can be used as a framework for the conference, (b) setting the environment for the conference in ways that will ensure physical comfort and two-way communication, and (c) following up on parents' requests.

The conference portfolio.   Documentation of a child's interests, developmental characteristics, and progress can be compiled in a conference portfolio. The portfolio can serve as a tool for authentic assessment and assist you as an adult in organizing your thoughts. It is one thing to be an observer of young children as most of us enjoy watching the wonderful ways children interact with their worlds. We move to another level of our development as teachers and caregivers, however, when we draw meaning from our observations of a child by relating the observed behaviors to developmental norms and to our expectations of that child. These expectations are generally based on our prior experiences with that child and children of similar age. The purpose of the developmental portfolio becomes threefold: (a) It provides you with an opportunity to learn more about the intricacies of the growth and development of the individual child; (b) it provides you with visually descriptive material that documents the child's development over time and in various situations that can be shared with the child, parents, and colleagues; and (c) it provides you with information about the types of opportunities for learning that will be developmentally appropriate for that child and be relevant to the child's experiences and learning style. These opportunities are designed to foster the child's growth, development, and excitement about learning.

The Portfolio and Its Use: Developmentally Appropriate Assessment of Young Children (Grace & Shores, 1992) serves as a very helpful guide in preparing an assessment portfolio. Materials should be arranged in a ring binder (2-inch is usually sufficient) with sections separated by dividers. In addition to your narrative comments, artifacts used to document the various aspects of the child's development and personality will include well-organized anecdotal notes; videotapes; audiotapes; photographs of block structures, dress-up activities, project activities, artwork, and so on; copies of dictated comments and stories; and samples of the child's writing and scribbling. Vinyl covers are useful in protecting the photographs and other documentation. Pages are organized as follows:

Section I: Title Page

Photograph of the Child

Brief Description

This will be typed below the photograph and will include the child's name, date of birth, information about the family, child's interests, personality characteristics, and so on. This page "introduces" the child to the reader.

Section II: Observer Sign-Off Sheet

The information collected that summarizes _____
(name of child)

development and interests was compiled during _____.
(date)

_____
(Name of the Observer)

_____
(Date)

Section III: Fine Motor Development

Overview Page

Photograph of the child (with date and description) that depicts fine motor development

Paragraph that summarizes the child's fine motor development, using specific examples

Supporting documentation

Typed and organized anecdotal records

Relevant sections of checklists

Overviews of video and audio recordings

Photographs depicting the child engaged in fine motor activity (with descriptions and dates)

Section IV: Gross Motor Development

Overview Page

Photograph of the child (with description and date) that depicts the child engaged in gross motor activities

Paragraph that summarizes the child's gross motor skills and interests, using specific examples

Supporting Documentation

Typed and organized anecdotal records

Relevant sections of checklists

Overviews of video and audio recordings

Photographs depicting the child engaged in gross motor activity (with descriptions and dates)

Section V: Concept Development

Overview Page

Photograph of the child (with description and date) that depicts the child engaged in concept development activities

Paragraph that summarizes the child's concept skills and interests, using specific examples

Supporting Documentation

Typed and organized anecdotal records

Relevant sections of checklists

Overviews of video and audio recordings

Photographs depicting the child engaged in concept activities (with descriptions and dates)

Section VI: Language and Literacy Development

Overview Page

Photograph of the child (with description and date) that depicts the child engaged in language and literacy events

Paragraph that summarizes the language and literacy skills and interests, using specific examples

Supporting Documentation

Typed and organized anecdotal records

Relevant sections of checklists

Overviews of video and audio recordings

Photographs depicting the child engaged in language and literacy events (with descriptions and dates)

Lists of children's books that the child seems to enjoy

Photographs or $8\frac{1}{2} \times 11''$ copies of the child's "writing"

Section VII: Personosocial Development

Overview Page

   Photograph of the child (with description and date) that depicts the child engaged in personosocial events

   Paragraph that summarizes the personosocial skills and interests, using specific examples

Supporting Documentation

   Typed and organized anecdotal records

   Relevant sections of checklists

   Overviews of video and audio recordings

   Photographs depicting the child engaged in personosocial activities (with descriptions and dates)

Section VIII: Suggested Program of Activities

Your in-depth observation of the child, conducted in the authentic environment of the classroom, yields a great deal of knowledge about the humanness of this child and his or her talents and joys. You may also discover areas that require more intense consideration. Do not ignore the talents and joys, however, because these are a vital part of the whole child. Plan for those areas as you would the child's areas of need or concern.

   In planning activities, "listen" to the child—with your ears and with your eyes. Visualize a scaffold on the side of a building where workers are positioned at different levels. Each one's work depends on the foundation being placed by other workers. Now, substitute learning experiences in the hands of each of those workers. Children have both experiences that are designed to meet their needs today (the foundation) and experiences that will come in the future to extend their learning and to challenge them to explore and investigate the wonders of new "worlds." The following is a very concrete example found in many early childhood settings.

◊ *Today, the child may be working a 4-piece puzzle with knobs on the handles of each piece. We provide several of these puzzles to help strengthen skills. However, we also place on the shelf several more difficult puzzles with interesting themes to interest the child and be available for exploration as he or she becomes more interested and developmentally capable of completing them.*

Preparing for the conference. In addition to the preparation of the conference portfolio, the teacher will need to prepare the conference schedule, allotting about 30 minutes for each conference. Conferences for the purposes of developing individualized education programs (IEPs) and individualized family service plans (IFSPs) will take much longer. Conferences will need to be scheduled to accommodate parents' work schedules. For a child who has two parents or more than one guardian, it is appropriate to include both parties. The physical space should be comfortable, with a table for displaying the conference portfolio. Adult-size chairs arranged around a round or oval table provides for comfort and prevents the feeling of a barrier between adults often caused by the teacher sitting behind a desk. Audiovisual equipment for playing audio- or videotapes should be set up and operable. Arrangements should be made to prevent interruptions by loudspeakers, children, or other adults.

Teachers preparing for a conference with a family of a child with disabilities should be cognizant of grief issues that may surface during the parent-teacher discussion. "Parental reaction to a handicapping condition is highly individualistic. Each parent will respond in his or her own way" (Gargiulo & Graves, 1990, p. 177). Teachers may encounter stages of emotional responses among families, including denial, anger, grief, guilt, and shame. These stages are often ongoing, with feelings resurfacing in reaction to changes, needs, and developmental milestones of the child (Bailey & Wolery, 1984).

Teachers will also need to be aware of cultural practices and expectations of the families participating in conferences. For example, a father may be seen as the only acceptable individual from the family unit to engage in conversation with the teacher. Teachers may also need to arrange for an interpreter if language is an issue.

Conducting the conference. Preparing the portfolio serves as a tool in directing the teacher's observations to each child. In a sense, it demands that the teacher relate his or her knowledge of child development to the actual behaviors and experiences of each child. Therefore, by the time the conference occurs, the teacher should feel confident that he or she knows the child. Generally, however, the parent knows the child best, and this must be kept at the front of the teacher's thoughts as the conference is conducted. The portfolio serves as a focus for describing the child's development in the context of developmentally appropriate practice and for fostering mutual discussion about the child's interests and possible experiences for promoting ongoing development.

Greet the family members in a culturally appropriate manner. Give the parents your attention both nonverbally (eye contact and unfolded arms) and verbally. Open the conference with a positive anecdote about the child. Outline the purpose of the conference. Review the portfolio, encouraging parental input. Remember that every child has strengths and that these should be discussed first. Acknowledge the parents' beliefs and concerns about their child. Reflective statements such as "It sounds like you are concerned about Susan listening to instructions" helps ensure that you have "heard" what the parent said. If you do not understand the meaning of a parent's comments, ask questions for clarification of meaning. Answer a parent's questions, being honest when you do not know answers. Use terms that can be understood by the nonteaching individual; professional jargon can be intimidating and inhibit the flow of discussion. Keep the focus on discussion of the child. Close the conference with concrete suggestions for continued work with the child, such as parent-child story times and positive ways to encourage the child's independence in the context of daily activities.

Teachers are often called to participate in meetings designed to develop programs for children with disabilities. Parents may participate in meetings with as many as five or more professionals giving information about their child. When working with families with children who have disabilities, remember that these families face great challenges that may be ongoing throughout their children's lives. Showing sensitivity and **respect** for the parents' perspective of their child's disability is essential for a partnership to be formed. In many cases, the parents know more about the child's disability and progress than the teacher because they have been so intimately involved in the child's life.

Gargiulo and Graves (1990) make the following suggestions for teachers working with parents of children with disabilities:

- Explain terminology.
- Send the message that it is acceptable and understandable to have negative feelings when confronted with news that a child has a disability.
- Listen to the parents' needs and concerns.
- Use a two-step process when initially informing parents that their child requires special education services. After presenting diagnostic information, allow parents time to comprehend and absorb what they have been told before working together to plan intervention strategies.
- Keep parents informed by using two-way communication techniques and demonstrating respect, concern, and a sincere desire to cooperate.
- Be accountable. If you agree to provide parents with specific information, follow through on your agreement. This assists in building trust.
- Recognize that all parents will not respond in the same way to intervention strategies, depending on family structures and parenting styles. Respect a parent's right to choose his or her level of involvement (p. 178).

Following up the conference.   Document the date and events of the conference. If you agreed to locate materials or resources for the family, do so in a timely fashion. Observe professional ethics by respecting the confidentiality of family-teacher communications.

Parent Meetings.   **Parent meetings** can serve a variety of purposes. Orientation meetings at the beginning of the year provide information to families about the program, including curriculum events, schedules, and policies and procedures. Other parent meetings may be held for the purpose of highlighting children's activities, including plays and parent nights to visit opened classrooms. Social activities provide opportunities for families to spend time getting to know one another in the context of the school environment.

The focus of this parent meeting discussion here is on those meetings designed to enhance parenting skills in such a way that the growth and development of the child is nurtured and the family unit is strengthened. Even though families have issues in common with their predecessors, such as what to do when a child bites or when siblings fight, today's families have issues that are unique to this time.

Some contemporary writers (e.g., Postman, 1985) believe that childhood is disappearing, with children and families being bombarded with information through various media including television, video games, computer networks, movies, and print materials. Through these media, children are exposed to violence, crimes, sexual practices, and adult situations that are far beyond the developmental capabilities of their understanding. Parents often complain that their child knows far more about certain subjects than they did when they were the child's age and more than they feel comfortable with the child knowing. Today, parents ask for information about teaching children to protect themselves from strangers, helping children adjust to divorce and remarriage, and helping the parents know as much about computers as their 5-year-old!

It is important to be aware of the needs of families when you plan meetings so that you can assist families in their dilemma. Consequently, families should be surveyed with respect to topics of critical importance, convenient times for meetings, needs for child care during meetings, and transportation concerns. Surveys can be both written and verbal communications between and among teachers and families. If written, surveys should be very brief. The rate of return on responses will be greater if surveys can be handed to school personnel, rather than mailed back to the teacher. Parent committees can also be formed to offer topics and ideas for parent education activities.

Whether planned by parents, teachers, or a team, meetings should follow certain guidelines:

- The topic should be family focused and reflect parents' concerns.
- Each meeting should have specific goals that are shared at the opening of the meeting.
- Each meeting should be organized with an agenda that is shared with participants.
- Meetings should begin and end on time. One hour is usually an appropriate length for meetings.
- Get-acquainted activities and icebreakers should be planned, and nametags should be used for both parents and teachers.

- The physical setting should be comfortable in terms of seating, lighting, and temperature.
- Seating should afford parents an opportunity to make eye contact with several other individuals; they will be more likely to engage in conversation.
- The presentation should include time for parents to be participants and not rely solely on a lecture format.
- Family members should be given ample opportunity to ask questions.
- Parents should be given opportunities to evaluate the meeting at its close. Written evaluations should be simple and to the point.
- Families should be provided handouts to reinforce those points stressed during the meeting.

If a team of teachers and parents is planning the meetings, it is important that they meet soon after each meeting to discuss its success and ways meetings can be improved. Written and oral comments of parents are critical to this process. "Involving parents in the planning process is just another of the many ways you show respect for them and their role" (Foster, 1994, p. 80).

Volunteers.   Parents and other family members, including grandparents (Latimer, 1994), can be very effective as **volunteers** within the classroom. Volunteers lend support to the classroom teacher while building their knowledge about child development and developmentally appropriate practice. Certainly, the Head Start model has provided many examples of the methods and successes of including family members as a part of the educational experiences of the school setting (DHHS, 1990).

In many schools, however, the term *parent volunteer* has been equated with a parent who makes photocopies, bakes cookies, organizes classroom parties, and supervises field trips. Even though these are important tasks, they do little to assist the parent in understanding what is going on in the classroom in terms of actual learning experiences or in recognizing the important role the parent plays in the education of the child. Parents are more likely to participate when they see that their involvement can benefit their child and that they are valued as a part of their child's education (Brand, 1996).

Participants in PITCH (Project Interconnecting Teachers, Children, and Homes) for Literacy used parent volunteers. Through class surveys, teachers learned that parents wanted more specific guidance and feedback from the teachers. They also wanted to know how their work as parents in the classroom was related to the teacher's curriculum goals (Brand, 1996, p. 77).

Kathleen Knowler (1988), director of the Unitarian Early Education Cooperative in Arizona, outlined eight steps to be used in orienting volunteers working in the cooperative nursery school. These can be adapted to many programs and are summarized as follows:

1. Parents are asked to visit the classroom before they enroll their child so that they can be accustomed to the hands-on experiences of the children.

2. Potluck luncheons are held prior to participation so that teachers and parents can discuss what is going on in the classroom and how the needs of the children are being met by the activities. An orientation handbook is distributed and discussed.

3. Before the beginning of school, parents are asked to participate in a workday of cleaning and organizing materials. This helps parents know where materials are located and why those locations are important.

4. A teacher makes home visits to parents before they begin their volunteer work. This gives the parents an opportunity to ask questions about their involvement.

5. Parents attend a day of class with their child so that they can be accustomed to the posted schedule and the routines followed by children and teachers.

6. After the first week, a parent orientation is held during which program participants are introduced and videos of the program are shown. Staff members engage in a panel discussion about the use of such materials as blocks or modeling clay.

7. Follow-up monthly meetings are held, with the first addressing issues of child guidance.

8. Orientation continues throughout the year via newsletters and telephone calls to parents. (p. 9)

Additional strategies for working with volunteers are the use of bulletin boards, file boxes of activities, and notebooks that outline daily assignments that may be conducted by volunteers. As described at the beginning of this chapter, each adult reflects particular styles of learning and interests. Teachers should be cognizant of these features and use the gifts of parent volunteers accordingly.

Decision-Making Boards and Councils.   Families should always be engaged in decision making with respect to their child's care and education. Organizations such as the Parent Teacher Association (PTA) and the Parent Teacher Organization (PTO) have offered avenues for parents to express concerns and ideas. More formal options, however, such as boards and councils, offer parents opportunities to have responsibility in the decisions that affect their children and families. Such decision making should mean "a process of partnership, of shared views and actions toward shared goals, not just a power struggle between conflicting ideas" (Epstein, 1995, p. 705).

Head Start is a historic example of a program that has delegated decision-making responsibility to three groups: the center committee, the parent policy committee, and the parent policy council. Both membership and leadership are democratically chosen. Each group has specific tasks and agendas. Through such efforts, family members have "ownership" in the decisions that affect the programs in which their children participate. These opportunities empower families in the care and education of their children (DHHS, 1990).

Public school programs are also making efforts to provide more direct involvement of parents in the decision making of policies and practices in the school. In Kentucky's version, known as *school-based decision making*, each council is composed of one administrator, two parents elected by the largest parent-teacher organization, and three teachers elected by the faculty. The councils make decisions in the following areas:

Selection of the school principal from a list; provided by the superintendent should a vacancy occur

Consultation with the principal with respect to hiring instructional and noninstructional personnel should vacancies occur

Determination of curriculum

Assignment of instructional and noninstructional staff time

Assignment of children to classes and programs within the school

Schedule of the school day and week within the context of the schedule and calendar established by the local school board

Use of school space during the school day

Planning and resolution of issues regarding instructional practices

Selection and implementation of discipline and classroom management techniques

Selection of extracurricular programs and policies regarding student participation

Procedures for aligning programs with state standards, technology use, and program appraisal in cooperation with the local board (Lindle, 1994, p. 21)

Even though they require additional time of the teachers involved, such councils provide opportunities for members of the community to work with school personnel in making collaborative decisions that affect the lives of children. In these cases, not only are children shared, but responsibility for important decisions are as well.

◊◊ Selecting Appropriate Strategies

You have already read a great deal about two categories of methods for communicating with families—one-way and two-way communication strategies. You have also had an opportunity to explore when specific strategies would be most appropriate. You may also want to consider additional aspects of the process of selecting the best methods for engaging family members in activities with their children in early childhood programs. We as teachers seem at times to assume that, because parents are adults, they can fully absorb the information we present to them through oral or written language. In fact, Dodge (1993), in her work with adult learners, notes that people generally remember 10% of what they read, 20% of what they hear,

30% of what they see, 50% of what they see and hear, 70% of what they say or write, and 90% of what they say as they do a thing. Therefore, the least effective medium for learning is verbal receiving and the most effective is the combination of hearing, saying, seeing, and doing.

In planning **collaboration** strategies, it is also important to remember that adults, like children, do not all learn in the same ways—nor do people all have the same interests and abilities. Perhaps Howard Gardner has been the most helpful in bringing teachers to understand the different ways that children learn in accordance with personalities and general personal characteristics. In his theory of **multiple intelligences,** Gardner (1985; Shores, 1995) outlines eight types of intelligences that are related to the natural **learning styles** of individuals: (a) bodily-kinesthetic, (b) intrapersonal, (c) interpersonal, (d) naturalistic, (e) musical, (f) logical-mathematical, (g) visual-spatial, and (h) linguistic. Some children show a natural inclination toward drawing and understanding spatial concepts, some toward music, some toward physical activities, and so on. Just as children show these interests and "talents," so do adults. Adults' learning styles are often depicted in their chosen careers and hobbies. Architects and builders have visual-spatial talents. Individuals who garden or enjoy encounters with nature are expressing their tendencies toward naturalistic learning.

As teachers and administrators select and implement strategies or engage families in work and play with their children at home and at school, it is important to remember that the child is the common bond that links the school, community, and family. "Our understanding of parent involvement needs to be on a continuum that allows for parent participation on a variety of levels and through a wide variety of activities" (Gage & Workman, 1994, p. 77). This understanding occurs when teachers become aware of the goals that families have for their children and when they are cognizant of the mutually identified strengths and concerns of the families and the individuals who make up those families. Finally, parent involvement activities must reflect the range of specific learning styles and talents represented by adults and the general ways in which people learn.

Summary Statements ◇

- The parent is the child's first and most important teacher.
- The success of parents in nurturing their children is affected by societal issues such as political and economic concerns, as well as by the personal growth and development of the individuals within the family.

- "Culture rules how we position our bodies, how we touch each other, what we regard as mannerly, how we look at the world, how we think, what we see as art, how we sense time and perceive space, what we think is important, and how we set immediate and lifelong goals" (Lyon, 1995, p. 51).

Professionals in early childhood have been pioneers in building partnerships with families.

- Schools, families, and communities have a **common goal:** to guide their children to adulthood.

- Schools, families, and communities must collaborate, with the focus remaining on the growth and development of the child.

- The early childhood field has been a pioneer in building partnerships with parents.

- Many cultures, lifestyles, and family practices are represented in school programs. Teachers must be cognizant of and respect such **diversity** in valuing each child.

- Many types of one-way communication strategies are designed to provide information to parents, including handbooks, newsletters, videos, and notes.

- Many types of two-way communication strategies are designed to provide parents with opportunities to engage in school-related aspects of the care and education of their children, including parent conferences, home visits, volunteering, parent meetings, and **decision-making councils.**

Activities ◇◇◇

1. The children in Ms. Anderson's kindergarten class have become very excited watching a house being built across from the school. They have watched the space being excavated, the foundation being prepared and poured, and the framework for the house being created. They have asked many questions about planning houses and the construction materials. Their interest could evolve into some type of project. How might

you involve family members in a related classroom project with the children?

2. Janet's mother is single and is caring for 6-year-old Janet and her two younger siblings. Recently, the mother has returned to college to improve her job skills so that she can support her family. Knowing how busy Janet's mother is, how can you assist her in becoming involved in Janet's school program?

3. Recently, the kindergarten class at your school celebrated Mother's Day with a tea for the mothers and their children. You are a student teacher in that class. You noted that some mothers were unavailable to attend the tea because of their work or lack of physical proximity to their children. Discuss how you think this experience might affect young children and whether you would repeat this activity in your classroom someday.

4. As the head teacher in the college preschool program, you often have children from other countries enrolled in your class. Their parents are completing degrees and want their children to have opportunities to be with other children and to practice English. This year, for the first time, you have several families from Saudi Arabia. How would you prepare for the enrollment of these children?

5. Cheyenne's mother volunteered to work with the 3-year-old class 2 days per week. You were delighted to have the extra help. After several weeks of volunteering, however, Cheyenne's mother still could not separate herself from her daughter. She was critical of her daughter's artwork, how she sat in a circle, and how she spoke to the teachers. Cheyenne was obviously not enjoying this experience. What strategies might you employ in working with this mother?

6. Dan's parents are divorced. They have joint custody, and Dan spends alternating weekends with his father. Recently, you saw Dan's father at the local grocery, and he expressed concern that he knew nothing about Dan's school life. All paperwork was sent to Dan's mother and not shared with him. As a teacher, what, if anything, would you do about this situation?

7. Recently, some migrant families from Mexico moved into the rural Midwest town where you teach first grade. On enrollment of the children, it is obvious that language is a barrier for adults and children. What might you do to ease this situation and to include the families in school experiences?

8. Four-year-old Rachel has difficulty with speech. At times, she becomes so frustrated that she points at what she wants, rather than uses her speech. You are preparing for a conference at which you will suggest that Rachel have a speech and language evaluation. How will you prepare for this meeting with Rachel's parents, who have indicated that she will "outgrow" this problem, and what strategies might you employ in conducting the conference?

Additional Exercises ◇◇◇◇◇◇◇◇◇◇◇◇◇◇◇◇◇◇◇◇◇◇◇◇◇◇◇◇◇◇◇◇◇◇

Exercise 1: How Do I View Families?

Individually or as a part of group discussion, complete the following:

1. Define *family*.

2. Describe what your family of origin is like.

3. Describe the way your family is like no other family.

4. What do you perceive as the strengths of your family with respect to parenting

skills and how you view those strengths as contributing to your personal goals for education, career, and personal growth?

5. In what ways were your parent(s) involved with the schools and/or caregiving situations in which you participated?

6. How do you think parents should be involved in school and/or caregiver situations?

7. As a parent, how are you, or how would you like to be, involved in your child's school?

Discuss your answers with other members of your class. Do you think your ideas are realistic or idealistic? What factors might change your answers?

Exercise 2: Designing a Family Bulletin Board

Sketch a sample bulletin board that contains information from parents. (Assume that parents will be picking up their children from school.) Evaluate your design for appeal to the eye, ease with which information can be seen, and general use to families. You may want to use a large poster board so that the design can be shared with others in the class for their input and feedback.

Exercise 3: A Collection of Happy Grams

Design three happy grams that use common themes for preschool programs (e.g., horses, trains, the sky, families). Share the happy grams with your classmates.

Exercise 4: Themes in a Bag

Choose a thematic topic or items of interest to young children. Examples are "colors," "shapes," and "bugs." In a large resealable bag, gather materials that will assist the par-

ent in enjoying this topic at home. Include an index card with clearly printed instructions for the adult. Share the bag with another early childhood professional or a child to ensure the materials are appropriate.

Exercise 5: "Lights, Camera, Action"

As part of a long-term project, videotape or collect videotapes of young children engaged in developmentally appropriate preschool activities. Write a script to accompany a portion of the videotape that enhances parent awareness of the importance of play in the developmental process.

Exercise 6: Planning a Home Visit Kit

Working with classmates as a team, select materials that would be used in a home visit kit. Decide on the age of the child, types of activities that might be appropriate, order of presentation, and ways to introduce the materials to the child and family members. Role-play enacting the home visit, rotating the persons serving as parent, visitor, and child. Discuss possible strategies for making the home visit more effective.

Exercise 7: Parent Meetings

Attend a parent meeting at a local school. Observe the physical arrangement of the meeting space. Were the parents comfortable and able to see the materials presented through audiovisuals? Did the arrangement of chairs facilitate parent participation? In what ways were parents encouraged to participate? What do you think was the outcome of the meeting? Did the purpose of the meeting seem to be met?

Exercise 8: Policy Handbooks

Collect policy handbooks from several programs. Compare their policies on immunization and health requirements. How are they alike, and how are they different? Can the information be easily understood by all parents? Why or why not? Practice writing your

own policy statement regarding health requirements for enrolling a child in a preschool program. Check for grammar. Share your policy statement with other members of the class.

References ◇◇

Bailey, D., & Wolery, M. (1984). *Teaching infants and preschoolers with handicaps.* Upper Saddle River, NJ: Merrill/Prentice Hall.

Brand, S. (1996). Making parent involvement a reality: Helping teachers develop partnerships with parents. *Young Children, 51,* 76–81.

Clifford, R. M. (1997). Partnerships with families. *Young Children, 52,* 2.

Dodge, D. T. (1993). *A guide for supervisors and trainers on implementing the creative curriculum for early childhood.* Washington, DC: Teaching Strategies.

Epstein, J. L. (1995). School/family/community partnerships: Caring for the children we share. *Phi Delta Kappan, 76,* 701–712.

Foster, S. M. (1994). Successful parent meetings. *Young Children, 50,* 78–80.

Fox-Barnett, M., & Meyer, T. (1992). The teacher's playing at my house this week! *Young Children, 47,* 45–50.

Gage, J., & Workman, S. (1994). Creating family support systems: In Head Start and beyond. *Young Children, 50,* 74–77.

Gardner, H. (1985). *Frames of the mind: The theory of multiple intelligences.* New York: Basic Books.

Gargiulo, R. M. & Graves, S. B. (1990). Parental feelings: The forgotten component when working with parents of handicapped preschool children. *Childhood Education, 67,* 176–178.

Grace. C., & Shores, E. (1992). *The portfolio and its use: Developmentally appropriate assessment of young children.* Little Rock, AR: SECA.

Greenwood, D. (1995). Home-school communication via video. *Young Children, 50,* 66.

Harding, N. (1996). Family journals: The bridge from school to home and back again. *Young Children, 51,* 27–30.

Harms, T. 0., & Cryer, D. (1978). Parent newsletter: A new format. *Young Children, 33,* 28–32.

Helm, J. (1994). Family theme bags: An innovative approach to family involvement in the school. *Young Children, 49,* 48–53.

Hildebrand, V., Phenice, L. A., Gray, M. M., & Hines, R. P. (1996). *Knowing and serving diverse families.* Upper Saddle River, NJ: Merrill/Prentice Hall.

Knowler, K. A. (1988). Caregivers' corner: Orienting parents and volunteers to the classroom. *Young Children, 44,* 9.

Latimer, D. J. (1994). Involving grandparents and other older adults in the preschool classroom. *Dimensions of Early Childhood, 22,* 26–30.

Lindle, J. C. (1994). Kentucky's reform opens doors to family involvement. *Dimensions in Early Childhood, 22,* 20–22.

Lyon, S. (1995). What is my culture? *Child Care Information Exchange, 51.*

Manning, M., Manning, G., & Morrison, G. (1995). Letter-writing connections: A teacher, first graders, and their parents. *Young Children, 50,* 34–38.

Postman, N. (1985). *The disappearance of childhood.* New York: Vintage.

Powell, D. R. (1994). Parents, pluralism, and the NAEYC statement on developmentally appropriate practice. In B. R. Mallory & R. S. New (Eds.), *Diversity and developmentally appropriate practices: Challenges for early childhood educators* (pp. 166–182). New York: Teachers College Press.

Quint, S. (1994). *Schooling homeless children: A working model for America's public schools.* New York: Teachers College Press.

Shores, E. F. (1995). Howard Gardner on the eighth intelligence: Seeing the natural world. *Dimensions of Early Childhood, 23,* 5–7.

Taylor, D., Dorsey-Gaines, C. (1988). *Growing up literate: Learning from inner-city families*. Portsmouth, NH: Heinemann.

U.S. Department of Health and Human Services (DHHS). (1990). *A handbook for involving parents in Head Start* (DHHS Publication No. 90-31187). Rockville, MD: Author.

II Profiles of Individual Families in America

4 Cross-Cultural Issues Involving Families and the Community

To be included is not merely to be present, but to participate, to influence, and to be influenced by the communities in which one lives, works, and learns.

Mallory & New, 1994, p. 11

Key Terms

antibias
bias
character
culture
developmentally appropriate
  practice
discrimination
diversity
emergent curriculum
enculturation
ethnocentrism
independence

interdependence
minority
morality
morals
multicultural
prejudice
Reggio Emilia
social cognition
sociocultural
stereotype
values
webbing

Across cultures, a young child's journey to adulthood is accomplished within the context of the family and surrounding community. The child's unique spirit, personality, interests, abilities, ways of knowing, and ways of seeing oneself in the context of the immediate world result from the meshing of genetic predispositions and the influences of parents, other family members, and other primary caregivers who have played significant roles in that child's young life.

As children grow, their near environment extends beyond that of immediate family, close friends of the family, and other primary caregivers. It encompasses the "community of the neighborhood" as children become involved with other children and families through informal play situations, sports activities, special-interest activities, and the building of lasting friendships. It also includes those influences found in more formal settings, including day care, schools, and places of worship.

In the best of worlds, children are valued and protected from influences that place their lives in jeopardy. In reality, however, many children are subjected to the abuse of adults, gang and drug violence, homes filled with chaos, and the "robbing" of their childhoods. These tragedies are depicted

Across cultures, a child's journey to adulthood is accomplished in the context of family and culture.

in graphic form in such contemporary writings as Jonathan Kozol's (1995) *Amazing Grace: The Lives of Children and the Conscience of a Nation.*

As children become young adults, many will move from the homes of their childhoods to experience new homes at college; in new cities where jobs are found; with husbands or wives; across the globe in the service of their country, their faith, or their jobs; or simply in another part of the neighborhood where their lives continue to intertwine with those of their families and childhood friends. Wherever the journey, their "humanness" urges them to seek the places where they feel a sense of connectedness with others and of "belonging." In these settings is a reciprocity as individuals influence, and are influenced by, others. The beliefs, **values,** attitudes, languages, and ideologies experienced in childhood will play a part in whatever path a child takes as she or he moves toward adulthood. Some practices of childhood will be cherished; others will be discarded as not in keeping with a new way of living. Added will be the beliefs, values, and practices "adopted" or taken in from the experiences with individuals and institutions on the road to adulthood.

In his ecological approach to explaining human development and behavior, Bronfenbrenner (1988) notes that development occurs in the context of daily lives. In its complexity, "the developmental processes taking place in the immediate settings in which human beings live, such as family, peer group, and workplace, are profoundly affected by conditions and events in the broader contexts in which these settings are embedded" (p. x). The conditions and events include:

> the material circumstances in which the person and his or her family live, the actual behaviors of other parties toward the person in question in face-to-face situations, and the actions and decisions taken in external, structurally-defined contexts, such as businesses, government agencies, social organizations, and other institutions in the public and the private sector. (p. xiv)

How does this discussion relate to the topic of culture? **Culture** helps determine who we are; the roles we take; the ways we seek to communicate with, and respond to, the world about us; and the values and attitudes we bring to our families, our work, our schools, and our communities. Our lives are also determined by the responses of others to our cultural practices and beliefs and to our presence. The willingness and ability to respond to the cultural aspects of the lives of the children and families whom we as teachers serve opens many doors to building the spirit of partnerships with families.

Not surprisingly, the topic of "culture" is frequently addressed in teacher preparation classrooms. The ultimate goal is to assist teachers in creating classroom climates that support and value the culture of each child. When asked to share something of their culture, however, many class participants may look surprised. It seems that culture is something only "those of color" or those from places foreign to us possess.

At Eastern Kentucky University, many students have roots deep in Appalachia, an area rich with heritage begun with the 18th-century settlers who came from Scotland, Northern Ireland, and northern England: "While Appalachians are not immigrants and are not necessarily racial minorities, they do share a cultural heritage with distinct childrearing patterns, attitudes, and expectations" (Klein, 1995, p. 10).

Fathers, grandfathers, great-grandfathers, and, yes, some women, worked the coal mines, spending hours deep underground and emerging exhausted and blackened with coal dust. For many, the time spent breathing dust from coal resulted in "black lung" disease and disability. Declining jobs and fear for health and safety sent many families away from the mountains. They moved north to the factories of large cities such as Detroit, Cleveland, Cincinnati, and Indianapolis but never lost contact with their Appalachian roots, making frequent trips home for holidays and family celebrations. They took with them the values and practices of their culture and became different in the world of the big city. Although many stayed in the big cities, many of these families eventually returned to the mountains or to cities nearer their mountain homes, including Cincinnati and smaller towns nearby. Why do individuals descending from a culture so rich in a spirit of connectedness and resolve seem puzzled when one asks them to discuss their culture? This same concept seems to apply to other individuals with roots in many parts of the United States, including both urban and rural environments.

Many explanations have been offered for why many of the nation's young people do not recognize themselves as part of a specific cultural heritage. This nation's history details the coming together of people from many countries, resulting in a "melting pot," or meshing of cultures and individuals to form families that may not represent any one geographic or religious heritage (Derman-Sparks & Ramsey, 1993, p. 276). Also, it may not have been acceptable to differentiate oneself as unique or set apart by one's origins. Being an "American" may have superseded one's heritage from another country. This has been particularly true during times of war with other countries. Many of us have heard stories from parents and grandparents who did not discuss their German roots with anyone else during World War II.

It is also important to consider the shifting patterns in geographic "connectedness" of families. Historically, members of one's extended family were close by, with grandparents, aunts, uncles, and cousins available for family dinners and celebrations and for helping one another. Several generations may have shared one household, as it was common for families to care for their elderly parents and grandparents. Grandparents and other older relatives were often looked to for advice in parenting children, as opposed to asking "experts" external to the family. Family businesses were common. Individuals experienced the "culture" of their families through time spent together, shared stories of the past, languages passed from one generation to the next, and the setting of common goals.

Today, people still search for a sense of community with others. Families, often fragmented by divorce, still struggle to provide for their children and to nurture their growth and development in healthy ways. As noted by

Margie Carter (1995), however, in her discussion of building community cultures, "A real experience of being raised and acculturated in community has been missing from most of our lives for several decades now" (p. 52). Today, people may have fewer opportunities to share the "culture" of their families or communities.

Families are more separated as their members pursue jobs and educational opportunities in various parts of the country and world. Children and elderly relatives are cared for outside the home as daughters, sons, mothers, and fathers pursue careers and support their families. Many individuals view their families as dysfunctional and look to those outside the family for "family-like" support.

Families are perpetually bombarded with external information about how they should act, how they should look, and what they should have. "We are primarily shaped by the media and commercialism" (Carter, 1995, p. 52). Furthermore, many families live in "homes without walls" as the media bring into living rooms violence and adult material from which families once protected their children. Through the media and the advertising that permeates the environment, children are educated to believe that products are what matter (Pipher, 1996).

Finally, we as Americans seem to be on a perpetual quest to have more, know more, and be more—to go beyond the world of our parents. This quest indicates (a) a healthy desire for growth and (b) attempts to exist and compete in the global marketplace. We must recognize, however, that our own growth is rooted in the cultures of our families and that culture is still an inherent part of who we are and what we bring to our worlds.

In keeping with our desire to respect the cultures of all individuals and to build bridges across cultures, this chapter examines the following:

- Definitions and role of culture
- Ways of defining one's own culture
- Goals of the multicultural perspective
- Developmental characteristics of young children that are related to developing an awareness of difference, including gender and race
- Characteristics of children with respect to the development of values, morals, and character
- Reflections on developmentally appropriate practice and diversity
- Characteristics of specific cultural groups
- Practices for inclusion of all families

◊◊ **Definitions and Role of Culture**

York (1991) notes that culture includes "[t]he behavior, values, beliefs, language, traits, artifacts, and products shared by and associated with a group of people" (p. 22).Perhaps we might consider the categories listed in Table 4.1 *as a part of* a group's culture.

Carol Brunson Phillips (1994) states, "The task of a society to prepare its children to take their place in the world of adults involves, in its broadest sense, the transmission of culture" (p. 137). Phillips further notes that, in U.S. society, the family and the educational system take primary responsibility for this transmission. Families do so through **enculturation**—"the things families do to enable children to know and understand society's shared ideas about values, attitudes, beliefs, and behaviors" (p. 137). Schools do this through *education*. Optimistically, the school and the family support one another in the complex task of bringing children to adulthood. At times, however, conflict arises between these two "giants" in the child's life because of differences in beliefs, values, and practices.

Perhaps of greatest interest to early childhood professionals are the views of children held by varying societies—for example, how children develop, what roles they take in the family, how they are nurtured. Many of these practices take root in broader political, social, economic, and religious beliefs viewed as necessary for the survival of that group.

Marian Zeitlin (1996), a nutritionist and adoptive mother of a Yoruban son, provides a provocative example in her account of the child-rearing

Table 4.1   Categories of cultural events in the lives of families

Communication	Families	Dress	Holidays	Foods
body language	roles	gender	types	who prepares
personal space	size	purpose	celebrations	types
eye contact	extended or nuclear	textiles	practices	meals
gestures		style	dates	religious issues
dialect		who makes or purchases	religious affiliations	
roles				

Religion	Leisure/Recreation	Work	Politics	Education
formal rituals	time spent	job roles	liberal	gender issues
belief in God or	games or events	training required	conservative	who educates
other spiritual	gender roles	gender issues	power issues	requirements
entities		role in life	gender issues	types
gender roles		status issues	role of government	responsibility for cost
written documents		pay	practices	who determines career path
which guide				
practices				
language				
selection of				
leaders				

practices of Yoruban (Nigeria) families. The Yoruba believe that the soul survives eternally in three states: the living, the ancestors, and the unborn waiting to be reincarnated with an ancestor from their own lineage. Before birth, a child is assigned by God or chooses her or his *ori,* or destiny. The family awaits the appearance of characteristics that will resemble the reincarnated ancestor. Motoric development is a priority, with children being encouraged to support their own weight from birth. By age 7, children are "expected to obey and respect their elders, care for themselves and younger siblings, assist in the home, and contribute to the family economy by providing assistance either on the farm or with trading activities" (Zeitlan, 1996, p. 413). The most valued skill possessed by the Yoruban child is the ability to complete errands for the family. Training begins with such tasks before age 1, and by age 2, children are sent on errands and given money to buy items for the family. Males are polygamous; women become heads of subunits of the family. In her role as head, the mother's nutritional status becomes more important than that of the child, with mothers given preference in food distribution. "Feeding more than remnants of these prestige foods (fish and meat) was feared to spoil the child's moral **character**" (Zeitlan, 1996, p. 419). In this agrarian society, economic flow is from child to parent, not parent to child.

As you can see, "The behaviors that parents exhibit toward their children and expect from them in daily interaction are complexly determined" (Gaskins, 1996, p. 345). Their notions about child rearing are embedded in cultural expectations and experiences.

Stated very simply, **culture** is about the roles we play in the context of our near environment and in response to the events of the outside world. It is about the things with which we surround ourselves and the ways in which we express ourselves. It is about how we see ourselves in relation to others. It is about how we care for others. It is about how we express our humanness and the goals we set for ourselves and our families. It is about what we value and hold dear.

What Is My Culture?

As teachers and caregivers, we must examine our attitudes and values with regard to our own heritage before we can value the **diversity** of the children within our care. We must begin with our near environment and work to that which is far. We must ask, What is my culture? We must be willing to share the experiences of our kin before we can effectively elicit the sharing of cultural experiences from others—children, families, and members of the community. You can create your own cultural grid by using the column listings shown in Table 4.1. Add other categories if they seem relevant. Complete the categories by using the cultural aspects of your life. Take some time with this activity, as you may be thinking about extended family members (e.g., grandparents) in doing so. If you like, share your cultural grid with

As teachers and caregivers, we must examine our own uniqueness by asking, "What is my culture?"

another member of the class. What are the similarities? What are the differences? What do you both see in common between your families of origin?

In her discussion of Appalachian families living in northern cities, Klein (1995) shares interesting anecdotes about the role of language in acclimating to a new environment. One of the most poignant is that of the school principal who attempts to elicit the help of families in providing cupcakes for a holiday party. The typical response was "I wouldn't care to do that" (p. 11). Thinking that parents were declining, the principal continued to call more parents. On the day of the party, the school was flooded with cupcakes. She realized that this statement by the parents indicated they would not mind providing cupcakes.

Language, whether oral or written, verbal or nonverbal, is used universally to communicate thoughts, ideas, desires, feelings, needs, and rules between individuals and across generations. Because this desire to communicate is common to all cultures, the use of language within and across cultural settings is of great interest to study. Case studies of preprimary children have shown that children acquire information about language and its forms and functions through their observations of language and how it is used in their near environments (Teale & Sulzby, 1989). The importance of written language within the context of use by the specific culture determines the extent that young children acquire information about the written word (Ferreiro & Teberosky, 1982). However, "[b]ecause the markings four year old children produce prior to formal schooling reflect the written language of their culture, we can no longer assume that children come to school without some knowledge of written language" (Harste & Woodward, 1989, p. 148).

Not only may children bring some knowledge of the forms and functions of the written language of their culture to the formal classroom setting, but they also bring their home rooted language with words and phrases used in culturally specific ways. As noted by Klein (1995), an understanding of the meanings and uses of phrases and words within cultural contexts is necessary for meaningful communication across cultures.

To make the concept of *home-rooted language* relevant to our experiences, it is helpful to begin with a discussion of language and the unique ways in which it is or was used within our home and community settings. An interesting place to begin is with words used to represent common objects. For example, the simple question, Where do you keep your clothes? elicits responses as diverse as the closet, the cupboard, the press, the chifforobe, the wardrobe, the chest, the bureau, the armoire, the highboy, the lowboy, the dresser, and more. One can also play with words for a couch—sofa, davenport, divan, daybed, and loveseat. Today, one might even say "futon"! You could add to these terms words from your personal experiences in "sitting."

Explore the words and phrases that are a part of your life experiences and cultural origins. You can make a list and share them with friends and colleagues. Language provokes discussions that allow us to begin identifying other cultural aspects of our lives, be it practices in child rearing, the culture of our schools and churches, the ways people greet each other or avoid greeting each other, what is seen as appropriate dress, and so on. In these discussions, the comments and love of a cherished grandmother may be revealed. It becomes okay, for example, to talk about helping with the planting of tobacco on a nearby farm or the way a family killed hogs every autumn for meat for the family. We talk about what we have learned from the experiences of our families and how our lives are affected today. Who we are and where our roots lie are accepted.

Interactions Among Family, School, and Community

Families are given the task of enculturation, but children also become *acculturated* as they encounter groups outside their *ethnic group* ("the commonality among people because of their ancestors; it includes race, religion, national origin, physical traits, values, beliefs, customs, language, and lifestyle" [York, 1991, p. 19]). Acculturation involves the transfer of culture from one ethnic group to another.

Among the earliest of these experiences within a formal setting comes with child care and/or schooling, where children are often expected to be and act like the majority of the population within that setting. This type of **ethnocentrism** (expecting others to think and act in the same way as a particular group) makes it difficult for children to ground their sense of self in who they are as they strive to be something desired by others. As explained by Saracho and Spodek (1983),

> [T]hey are expected to make major changes in what they do and how they speak, they may be forced to use a language that is foreign to them, and the social patterns and interactions expected of them may be equally foreign. These children must not only learn their own family language and culture but they must also learn to be competent in an alien language and culture. Often they are made to feel that they have to reject their own language and culture and adopt those of the school. This can result in a sense of bewilderment, in rejection, and in a loss of ethnic identity for the child. (p. viii)

Schools and other early childhood programs are vehicles for helping children build bridges between the cultures of their families and the cultures of broader communities where they may someday live and work. Through practices that respect and respond to diversity, teachers can take children from near to far experiences and assist them in building the type of cultural reciprocity that is needed to make sense of, and fully participate in, a changing world.

Teachers, administrators, child care providers, families, and communities must work together to build a climate for children that encourages knowledge of, and respect for, the diversity of families. The early childhood profession has historically been the strongest nurturer of relationships with families regardless of the diversity represented. The idea of the parent as the most important teacher in a child's life has long been held by early childhood advocates. One clear example of this is found in the Head Start program, which began as a part of the war on poverty in 1965 and continues to grow some 30 years later. The involvement of the parents and the community in the program is fundamental to the success of Head Start in making a difference in the lives of children.

"A central part of the professional early childhood community's ethos is that continuity should exist between family and program" (Powell, 1994, p. 167). U.S. society holds the fundamental belief that the family is the child's first and most important teacher and has the right to determine what is in the best interest of that child, given that families do not abuse those rights. Quality programs require continuity between home and school. "Program-family discontinuities, which are of the greatest magnitude for children from low-income and ethnic minority families, are thought to have negative effects on children's academic outcomes and socialization experiences" (Powell, 1994, p. 167). "When children are in early childhood programs that are not culturally sensitive to and consistent with their home cultures, they are at risk" (Derman-Sparks & Ramsey, 1993, p. 285).

◇◇ **Multicultural Education**

We participate in many communities, including those where we work, those where we live, those where we or our children go to school, those where we worship, and those where we experience fellowship with a group of friends. Everyone, regardless of race or color, gender or ability, religion or education, brings a rich heritage to that community or group. These heritages blend to form the culture of that group and the culture of the families. "Cultural pluralism is the notion that groups in the United States should be allowed, even encouraged, to hold on to what gives them their unique identities while maintaining their membership in the larger social framework" (Gonzalez-Mena, 1993, p. 2). Our role as teachers, caregivers, and administrators is to build a culture within our classrooms that shows that we

- Recognize and value the uniqueness of the life experience of each child and her or his family
- Assist each child in recognizing and valuing her or his heritage
- Assist each child in valuing and respecting the uniqueness of each individual even though that individual may not be just like that child
- Recognize the need to help children acquire those skills needed to live in a diverse world

Everyone brings a rich heritage to that community or group.

One avenue for accomplishing these tasks is to engage in educational and caring practices that are multicultural in nature. "Multicultural education is neither a unique phenomenon nor a recent innovation. . . . The socialization of young children into the larger society has long been considered an appropriate goal of early childhood education" (Saracho & Spodek, 1983, p. viii). **Multicultural** education is more than teaching children about the artifacts of various cultures (e.g., dress, customs, holidays, foods). It also means exposing children to other cultures and helping them be comfortable with and respect all the ways people are different from each other. It is teaching children how to relate to one another and how to play fair (York, 1991, p. 22).

In her book *Teaching and Learning in a Diverse World: Multicultural Education for Young Children*, Patricia Ramsey (1987) concludes that multicultural education involves a way of thinking. This way of thinking is characterized by respect for oneself and respect for others regardless of the ways others are different from oneself (e.g., gender, race, religion, wealth). It also reflects a concern for helping children acquire those skills that will help them build and maintain healthy relationships in the context of communities near or far. Ramsey set broad goals for teaching from a multicultural perspective. Taken directly from her text, these goals are:

1. To help children develop positive gender, racial, cultural class, and individual identities and to recognize and accept their membership in many different groups.
2. To enable children to see themselves as part of the larger society; to identify, empathize, and relate with individuals from other groups.
3. To foster respect and appreciation for the diverse ways in which other people live.
4. To encourage in young children's earliest social relationships an openness and interest in others, a willingness to include others, and a desire to cooperate.
5. To promote the development of realistic awareness of contemporary society, a sense of social responsibility, and an active concern that extend beyond one's immediate family or group.
6. To empower children to become autonomous and critical analysts and activists in their social environment.
7. To support the development of educational and social skills that are needed for children to become full participants in the larger society in ways that are most appropriate to individual styles, cultural orientations, and linguistic backgrounds.
8. To promote effective and reciprocal relationships between schools and families. (p. 5)

These goals reflect a concern for assisting children in the development of attitudes and values that demonstrate concern for humanity. They also reflect a concern for promoting a perspective on living with other people, which is **antibias,** defined by Louise Derman-Sparks (1989) as "an active/ist approach to challenging **prejudice,** stereotyping, bias, and the 'isms'" (p. 3). These **biases** or **stereotypes** refer to gender, race, religion, disability, or any other aspect of one's life that is used to set one apart from and by others.

The actions teachers take to meet these goals should also be designed to eliminate some myths and misconceptions that tend to influence attitudes toward individuals who are in some way different from what is familiar and that have become accepted (Battle, Black, Guddemi, & O'Bar, 1992). Such misconceptions include that (a) all children of the same ethnic background have the same abilities and interests (e.g., physical and intellectual); (b) all children who do not speak Standard English are intellectually inferior; (c) all ethnic minorities receive government assistance and are content to be "on welfare"; (d) all Asian children are academically gifted; (e) all children growing up in rural environments are "rednecks"; and (f) all children growing up in mountainous areas are "hillbillies."

In her book *Black Children: Their Roots, Culture, and Learning Styles*, Janice Hale (1982) argued that American social scientists view African American families as pathological and incapable of preparing their children for school. Denny Taylor and Catherine Dorsey-Gaines (1988) are among the ethnographers whose work has dispelled this myth. Their fieldwork involved the study of the contexts in which African American families living in the inner city of a major metropolitan area in the Northeast accomplished literacy. From their ethnographic research, they concluded that gender, race, economic status, and setting cannot be used to determine literacy (p. 194). In fact, "a person who is poor must certainly be 'bright' as well as determined in order to survive in the face of potentially overpowering odds" (Bishop, 1988, p. ix).

These families spent time with their children, encouraging them to write by providing writing and drawing materials, space, time, and themselves as participants. The children spontaneously engaged in writing notes containing many "I love yous" and labeled the pictures of the family members they drew with care. Interestingly, their budding knowledge of the functional uses of print was diminished in formal schooling when rote exercises in writing letters of the alphabet and in copying work from the chalkboard was shown to be of significant importance (Taylor & Dorsey-Gaines, 1988, p. 91).

Perhaps the most poignant of these stories is of a young mother living in a building with no heat or running water. Driven from the building by the cold, this mother, ill and in search of a home for her children, was very concerned about their education. She described how she helped her young daughter learn to read:

> I have some cue cards with sentences and words that I thought she should know in kindergarten . . . I bought them at the store. And, um, we go over them. I try maybe a half hour a day to spend some time with her going over them . . . That was more so in kindergarten or first grade. Now she's starting to read. (Taylor & Dorsey-Gaines, 1988, p. 6)

In summary, Taylor and Dorsey-Gaines's (1988) conclusions about the family characteristics of these families included the (a) sense of conviction about their own abilities as parents and determination to raise healthy children; (b) loving environments in which children were cared for with affection; (c) structured home environments with expectations for cooperation and a framework of rules understood by children and reinforced by parents; (d) concern for the safety and well-being of the children at home, in the neighborhood, and to and from school; and (e) the value that parents and family members placed on the growing sense of competence and independence demonstrated by the children as they participated in the events of the family and the neighborhood (p. 194).

Helen Klein (1995) worked to dispel similar myths about children from Appalachia whose families had migrated to northern cities, looking for work. When Klein asked professionals working with these children, "Who are these people?" responses included the following: (a) They're poor Whites from the South, (b) hillbillies, (c) I think they beat their kids, (d) briars, and (e) they live in shacks and make moonshine (p. 10).

These individuals who spoke with a different dialect, had different mannerisms, and had different customs were labeled with such characteristics as ignorant, lazy, unclean, and immoral (Klein, 1995, p. 10). In her efforts to make sense of and remove the stereotypes associated with these children and their families, Klein (1995) turned to their history and wrote about the strong and proud heritage these families brought from their Appalachian homes. "Deeply rooted in the history of the Appalachians was a sense of individualism and self-reliance" (p. 13). This sense of self-reliance served these families well as they journeyed to new homes with new ways.

Appalachian culture is rooted in a sense of traditionalism and kinship. Children benefited from being raised in, and cared for by, the extended family. "The Appalachian family was multigenerational, and it was not unusual for children to be cared for by grandparents, elders to be cared for by teens, and so on" (Klein, 1995, p. 14). Given this strong sense of kinship, it was not surprising that families traveled home to visit relatives and the cemetery for Memorial Day regardless of the number of days remaining in the school year.

Appalachian families brought a history of hard labor as they worked their land and the mines. Strength and stamina were also of crucial importance as they entered the factories of the North. Honesty was very important in their interactions with people. "Appalachians were not impressed with status and degrees but rather looked to inner characteristics" (Klein, 1995, p. 14).

Both the African American families studied by Taylor and Dorsey-Gaines and the Appalachian families whose history was chronicled by Klein may have easily been stereotyped as not willing or able to care for and educate their children. In fact, determination and resolve were pervasive in both situations.

As educators and caregivers, we can create climates that address multicultural education and discourage the development of ideas that are biased. As parents, teachers, and caregivers, it is imperative that we understand how young children acquire social knowledge because such knowledge "provides a basis for all communication and interaction, for all learning and problem solving, at home and school (Edwards, 1986, p. 5).

◊◊ Development of Social and Moral Knowledge in Early Childhood

"In all cultural communities worldwide, the years from two to six are a time of rapid changes in the development of social and moral knowledge" (Edwards, 1986, p. 3). Indeed, this is a time when children begin to develop their ideas and beliefs about the equality or inequality of individuals with regard to differences, including gender, race, and disability. "[D]espite legal and educational efforts to diminish racial **discrimination,** the cycle of prejudice is still strong and easily takes root in the minds and feelings of young children" (Ramsey, 1986, p. 1). "Our children add up, imitate, file away what they've observed and so very often later fall in line with the particular moral counsel we wittingly or quite unself-consciously have offered them" (Coles, 1997, p. 7).

This is also a time when children begin to act out some of their beliefs about what is fair and what is appealing in other individuals. In your work with young children in classroom settings, you have no doubt experienced the

Children become aware of differences in race, gender, and economic status prior to entering kindergarten.

"cliques" that can so easily form, leaving individual children isolated, lonely, and often angry at the exclusion. The sound of "You can't play" is brutal to the ears of the young child and to the caring adult who overhears. In her provocative book *You Can't Say You Can't Play*, Vivian Gussin Paley (1992) notes:

> By kindergarten . . . a structure begins to be revealed and will soon be carved in stone. Certain children will have the right to limit the social experiences of their classmates. Henceforth, a ruling class will notify others of their acceptability, and the outsiders learn to anticipate the sting of rejection. Long after hitting and name-calling have been outlawed by the teachers, a more damaging phenomenon is allowed to take root, spreading like a weed from grade to grade. (p. 3)

How does one get to be in the "in-group"? Is it gender, skin color, the color of a child's hair, the child's personality, or some other personal feature? Is it the occupation of the parent or the types of clothes the child wears? Is it the toys the child brings for show-and-tell? Is it the ability of the child to read or draw or paint or run fast? How do we know the rules?

We have already discussed examples of myths and misconceptions that may be held about cultural groups. Many misconceptions may also be held about what one needs to "fit." Consider the encounters that many children experience in the "culture of America" that suggest rules for stereotypes and about what is desirable in order to "belong."

Thin is beautiful.   Commercial weight-loss programs find their way into homes through the media and to parents whose busy schedules seem to afford little time for healthful eating and exercise. The "lean look" graces magazines and billboards with young girls and boys who model the latest lean fashions.

Busy is best.   The child who is involved in several after-school sports activities, dance, gymnastics, choir, and service activities is seen as achieving, popular, talented, and bright.

More is better.   Religious celebrations that involve the giving and receiving of gifts, including Hanukkah and Christmas, have become more and more commercial, with children's expectations for bigger gifts increasing.

You'd better go into debt to be on the Net!   Technology has brought many wonderful opportunities to children in helping broaden their knowledge of the world. Many parents, however, feel as though they must have the latest in computer technology at home in order for their children to "succeed."

My sons invited a neighbor child to play at our house on a rainy summer afternoon. First, they went to the computer in my son's room. I heard, "You mean you're not on the Net!" "No," was my son's quiet reply. Later, they moved to the den to watch television. "Where's the box in the corner?" was the friend's outcry. (I later realized he was talking about the "picture in a picture" feature of many televisions.) "No," was, again, my son's quiet reply. Had I failed my children?

It's in the name.   Children are convinced by the media that they will jump higher, run faster, and "be cool" if they just have a particular insignia on their shoes. In the United States, children have murdered other children for their athletic shoes! The labels of popular brands of jeans are prominently displaced on rear pockets, and, yes, even socks carry the appropriate "sign."

It's time to circle the wagons.   In schools, we attempt to help children acquire accurate information about Native Americans and to avoid the stereotypes that have prevailed for years. Yet, the commercial aspects of U.S. society continue to characterize Native Americans in very stereotypical ways. This is particularly true during Thanksgiving, when posters and displays are made available for purchase and to accompany holiday sales promotions.

Career Days are for doctors, lawyers, veterinarians, and basketball players.   Asking parents to be visitors to our classrooms in order to share their careers has been a part of school programs for years. Do we truly represent the broad spectrum of employment possibilities, however, or do we focus on such professions as law, medicine, and sports? How many children have parents whose jobs represent these careers? Are we shutting out parents and children when we exclude the auto mechanic, the appliance repair technician, the day care worker, the workers who pave roads and build homes, and, yes, the mother or father who makes a life choice to spend time caring for her or his child at home?

These scenarios represent the subtle and not so subtle ways we as adults have responsibility in various ways for the biases that children exhibit in their behaviors. Perhaps, as parents and teachers, we have three considerations in helping our children acquire antibias attitudes and beliefs:

1. To examine together what is in our hearts and minds and, ultimately, our actions

2. To become more cognizant of how young children acquire social information and moral knowledge

3. To provide guided experiences for children to engage in moral reasoning and to practice antibias behaviors

Adults as Moral Figures in the Lives of Children

The topic of adults as moral figures in the lives of their children has been addressed through our discussion of myths and stereotypes. It seems necessary, however, to continue to stress the ways we teach children about **morals** and about caring for other people. As psychiatrist Robert Coles stated in his book *How to Raise a Moral Child: The Moral Intelligence of Children* (1997):

> The child is a witness; the child is an ever-attentive witness of grown-up **morality**—or lack thereof; the child looks and looks for cues as to how one ought to behave, and finds them galore as we parents and teachers go about our lives, making choices, addressing people, showing in action our rock-bottom assumptions, desires, and values, and thereby telling those young observers much more than we may realize. (p. 5)

The following are real-life examples collected through informal conversations with friends and parents.

◊ *A young child accompanies his father to the grocery store. The father pays for the groceries and receives change from the clerk. The father and child leave the store, and the father, counting his change, comments that he has been given too much change. The child also hears, "This is my lucky day!" from the father, and they begin their trip home. What did the child learn?*

◊ *A child is playing with her friend one evening while their mothers talk over coffee in the kitchen. One mother is overheard complaining that the little boy in her daughter's classroom takes too much of the teacher's time and distracts the teacher from paying attention to her daughter. The mother thinks that children with "those kinds" of disabilities should be removed from the classroom. What did the little girl learn?*

◊ *A little girl whose family is Jewish learns that other girls in the classroom have been invited to a friend's party. After investigating, the mother and the teacher discover that the only girls not invited to the party were her daughter and two African American girls in the class. What did these little girls learn?*

◊ *A young boy is repeatedly taunted because he is not thin. Finally, the offender is confronted by the boy's mother, who had become exasperated at seeing her child hurt and in tears. The offender quickly denies the taunt and says he feels sorry for the boy because the boy is "fat." What has the offender learned?*

◊ *A little girl comes crying to her father; she has been teased by other girls because her clothes don't match. She tells her father that she just wants to be "herself" but that others don't like her that way. How does the girl maintain her spirit of individualism?*

◊ *Hurrying to get into the car and get the children to their activities, a mother becomes frustrated. In her frustration, she uses profane language, which is overheard by her two young sons. Later, one son uses the same language in front of the mother's friend. The mother, embarrassed, criticizes the child in front of the other adult, saying, "I don't know where you hear such language!" How will this child deal with the confusion created by this mother?*

How Young Children Construct Knowledge

Young children construct knowledge about what is right and wrong from what they see, hear, and experience. Their **social cognition**—that is, "an ability to read social situations and to interpret the feelings, motives, and intentions of others" (Trawick-Smith, 1997, p. G–9)—requires "systems for identifying and classifying self and others; for making inferences about people's thoughts, feelings, and intentions; for understanding institutions such as the family and the government; and about learning about rules and values that define right and wrong" (Edwards, 1986, p. 4).

A "constructivist," Piaget (1983) believed that young children construct their knowledge about people, places, and events through their interactions with individuals, objects, and situations. Children bring their unique ways of thinking to encounters with the social aspects of their environments. For the young child, this way of thinking follows a process of development that proceeds in an orderly and predictable sequence, with children moving from thinking based on that which is concrete to thinking based on that which is more abstract. This concrete way of thinking also relates to the child's growing sense of "right" and "wrong."

Piaget (1932) used techniques in observation and play to understand the development of moral thinking in children. He asked children, during their sessions of play, a series of questions that posed moral dilemmas. Studying their answers, Piaget concluded that most preschool (preoperational) children are *premoral*, meaning that they would change the rules of the game in their favor. Similar experiences may be found with young children in sorting objects by various attributes when the rules being followed in sorting change periodically.

This way of thinking is also in keeping with what is known about the egocentric nature of the young child who believes that all actions are centered about her or his being. The child who believes that a parent died because the child was "naughty" or that a parent left the family because the child did not eat her vegetables as told by the parent exhibits such egocentrism. This behavior does not indicate that something is "wrong" with the child, but is simply a reflection of that child's level of thinking at this particular stage of development.

A sense of moral realism appears during the primary years (concrete), with children exhibiting behaviors that are very rule-bound. Authority figures such as parents, teachers, and God, or the child's higher power, become very important. Rules are unchangeable, regardless of the situation. Think about the exclamations of "You're not supposed to do that!" you've heard from children when they see another child break a rule.

Individuals may not reach the final stage of moral development—*moral relativism*—until adolescence or adulthood (formal thought). Although rules are respected, it seems to be understood that exceptions can be made. The intent of the action may be taken into account. For example, the driver of a car does not usually intend to back into another car in the parking lot. This act, though unfortunate and costly, does not generally indicate an immoral act as can be understood by someone in the stage of moral relativism.

Although these stages represent the sequential aspects of the child's acquisition of moral reasoning, caution should be employed in predetermining a child's level of moral reasoning at specific ages. For example, some primary children are, in fact, capable of making exceptions to the rules of games to accommodate their classmates who have disabilities. Observations of individual children in given situations should be used to determine each child's abilities to engage in moral reasoning. Consideration should also be given to the types of activities that serve to foster the child's development of moral reasoning. These activities are discussed in a later section of this chapter.

Children also experience developmental shifts in their understanding of issues regarding diversity (e.g., gender, race, social class) by using physical characteristics to make their judgments. Although children label people as girls or boys by such features as length of hair and gender-specific clothing, they generally do not understand that gender will not change (e.g., that boys cannot become mommies) until the end of the preschool period.

Children appear to notice racial cues during infancy (Katz, 1976). By age 3 or 4, children can label people by racial group (Goodman, 1952). By age 5, children begin to relate to, and identify with, people of their own culture and race (Aboud, 1988). Until somewhere around age 7, however, children may think that race can be changed by washing the skin or by changing clothing (Ramsey, 1987).

Even though preschoolers do not understand the concept of *social class*, they do understand that there are differences in what people have in terms of material goods. They are also beginning to be able to discuss what is fair and unfair in terms of distribution of those goods (Ramsey, 1995).

◇◇ Reflections on Developmentally Appropriate Practice and Diversity

Even though young children may not yet have acquired the cognitive capacity for engaging in complex mental actions with regard to issues of diversity, they are capable of participating in concrete events and experiences that will assist them in acquiring social knowledge. As noted by Edwards (1986) in her discussion of facilitating social and moral knowledge of young children,

> Any early childhood setting presents many opportunities for adults and children to talk together about social and moral issues. Conversation can help children to organize their thinking about questions that are interesting to them. It gives teachers the kind of concrete information that they need in order to understand children's developmental needs and communicate effectively in guidance and disciplinary situations. (p. 21)

Much conversation results from the spontaneous play of children. Teachers, however, can provide activities about various social issues that will further stimulate and focus discussion. Edwards (1986) calls such activities "thinking games." An example is a stereotype expressed by a child that all Chinese people eat in restaurants (this was the child's experience in seeing Chinese people). This type of overgeneralization is common in young children. Ramsey (1986, p. 97) suggests the following ideas for helping children broaden their ideas about the Chinese culture through specific activities: (a) Provide photographs of Chinese Americans in their home settings and (b) set up role-play areas of eating at restaurants and eating at home (chopsticks, bowls, and rice can be used in both settings).

Developing and implementing such activities provide many opportunities for teachers and parents to collaborate. In doing so, the adults engage in their own developmental growth as they share information and ideas and implement strategies for assisting children in their thinking about various topics. New (1994) notes that this type of work provides many opportunities for teachers to be engaged as researchers as they "not only seek out opportunities to learn from the diverse children in their classrooms, but incorporate parents into a partnership affiliation that is denied by such concepts as 'parent education'"(p. 79).

Adults can guide children in their awareness of diversity and their understanding that each individual has a common need for love and caring.

◊◊ **Understanding Characteristics of Diverse Groups**

The child walking through a classroom door must first be viewed as an individual whose life is embedded "in a family, a community, a culture, and a society" (Mallory & New, 1994, p. 8). The child and the family bring specific competencies, viewpoints, and practices that will become a part of the culture of the classroom. The teacher who regards children and families with inquiry rather than with predetermined attitudes will be better able to understand each child's learning characteristics; styles of interacting with children, adults, and materials; and social, physical, and cognitive competencies. In doing so, the teacher will be better prepared to support each child's development within the context of the family and the community.

Teachers must see children as individuals within the context of their **sociocultural** settings. Noted African American author Janice Hale encourages teachers to broaden their awareness of the characteristics and competencies of specific groups so that children's development can be nurtured in the classroom setting. Teachers and caregivers are also encouraged to become aware of cultural differences in the way children's needs are met—"in how teachers and caregivers interact and relate to children, in the nitty-gritty of body language and nonverbal communication" (Gonzalez-Mena, 1993, p. 4).

One can learn about other cultures in many ways, but four strategies seem most effective:

1. Studying and reading about the culture
2. Working with individuals from the culture who can serve as guides
3. Participating in daily living experiences of the culture
4. Learning the language of the culture (Lynch & Hanson, 1992)

Each of these strategies, particularly learning the language of the culture, is helpful in increasing one's ability to communicate effectively with children and families of differing cultures. Further, communication effectiveness is significantly improved when the teacher:

Respects individuals from other cultures

Makes continued and sincere attempts to understand the world from others' points of view

Is open to new learning

Is flexible

Has a sense of humor

Tolerates ambiguity well

Approaches others with a desire to learn (Lynch & Hanson, 1992, p. 51)

Let's begin our discussion of cultural variations with the Anglo European culture, keeping in mind that we are speaking in generalizations and that families will have their specific idiosyncrasies and characteristics. Time and space do not permit complete discussion of any one group. Characteristics will primarily relate to views of child rearing and communication strategies. For further information about lifestyles, beliefs, and practices of specific groups, we suggest that you read such texts as *Developing Cross-Cultural Competence: A Guide for Working With Young Children and Their Families* (Lynch & Hanson, 1992) and *Knowing and Serving Diverse Families* (Hildebrand, Phenice, Gray, & Pines, 1996).

Families of Anglo European Descent

Families of European descent are dominant in the United States. Their ancestors were among those who explored and settled in this country during the 19th and early 20th centuries. The first group was composed mainly of individuals from England, Ireland, and Germany. The second group, in the 1860s to 1890s, brought many Scandinavians. A third major group of immigrants, after the 1890s, came from Italy, Russia, and the Austrian-Hungarian empire (Hanson, 1992). Values and assumptions that have evolved from the Anglo European background are as follows:

A high regard for individualism and privacy

A belief in equality of all individuals

A preference for informality in interactions

A focus toward future, change, and progress

A belief in the goodness of humanity

A focus on time

A focus on achievement and a strong work ethic

A focus on materialism

Directness and assertiveness in interactions (Althen, 1988)

Although these values speak to a general population from Europe, families may bring more specific practices from their own countries and communities.

Families appear more concerned with developing autonomy and **independence** in young children than in the **interdependence** of the family. One example is in the sleeping patterns and customs of families. Young children are generally expected to go to bed before adults, to comfort themselves in going to sleep, and to sleep by themselves from infancy. This is in contrast with today's Italian and Japanese families, who believe that parents should respond to their young children's needs to want to remain close to family members (New, 1994; Wolf, Lozoff, Latz, & Paludetto, 1996). Education and achievement are highly regarded among families of Anglo European descent, with parents expecting to be involved in their child's education and to be kept informed by teachers of the child's progress. Families also expect to be involved in decision making within the schools through boards, councils, and parent-teacher groups.

Families of African Descent

More than 4 million Africans from the Mandingo, Ibos, Efiks, Hausas, Krus, Yorubas, Ashantis, and Senegalese (Bennett, 1966) were brought against their will to North America. As slaves and later in freedom, they played a critical role in the development of the building of America. Both plantation economies and the mercantile systems depended on slave labor. "Their contribution to trade, industry, and agriculture was significant and immeasurable, and they distinguished themselves in the major wars of their new land as well" (Willis, 1992, p. 123).

Through the years, many African Americans have been able to move beyond the legacy of slavery. A history of slavery, oppression, and abandonment by a society that enslaved them, however, has had overwhelming long-term effects for many families. In 1991, 30 million (12.1% of total population) African Americans lived in the United States—the largest ethnic **minority** (Hildebrand et al., 1996), and 28% of their families had incomes below the poverty level (U.S. Bureau of the Census, 1990). In addition, 43% of children in African American families live in homes where the father is absent (U.S. Bureau of the Census, 1987). Most (84%) live in major inner-city areas where crime is prevalent and poor housing, unemployment, and limited resources are common (O'Hare, Pollard, Mann, & Kent, 1991).

According to Hildebrand et al. (1996), "Endurance of suffering while moving ahead is a major theme found in Black families" (p. 59). How have African American families been able to survive and move forward under such economic and social constraints?

Strong kinship bonds among a variety of family households

Strong work, education, and achievement orientation

High level of flexibility in family roles

Strong commitment to religious values and church participation

A humanistic orientation for perceiving the world and relationships (p. 59)

Teachers can build on family strengths by respecting the strong sense of kinship experienced by children. Within this system, children are expected to show respect for their elders and to obey their parents and older members of the family and community. Appropriate titles are preferred. The parents' style of interacting may be more authoritative, and showing an individual that you care about her or him through your actions may be more important than the verbal expression of love (Willis, 1992).

Teachers will also note a strong oral tradition in families of African descent, characterized by proverbs, songs, stories, and fables (Hale, 1991).

As slaves, traditional ways of communicating (e.g., drumming) were often prohibited. Slaves used other ways to communicate the rich traditions of their African cultures and to transmit wisdom necessary for dealing with adversity across generations. Stories, proverbs, spirituals, and folktales were all sources of teaching for African families in bondage to their owners. Today, this oral tradition continues among African American families. In encouraging teachers to make use of this tradition, Hale (1991) notes:

> These stories transmit the message to African American children that quick-sand and landmines characterize the road to becoming an African American achiever in America; however, they also transmit the message that it is possible to overcome obstacles. (p. 13)

Families of Asian Descent

Asian Americans represent more than 29 distinct subgroups that differ in language, religions, and cultural practices (Feng, 1994). This population, characterized by great diversity, originates from three major geographic areas: (a) East Asia (China, Japan, and Korea), (b) Southeast Asia (Cambodia, Laos, Vietnam, Burma, Thailand, Malaysia, Singapore, Indonesia, and the Philippines), and (c) South Asia (India, Pakistan, and Sri Lanka; Chan, 1992).

Asian Americans are the fastest growing minority group in the United States, representing about 3% of the population (Hildebrand et al., 1996). Despite the many variations in practices and beliefs because of the great diversity of the origins, languages, and sociocultural experiences of these families, some practices, values, and beliefs are shared (Feng, 1994).

Many Asian cultures have been influenced by "the three teachings," or the philosophies of Confucianism, Taoism, and Buddhism. In his philosophy of humanity, Confucius (551–479 B.C.) prescribed a way of living that reflected virtue and wisdom. Being moral, trustworthy, and benevolent to one's fellow human beings was highly valued. Loyalty and obedience to one's parents and reverence for one's ancestors were also taught.

Taoism focused on the value of meditation and transcending that which is worldly. Its legendary patriarch, Lao Tzu (born in 604 B.C.), advocated inner strength, selflessness, spontaneity, and harmony with nature and humanity.

Buddhism, founded by Prince Siddhartha Gautama (560–480 B.C.), entered China from India following the establishment of Confucianism and Taoism. This religion also focused on self-discipline, meditation, and the renouncing of that which is worldly (Chan, 1992). "The traditional collectivist values of Chinese, Koreans, Cambodians, Laotians, and Vietnamese in particular are rooted in the 'three teachings'" (Chan, 1992, p. 212).

The concern for maintaining the interdependence of the family and the individual's loyalty to the family is seen in child-rearing practices. Behaviors of the individual are seen as reflecting on one's ancestors and one's race. "While striving to defend the family's honor and enhance its reputation, one must properly observe historical events and maintain family traditions" (Chan, 1992, p. 212).

Whereas American schools emphasize individualism and competition, Asian children have generally been taught to think first of the group. "Most Asian-American parents teach their children to value education, respect authority, feel responsible for relatives, and show self-control" (Feng, 1994, p. 1). Consequently, informality among teachers and students may be confusing, and a quiet, structured environment with a good deal of teacher reinforcement valued (Feng, 1994).

Families of Hispanic Descent

During the 15th century, explorers from Spain conquered and exploited many parts of the New World, including what is now the southern part of the United States, Mexico, and Central and South America. Three Hispanic groups now compose the majority of Hispanics in the United States: Mexicans, Puerto Ricans, and Cuban Hispanics. The remainder are from Central and South America and the Caribbean. Composing the second largest minority group within the United States (9% of the population), Hispanics living in this country are expected to undergo a rapid increase in number into the next century (Hildebrand et al., 1996) as individuals seek freedom from economic and political oppression.

Even though their geographic origins are varied, as with other groups, Hispanics share numerous cultural values, practices, and beliefs. Many are related to Catholicism as the dominant religion. In Hispanic or Latino cultures, marriage is for the purpose of having children, with the relationship of parent and child of more importance than the relationship of husband and wife. The attitude toward children is nurturing, and parents may be indulgent and permissive with young children. Children are taught to interact with others with respect and dignity and are expected to take up work roles within the family. Children are reared within the context of the extended family, and respect for their elders is an important aspect of their teaching (Zuniga, 1992). Although education is valued, its goal is for the benefit of the family and not simply for the individual. Should education come between the individual and the family, it may receive a low priority. Consequently, the message that people are valued should be a high priority for the teacher working with these children (Hildebrand et al., 1996).

Families of Native American Descent

In 1990, approximately 1.9 million people in the United States identified themselves as American Indians, Eskimos, or Aleuts (Johnson, 1991). They make up only slightly more than 0.75% of the total U.S. population (Joe & Malach, 1992). These individuals, descendants of people indigenous to North America, represent many tribes and many languages. "European immigrants, explorers, traders, missionaries, soldiers, colonists, and trappers changed forever the culture and world of the native peoples and most of these changes were negative" (Joe & Malach, 1992, p. 93).

As noted, there are many tribes and, therefore, many different practices. Beliefs about the need for interdependence of the group and a focus on the collective are shared, however. These people also hold a desire for attaining harmony with nature. Hildebrand et al. (1996) concluded that four traits characterize the cultural expression of values:

Self-reliance

Noninterference

Nonconfrontation

Respect for elders (p. 143)

Children are viewed as gifts with unique characteristics that will help determine their place in the tribe. A period of time will pass to observe a child before a name is chosen that represents these characteristics. Elders are given the task of sharing the oral traditions of the tribe with the younger members by passing on stories and songs. Child-rearing responsibilities may be spread to extended family members, and parents may ask advice from older family members in matters relating to child rearing.

Given a history of oppression, Native Americans may have concerns relative to dealing with governmental agencies. Individuals are observed for their behaviors and what they do, rather than what people say.

The diversity of this group makes it particularly important that teachers carefully research the cultural practices of the family with regard to child-rearing, participation in the child's education, and style of communication. The rich cultural heritage of this group also provides wonderful opportunities for shared experiences within the classroom setting.

Families of Children with Dual Heritage

In the preceding discussions, the cultures of specific groups were addressed. A growing number of children in this country, however, are born into families that are biracial or multiracial. In coming years, these children may be regarded as "children," not as belonging to a representative ethnic group (e.g., Black, White). Parents may identify their child with one ethnic group, with both groups, or with little regard for cultural origins. Teachers should work with parents to determine the wishes of the family in acknowledging the heritage(s) of the child. In this way, the teacher can be more responsive to the child and the family in planning daily classroom experiences (Morrison & Rodgers, 1996).

◊◊ Summary of Practices for Inclusion of All Families

This chapter has taken us many places in our search for understanding how to build partnerships with families and within communities by regarding, respecting, and building on people's differences. We have attempted to define culture by beginning with that which is unique to our near environment and moving to "worlds" that are "foreign" to us. We have explored the role that culture plays in shaping our lives as we move into diverse worlds. We have tapped the roots of multicultural education—its meaning, value, and applications. We have given thought to the moral implications of valuing the diversity of our neighbors and looked into ways we can foster such responsibility in our children. We have "wandered" through various cultures, with possibilities for their uniqueness and sense of family. This brings us to what we need as teachers and caregivers—practical ideas for implementing this perspective with families and within communities.

Before we begin to explore these ideas as shared in printed materials and through an interview with a respected teacher, keep in mind that our focus is always on the strength of the family. As suggested by Garcia (1997), in his work with Hispanic families, we should move away from a needs assessment viewpoint, which in particular sees native language as a problem, to the "asset inventory" that focuses on native language as a resource (p. 12). Garcia lists five practical applications that teachers can use in regarding the roots and wings of children:

1. Take the role of the ethnographer in learning about the linguistic and cultural diversity of children. Learn to pronounce the child's name as it is pronounced at home. Keep written notes about this information.
2. Demonstrate your willingness to learn about the language by learning some of the language that you will find useful in working with the child and the family.
3. Be up to date on new information about cultural inclusion. Incorporate songs, games, and poems from various cultures into the curriculum.
4. Share the knowledge you acquire with both the educational and non-educational community.
5. Be an advocate for the children "by nurturing, celebrating, and challenging them" (Garcia, 1997, p. 13).

This celebration of children and their families can be represented in the physical, cognitive, and social or interpersonal aspects of the classroom environment.

Designing the Learning Environment: Possibilities for the Inclusion of Families and the Community

Some controversy always surrounds bringing materials and information from other cultures into the preschool classroom because those cultures and ethnic groups might not be represented in the classroom. Children who are a part of homogeneous groups, however, need this type of experience even more than those who have opportunities to experience other cultures in the course of their daily living experiences as they move into a diverse world.

Ramsey (1987) suggests that the physical setting should be designed to foster children's (a) positive views of others from different races, cultures, and classes; (b) abilities to empathize and identify with children from other groups; (c) respect and appreciation for other ways of life; and (d) awareness of a larger social environment (p. 59).

Perhaps one of the most interesting ways for children and adults to participate in experiences designed to meet such goals is found in an approach to curriculum development known as **webbing.** In this approach, children's questions and ideas serve as prompts for possible curriculum adventures. As active participants in the learning experiences of the classroom, children engage in activities that are relevant to their interests and experiences. Teachers listen to the children, plan experiences, and watch learning events emerge from the children's active explorations with materials and individuals.

Some teachers have become interested in this type of **emergent curriculum,** including those teachers at the Burrier Child Development Center at Eastern Kentucky University. In helping the teachers take on the roles of researcher and developer of curricula, course instructors and preschool administrators introduced the work of teachers in **Reggio Emilia,** Italy. Information from *The Hundred Languages of Children: The Reggio Emilia Approach to Early Childhood Education* (Edwards, Gandini, & Forman, 1993) was shared along with videos depicting the project work of the Italian children (*To Make A Portrait of a Lion* [Comune di Reggio Emilia, 1987]; *The Long Jump* [Forman & Gandini, 1991], and *An Amusement Park for Birds* [Forman et al., 1993]). Provocative work on emergent curriculum via webbing as shared by Elizabeth Jones and John Nimmo (1994) was also introduced.

Of course, the incredible graphic representations created by the children are of primary interest, as is the research these youngsters do as they create and re-create images. The role of the adult, both parent and teacher, however, is very significant in these schools of northern Italy. Teachers stay with the same group of children across the 3 years of their participation in the program, building strong bonds with the children and their families. Families participate in the children's projects, lending their opinions to selected school projects and participating in the projects by providing both human and materials resources.

One of the most community based of these projects comes with the harvesting of grapes each year. The farmers come to the school to visit with the children and to discuss the process of the harvest. This gives the children an opportunity to build relationships with the farm "family" and to ask questions, predict, and begin investigations into the process of the harvest—a tradition of this Italian countryside.

The children are then taken to a farm, where they pick, sort, mash, and in every way seem to become active participants of the process of the harvest. After the tasks are completed, the children return to their classrooms, where they are again visited by the farmers to share in the celebration of harvest—to drink the grape juice and to share food and memories. All events are documented in photographs and in the children's graphic depictions of the days of work and the time shared together (Department of Early Education, City of Reggio Emilia, 1987).

As a team of teachers, we watched these videos, shared our readings and impressions, and began the work of implementing a project approach in our classrooms, always watchful of ways to keep the families involved. Not yet ready to give up completely the control of selecting a topic, we decided to work on the topic of "homes" because this seemed to be a common denominator to our group of children (none were homeless). The topic also seemed to provide many ways to go with cultural activities—different locations, types, arrangements, and so on. Our original web of homes looked something like that shown in Figure 4.1.

Teachers and children took walks around our campus to see what the buildings were made of and how they were constructed. These walks served as provocations for creating homes. The children experimented with ways to build homes by using cardboard boxes and other trashables. We placed materials in our dramatic play center that might be used for taking care of homes. We invited parents in to talk about construction and took a field trip to a

Figure 4.1   A web of subtopics related to homes

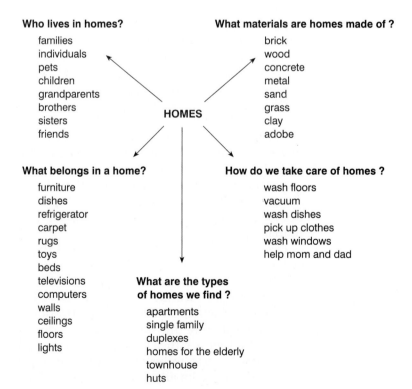

Who lives in homes?
families
individuals
pets
children
grandparents
brothers
sisters
friends

What materials are homes made of ?
brick
wood
concrete
metal
sand
grass
clay
adobe

HOMES

What belongs in a home?
furniture
dishes
refrigerator
carpet
rugs
toys
beds
televisions
computers
walls
ceilings
floors
lights

How do we take care of homes ?
wash floors
vacuum
wash dishes
pick up clothes
wash windows
help mom and dad

What are the types of homes we find ?
apartments
single family
duplexes
homes for the elderly
townhouse
huts

building center to explore building materials. Even after all that, much more was still to be done as we explored books with pictures of homes from other parts of the world (Maya Angelou's *My Painted House, My Friendly Chicken, and Me* [1994] is a wonderful resource), built homes with blocks and other manipulatives, and shared the types of homes that our families shared.

We as teachers learned from this experience and made plans to work with the children again on this topic that caught and kept their interest for weeks. We also made plans to learn more about homes in cultures across the world and to explore possibilities for extending this project. Figuring the cost of homes would be a possibility for older children, as would more sophisticated forms of measuring and construction.

Topics such as the home can be a wonderful focal point for discussions among teachers and families and children. Wellhousen (1996) and Harris and Fuqua (1996) have presented many possibilities for exploring diversity through a study of homes across the preschool and primary years. Still, some teachers are concerned that children will feel uncomfortable that their homes are too small, too unkempt, or too "something" to share with others or that comparison will make children feel "less than" in some way. Such a case is a rich opportunity for teachers to put into practice the valuing of diversity and respect for each other. Even though we know that young children are aware of these differences, perhaps the prejudices created are those projected by well-meaning adults.

Edwards and Springate (1995) provide suggestions on how teachers can support the work of children in their emergent interests and creativity. These suggestions (which follow) can also be related to the ways teachers can include families and the community in their work with young children:

Time. Children need time to explore, investigate, and reflect on the topic being studied. Our work on homes took place over several weeks, and still many avenues were left untraveled. If teachers take time to present for study those relevant topics of interest to children, more time will be available for parents and community members to become involved. For example, our study of homes presented opportunities for bricklayers, carpenters, roofers, concrete suppliers, and so on to become involved. Opportunities for community field trips to relevant locations would also be more viable. Word-of-mouth experiences also bring more ideas for input from families when time is given to share.

Space. Children need space to work where materials and projects under construction will not be disrupted. Similarly, adults may need some space in the classroom to leave materials they may be sharing for further discussion and exploration. A table or other space to house the T square and blueprints shared by the architect or the photographs of homes in other lands shared by a parent or community member lends continuity, allowing for children to revisit the resource person's information.

Materials.   Children need materials with which to work. In our exploration of homes, we found trashables to be wonderful resources for building. It was also helpful when community members and parents could share
brick, mortar, stones, and so on so that the children could see and feel
some actual textures of materials. Even more interesting would have been
some assistance in making adobe and exploring thatch and other forms of
materials alternative to our area.

Climate for Learning.   A climate that supports open-ended investigations is desirable, if not essential, to the success of project work. For example, in Italy, the Reggio Emilia parents meet together with teachers to discuss the work of projects. Perhaps communication with families about
possible projects for the year and suggested meetings for those who are
interested in collaborating on these projects would be helpful. It is also
helpful to "interview" the families in an informal way during home visits
and conferences to discover the interests and skills of the parents and
whether they would like to share in the school setting. In this environment,
the ways of knowing and contributions of all participants are valuable.

Occasions.   Which occasions provoke a desire to learn about something
unexplored—for children and for adults? Perhaps a new building is going up
in town or some child is moving to a different home. Perhaps the school is
being renovated or a barn is being raised. Whatever the topic, events and occasions about it will excite and attract the attention of both children and adults.
Whether it is the harvest of the grapes in Italy or the harvest of another crop in
the United States, many real-life experiences, when looked at with open eyes,
can be used for learning and for bringing communities together.

An Interview with a Teacher

Several years ago, one of the authors of this book was searching for a
preschool for her children that exemplified respect for, and appreciation of,
the diversity of families and their children. None seemed to be in place, and
she, along with several other mothers, decided to open her own preschool.
Dr. Anne Brautigam, a long-time advocate and supporter of programs for children from diverse populations, served as the director. Seven years later, the
program continues and serves as a model to the community of how families
of diverse cultures and languages come together for the purpose of loving and
nurturing their children. Accredited by the National Association for the Education of Young Children and having been highlighted in news articles and a
national news show, Ecumenical Preschool is truly multicultural. It is also
multiage so that children experience the sense of family as they share experiences with younger and older, brothers and sisters, and yes, grandmas and
grandpas. The school is housed in the same church facility as the Helping
Hands program, a local program for individuals with Alzheimer's disease.

Ms. Kathy Healey has served as the head teacher of Ecumenical Preschool for 6 years. She now also serves as director. Her work, as that of many other teachers, is worthy of an interview in a text for those preparing to work with diverse families.

Question: Tell me about the children enrolled at Ecumenical.

Answer: This year, we had children from Zaire [Congo], Liberia, and Korea. We had children from the U.S. who were White and African American. We also had one child whose mother was from the Philippines and father from the U.S. All children had some, if limited, English.

Question: How do you find out about the cultural practices and, perhaps, expectations of the families with regard to their children?

Answer: We [Ms. Kathy and assistant teacher Mary Ann Jolly] talk to the family at the time of enrollment and ask them to share information about their culture which would be helpful to us. We ask about special holidays which they celebrate and tell them about holidays which we celebrate, such as Thanksgiving. We also ask them if they would like for their children to learn about and participate in such events. Many of these families are in the United States for a short period of time and want their children to know as much about our culture as possible before they return home.

We learn about the families when they include us in their lives at home. Recently, a mother of one of the children from Korea called Mary Anne to invite her to dinner. As is our custom, Mary Anne asked what she could bring. The mother was surprised and shared that, in her country, it would be unacceptable to make such an offer as it is the responsibility of the host to provide all food. Nevertheless, she was interested in participating in an American custom and suggested something for Mary Anne to bring. When she called me, I made the same offer, and we agreed upon something for me to bring.

Question: How do you include cultural events in the classroom?

Answer: We ask the families to share information about special foods, recipes for foods, photos, special clothing and to come to school and share.

Question: How do you involve families in school activities?

Answer: As I said, we ask families to come to school and share. This year, the father of the child from Zaire came to school and shared with the children what it was like for him to go to school as a child in Zaire. The children were fascinated by his story. We also hold programs with potlucks where many ethnic foods are shared, a spring art show of the children's creations, parent conferences, and an end-of-year celebration.

Question: What do you find most difficult about working with families of so many different cultures?

Answer: The expectations of parents about what teachers can do are often unrealistic. Parents seem to expect teachers to have all the answers. Often, there are unrealistic expectations of what children should be able to accomplish.

Question: What do you find most valuable in being in this environment as a teacher? for the children? for the families?

Answer: This type of environment opens up the world to children and families. It is a learning experience for adults and for the children. The American children benefit because of their exposure to different languages and customs. One little boy was thrilled to be teaching his dog to "sit" in Korean, which he had learned from the Korean children at school. All children feel they are teachers as they share their language with other children. Each child makes a personal contribution. The children in the school give the observer a sense of the United Nations "look." I hope that when these children return to their own countries, they will have positive memories and that all children will remember those experiences in times of controversy. It is our contribution to world peace.

Summary Statements ◊

- Across cultures, a young child's journey to adulthood is accomplished within the context of the family and surrounding community. The beliefs, values, attitudes, languages, and ideologies experienced in childhood will play a part in whatever path the child takes as she or he moves toward adulthood.

- The willingness and ability of teachers to respond to the cultural aspects of the lives of the children and families they serve opens many doors to building the spirit of partnerships with families.

- Many individuals in this country do not recognize the characteristics of their own cultures; they believe instead that one has to be from another country or race in order to be considered of another culture.

- Although we believe that certain developmental milestones are reached by children at certain ages, attainment of these milestones and the ages at which they are reached are dependent, in part, on the cultural practices and beliefs of families and the societies in which people live.

- Teachers and caregivers must work with families to understand the caregiving beliefs of the family with regard to sleep patterns, feeding patterns, and comforting patterns.

- American families generally strive for the independence of the child. Families from some other cultures, including those of Hispanic and Asian descent, generally strive for interdependence, with less focus on autonomy. This is one way families from different cultures may be different, although some differences among families are representative of the same cultures.

- As teachers and caregivers, we must examine our attitudes and values with regard to our own heritage before we can value the diversity of the children within our care. We must ask, What is my culture?

- Children are aware of, and talk about, differences in race, gender, and economic status prior to entering kindergarten.

- Adults pass along the stereotypes that exist across time about various cultural and ethnic groups both knowingly and unwittingly to their children.

- Children can engage in thinking games that are designed to foster an awareness of diversity and an appreciation for that which is different from oneself.

- Teachers, administrators, child care providers, families, and communities must work together to build a climate for children that encourages knowledge of, and respect for, the diversity of families.

- Everyone, regardless of race or color, gender or ability, religion or education, brings a rich heritage to the community or group.

- Schools in Reggio Emilia, Italy, provide a wonderful example of the role of the community in supporting the work of the schools.

- Families can become involved in collaborative efforts with schools and community members by engaging in projects with children that emerge from the interests of the children and events of the community.

- The world is in a constant state of change. Children will need to be prepared to meet the challenges of those changes, which include meeting, working, and coping with individuals who have different beliefs, values, and practices in living. Helping children learn about and understand that people are different assists them in making choices appropriate for themselves and in dealing with the world in the context of an ever-changing society.

Activities ◊

1. One family in your nursery school has a 4-year-old child whom they adopted as an infant. Both parents are White, and the child is of African American descent. The mother asks a young teacher, who is also African American, to give her ideas about caring for the little girl's hair. The teacher shares this during a staff meeting and also expresses her discomfort with the situation. As a director, how might you address this situation for the benefit of the teacher, the child, and the family?

2. A father has enrolled his child in your center. You notice on the enrollment application that the mother's name is not mentioned. On further investigation, you discover that, in this particular culture, the mother will remain in the background, with the males and the

father interacting with school personnel. What might your feelings be in this situation, and how might you best address involving the family in the child's school experience?

3. The teacher has been told by the family that one child in the classroom is not allowed by the rules of his religion to celebrate holidays or his birthday. Halloween comes soon after he enrolls, and the children are busy preparing for a Halloween party. The room is being decorated, snacks prepared, and costumes collected. The teacher feels bad about excluding this child and, in fact, has no one to watch the child outside the classroom. What ideas or suggestions do you have for this teacher?

4. You have been working with several other teachers to plan tentative project activities for the year for kindergarten children. You are aware that the children may have taken short or long trips during their summers away from school. These trips may have involved camping, going to a family reunion, visiting a relative in a nearby community, or taking a trip to the beach. You decide to build a curriculum unit based on a travel theme and will introduce prompts for the children, including luggage, maps, camping equipment, and so on. Subsequent activities will depend on the emergent interests of the children. How can families and members of the community be involved in this type of thematic experience?

5. You are teaching primary school in a midwestern community. In recent years, some migrant workers of Hispanic descent have spent a portion of the school year in the community. Several children of the families have been enrolled in your class for as long as 4 months. You have little experience in working with children who are Hispanic and are also frustrated by the brief amount of time the children spend with you. It almost seems pointless to attempt to involve these families. What suggestions might you have for dealing with your feelings and in working with the children and their families?

6. You notice that one girl in your primary class continues to shy away from children not of her race in your classroom. She asks to be moved to other groups of children during group assignments and seeks other places to sit at lunch and during school activities. You finally ask her whether she has a problem, and she divulges that she is acting on the advice of her family. How might you address this situation?

7. A team of teachers has been asked to prepare a list of holidays that might be celebrated in the classrooms and that are representative of various cultures. The team will also be researching and providing background materials to the teachers. Which holidays do you think might be appropriate for the team to select, or do you think this is an appropriate topic to address within the school setting?

8. A local church has "adopted" a family fleeing political strife in another country. The family will rely on contributions for all their needs for a period of time until they can find employment. Both parents held prestigious jobs in their homeland but, because of differing credentials, practices, and language, will be forced to work in low-paying jobs. Their two young children are enrolled in your program and often seem sad. You do not speak the family's language but do want to build a relationship with them in working with their child. What steps might you take to deal with this situation and to assist

the child and the family in this dramatic change in their lives?

9. Two boys in your class are arguing over who has the next turn at the computer. One boy calls the other a "redneck," and the argument continues. How might you handle this situation? What is a "redneck"?

10. One teacher in the preschool program you direct is of Asian descent. She is loved by the children as she works with them in her quiet, shy way. You are a bit more outgoing and want her to "express herself" in a more assertive manner. You suggest that she take some classes that focus on assertiveness in dealing with others. As a director, is this an appropriate recommendation? Why? Why not?

Additional Resources ◊

Beaty, J. J. (1997). *Building bridges with multicultural picture books for children 3–5.* Upper Saddle River, NJ: Merrill/Prentice Hall.

Bete, T. (1997). Finding cultural information on the Internet. *Early Childhood News, 9,* 31.

Cech, M. (1991). *Global child: Multicultural resources for young children.* Menlo Park, CA: Addison-Wesley.

Chang, H. (1996). Many languages, many cultures: Ideas and inspiration for helping young children thrive in a diverse society. *Scholastic Early Childhood Today, 11,* 60–66.

Leister, C. (1993). Working with parents of different cultures. *Dimensions of Early Childhood, 21,* 13–14.

Levin, D. E. (1995, January). Getting to know us: Building classroom culture through our diversity and history. *Child Care Information Exchange Beginnings,* pp. 39–42.

Levy, A. (1997). Culture in the classroom. *Early Childhood News, 9,* 28–30, 32–33.

Mesa-Bains, A., & Shulman, J. H. (Eds.). (1994). *Diversity in the classroom: A casebook for teachers and teacher educators.* Mahwah, NJ: Erlbaum.

Mesa-Bains, A., & Shulman, J. H. (1994). *Diversity in the classroom: Facilitator's guide.* Mahwah, NJ: Erlbaum.

National Association for the Education of Young Children (NAEYC). (1996). NAEYC position statement: Responding to linguistic and cultural diversity—Recommendations for effective early childhood education. *Young Children, 51,* 4–12.

Neugebauer, B. (1997). Parents' perspectives on mealtimes: Based on interviews by Cecelia Alvarado, Cam Do Wong, Robin Gadsen-Dupree, and Karen Kelly. *Child Care Information Exchange* (Issue 117), 56–58.

References ◊

Aboud, F. E. (1988). *Children and prejudice.* New York: Basil Blackwell.

Althen, G. (1988). *American ways: A guide for foreigners in the United States.* Yarmouth, ME: Intercultural Press.

Angelo, M. (1994). *My painted house, my friendly chicken, and me.* New York: Clarkson Potter.

Battle, J. L., Black, J. K., Guddemi, M., & O'Bar, A. (1992). *Multicultural education: A position statement.* Little Rock, AR: Southern Early Childhood Association.

Bennett, L., Jr. (1966). *Before the Mayflower.* Baltimore: Penguin Books.

Bishop, R. S. (1988). Foreword. In D. Taylor & C. Dorsey-Gaines, *Growing up literate: Learning from inner-city families.* Portsmouth, NH: Heinemann.

Bronfenbrenner, U. (1988). Foreword. In A. R. Pence (Ed.), *Ecological research with children and families: From concepts to methodology.* New York: Teachers College Press.

Carter, M. (1995). Building a community culture among teachers. *Child Care Information Exchange, I,* 52–54.

Chan, S. (1992). Families with Asian roots. In E. W. Lynch & M. J. Hanson (Eds.), *Developing cross-cultural competence: A guide for working with young children and their families* (pp. 181–258). Baltimore, MD: Brookes.

Coles, R. (1997). *How to raise a moral child: The moral intelligence of children.* New York: Random House.

Comune di Reggio Emilia, Centro Documentazione Ricerca ducativa Nidi e Scuole dell'Infanzi. (1987). *To make a portrait of a lion (Per Fare il Ritratto di un Leone)* [Video]. Available through Baji Rankin, 346 Washington St., Cambridge, MA 02139.

Department of Early Education, City of Reggio Emilia, Region of Emilia Romagna. (1987). *I centro linguaggi dei bambini (The hundred languages of children: Narrative of the possible).* Catalog of the Exhibit, "The hundred languages of children," in Italian and English. Assessorate Scuole Infanzia e Asili Nido, Via Guido da Castello 12, 42011 Reggio Emilia, Italy.

Derman-Sparks, L. (1989). *Antibias curriculum: Tools for empowering young children.* Washington, DC: National Association for the Education of Young Children.

Derman-Sparks, L. & Ramsey, P. G. (1993). Early childhood multicultural, antibias education in the 1990s: Toward the 21st century. In J. L. Roopnarine & J. E. Johnson (Eds.), *Approaches to early childhood education* (pp. 275–294). New York: Macmillan.

Edwards, C., Gandini, L., & Forman, G. (1993). *The hundred languages of children: The Reggio Emilia approach to early childhood education.* Norwood, NJ: Ablex.

Edwards, C. P. (1986). *Promoting social and moral development in young children: Creative approaches for the classroom.* New York: Teachers College Press.

Edwards, C. P. & Springate, K. W. (1995). The lion comes out of the stone: Helping young children achieve their creative potential. *Dimensions of Early Childhood, 23,* 24–29.

Feng, J. (1994, June). Asian American children: What teachers should know. *Eric Digest* (EDP-PS-94-4). Urbana, IL: ERIC.

Ferreiro, E., & Teberosky, A. (1992). *Literacy before schooling.* Portsmouth, NH: Heinemann.

Forman, G. E., & Gandini, L. (1991). *The long jump: A video analysis of small group projects in early education as practiced in Reggio Emilia, Italy* [Video]. Available from Performanetics Press, 19 The Hollow, Amherst, MA 02139.

Forman, G., Gandini, L., Malaguzzi, L., Rinaldi, C., Piazza, G., & Gambetti, A. (1993). *An amusement park for birds* [Video]. Available from Performanetics Press, 19 The Hollow, Amherst MA 01002.

Garcia, E. E. (1997). The education of Hispanics in early childhood: Of roots and wings. *Young Children, 52,* 5–14.

Gaskins, S. (1996). How Mayan parental theories come into play. In S. Harkness & C. M. Super (Eds.), *Parents' cultural belief systems: Their origins, expressions, and consequences* (pp. 345–363). New York: Guilford Press.

Gonzalez-Mena, J. (1993). *Multicultural issues in child care.* Mountain View, CA: Mayfield.

Goodman, M. E. (1952). *Race awareness in young children.* Cambridge, MA: Addison-Wesley.

Hale, J. (1982). *Black children: Their roots, culture, and learning styles.* New York: Springer.

Hale, J. (1991). The transmission of cultural values to young African American children. *Young Children, 46,* 7–15.

Hanson, M. J. (1992). Families with Anglo European roots. In E. W. Lynch & M. J. Hanson (Eds.), *Developing cross-cultural competence: A guide for working with young children and their families* (pp. 65–88). Baltimore, MD: Brookes.

Harris, T. T. & Fuqua, J. D. (1996). To build a house: Designing curriculum for primary-grade children. *Young Children, 52,* 77–83.

Harste, J. C. & Woodward, V. A. (1989). Fostering needed change in early literacy programs. In D. Strickland & L. M. Morrow (Eds.), *Emerging literacy: Young children learn to read and write* (pp. 147–159). New York: Springer.

Hildebrand, V., Phenice, L. A., Gray, M. M., & Hines, R. P. (1996). *Knowing and serving diverse families.* Upper Saddle River, NJ: Merrill/Prentice Hall.

Joe, J. R. & Malach, R. S. (1992). Families with Native American roots. In E. W. Lynch & M. J. Hanson (Eds.), *Developing cross-cultural competence: A guide for working with young children and their families* (pp. 89–120). Baltimore, MD: Brookes.

Johnson, D. (1991). *1990 census: National and state population counts for American Indians, Eskimos, and Aleuts.* Washington, DC: U.S. Department of Commerce, Bureau of the Census.

Jones, E., & Nimmo, J. (1994). *Emergent curriculum.* Washington, DC: National Association for the Education of Young Children.

Katz, P. A. (1976). The acquisition of racial attitudes in children. In R. P. Katz (Ed.), *Toward the elimination of racism* (pp. 125–154). New York: Pergamon.

Klein, H. A. (1995). Urban Appalachian children in northern schools: A study in diversity. *Young Children, 50,* 10–16.

Kozol, J. (1995). *Amazing Grace: The lives of children and the conscience of a nation.* New York: Harper Perennial.

Lynch, E. W., & Hanson, M. J. (1992). *Developing cross-cultural competence: A guide for working with young children and their families.* Baltimore, MD: Brookes.

Mallory, B. L., & New, R. S. (1994). Introduction: The ethic of inclusion. In B. R. Mallory & R. S. New (Eds.), *Diversity and developmentally appropriate practices: Challenges for early childhood education* (pp. 1–13). New York: Teachers College Press.

Morrison, J. W., & Rodgers, L. S. (1996). Being responsive to the needs of children from dual heritage backgrounds. *Young Children, 52,* 29–33.

New, R. S. (1994). Culture, child development, and developmentally appropriate practices: Teachers as collaborative researchers. In B. L. Mallory & R. S. New (Eds.), *Diversity and developmentally appropriate practices: Challenges for early childhood education* (pp. 65–83). New York: Teachers College Press.

O'Hare, W., Pollard, K., Mann, T., & Kent, M. (1991, July). African Americans in the 1990s. *Population Bulletin.*

Paley, V. G. (1992). *You can't say you can't play.* Cambridge, MA: Harvard University Press.

Phillips, C. B. (1994). The movement of African American children through sociocultural contexts. In B. R. Mallory & R. S. New (Eds.), *Diversity and developmentally appropriate practices: Challenges for early childhood education* (pp. 137–154). New York: Teachers College Press.

Piaget, J. (1932). *The moral judgement of the child.* New York: Free Press.

Piaget, J. (1983). Piaget's theory. In P. H. Mussen (Ed.), *Handbook of child psychology: Vol. 1. History, theory, and methods.* New York: Wiley.

Pipher, M. (1996). *The shelter of each other: Rebuilding our families.* New York: Putnam.

Powell, D. R. (1994). Parents, pluralism, and the NAEYC statement on developmentally appropriate practice. In B. R. Mallory & R. S. New (Eds.), *Diversity and developmentally appropriate practices: Challenges for early childhood education* (pp. 166–182). New York: Teachers College Press.

Ramsey, P. G. (1986). Racial and cultural categories. In C. P. Edwards, *Social and moral development in young children.* New York: Teachers College Press.

Ramsey, P. G. (1987). *Teaching and learning in a diverse world: Multicultural education for young children.* New York: Teachers College Press.

Saracho, O. N., & Spodek, B. (1983). Preface. In O. N. Saracho & B. Spodek (Eds.), *Understanding the multicultural experience in early childhood education* (pp. 3–15). Washington, DC: National Association for the Education of Young Children.

Taylor, D., & Dorsey-Gaines, C. (1988). *Growing up literate: Learning from inner-city families*. Portsmouth, NH: Heinemann.

Teale, W. H., & Sulzby, E. (1989). Emergent literacy: New perspectives. In D. Strickland & L. M. Morrow (Eds.), *Emerging literacy: Young children learn to read and write* (pp. 1–15). New York: Springer.

Trawick-Smith, J. (1997). *Early childhood development: A multicultural perspective*. Upper Saddle River, NJ: Merrill/Prentice Hall.

U.S. Bureau of the Census. (1987). *Statistical abstract of the United States, 1988* (108th ed.). Washington, DC: U.S. Department of Commerce.

U.S. Bureau of the Census. (1990). *Statistical abstract of the United States, 1990* (110th ed.). Washington, DC: U.S. Department of Commerce.

Wellhousen, K. (1996). Be it ever so humble: Developing a study of homes for today's diverse society. *Young Children, 52*, 72–76.

Willis, W. (1992). Families with African American roots. In E. W. Lynch & M. J. Hanson (Eds.), *Developing cross-cultural competence: A guide for working with young children and their families* (pp. 121–150). Baltimore, MD: Brookes.

Wolf, A. W., Lozoff, B., Latz, S., & Paludetto, R. (1996). Parental theories in the management of young children's sleep in Japan, Italy, and the United States. In S. Harkness & C. M. Super (Eds.), *Parents' cultural belief systems: Their origins, expressions, and consequences* (pp. 407–427). New York: Guilford Press.

York, S. (1991). *Roots and wings: Affirming culture in early childhood programs*. St. Paul, MN: Red Leaf Press.

Zeitlan, M. (1996). My child is my crown: Yoruba parental theories and practices in early childhood. In S. Harkness & C. M. Super (Eds.), *Parents' cultural belief systems: Their origins, expressions, and consequences* (pp. 407–427). New York: Guilford Press.

Zuniga, M. E. (1992). Families with Latino roots. In E. W. Lynch & M. J. Hanson (Eds.), *Developing cross-cultural competence: A guide for working with young children and their families* (pp. 151–180). Baltimore, MD: Brookes.

5 Creating Community and School Linkages for Children with Special Needs

Interactions between very young children and their caregivers provide a powerful context for early learning and development, and in many ways set the stage for what comes later. It is within this context that children first develop views of themselves and others that are carried forward to later relationships.

Field, 1986, p. 47

Key Terms

ADA
at-risk children
autism
cerebral palsy
child advocacy
crack/cocaine/heroin effects
DAP
Developmental Disabilities Act
developmental disability
emotional disturbance
family support programs
formal community resources
giftedness
handicapping conditions
hearing impairment
HIV/AIDS
IDEA legislation
incidence of disability

inclusion movement
individualized education program
    (IEP)
interagency collaboration
LRE
mental retardation
multifactored assessment
normalization
orthopedic impairment
parent advocacy group
parent education programs
parent empowerment
P.L. 94-142
P.L. 99-457
screening and referral
speech and language disorder
superbaby
visual impairment

Meeting the unique and individual needs of families of children with special needs requires special planning and teamwork between parents and professionals (Dunst, Johanson, Trivette, & Hamby, 1991; Mallory & New, 1994; Safford, 1989). The collaborative services of teachers and caregivers, along with such specialists as special education teachers, curriculum specialists, social workers, and physical, occupational, or speech and language therapists, are often required.

The emerging movement toward educational inclusion in the United States, evidenced through **P.L. 99-457** (the Education of the Handicapped Act Amendments of 1986; see Figure 5.1), has brought together law and logic to ensure that families of children with special needs will receive the greatest possible normality in the educational experiences of the children. Thus, the goal of services for families of children with special needs should be to provide intervention appropriate to the needs of each exceptional child but, at the same time, to promote normalization (Dunst et al., 1991; Mallory & New, 1994; Rose & Smith, 1993).

This chapter addresses the unique needs of families of children with special needs as they interface with early childhood teachers in school and child care arrangement settings. Included in this chapter are the following topics:

- Definitions and rates of **incidence of disabilities** and special needs in the United States, including giftedness
- Psychological, emotional, and social adaptations of families of children with special needs
- Descriptions of disabilities, special needs, and special gifts or talents of young children
- The role of the early childhood teacher in assessing, planning, implementing, and evaluating educational and developmental individualized plans and programs for families and children with special needs
- Community resources, financial resources and funding avenues, and interagency collaboration strategies for children and families with special needs
- Public laws and advocacy initiatives related to childhood disability

◇◇ **Definitions and Incidence of Special Needs Children**

Families of children with special needs face many challenges that are different from those of typically developing children. This is reflected in simply defining the terminology in the area of early childhood special education, which is an ongoing process. *Special needs* is often defined through societal consensus: A person considered "normal" in one culture may be considered "special needs" in another (Mallory & New, 1994; Rose & Smith, 1993; Safford, 1989). Even specialists cannot agree on specific criteria for diagnoses and classification, and the definition of *special needs* or *at-risk* is confounded for younger children because some diagnoses or definitions do not apply until children reach school age (Marozas & May, 1988). In addition, early childhood development occurs rapidly and unevenly and is not clearly defined in terms of "typical" versus "atypical."

In general, children with special needs are those whose mental, communicative, social-emotional, or physical characteristics require some adaptations in the educational program in order for them to learn optimally (Mallory & New, 1994; Safford, 1989). Approximately 10% of all children are assumed to have special needs significant enough to qualify them as exceptional, whereas another 2% to 3% constitute gifted and talented children. Children with special needs display characteristics that involve disabilities or delays in one or more areas of functioning.

An estimated one million special needs children of preschool age live in the United States. **P.L. 94-142** (the Education for All Handicapped Children Act [EHA] of 1975) defines children with special needs in the following way:

> [Special needs] children are those children evaluated as being mentally retarded, hard-of-hearing, deaf, speech impaired, visually handicapped, seriously emotionally disturbed, orthopedically impaired, other health impaired, deaf-blind, multi-handicapped, or having specific learning disabilities, who because of these impairments need special education and related services. (Sec. 121a.5 [42 Fed. Reg.], p. 12478)

Politically Correct Terminology

Being aware of current politically correct terminology related to special needs children is very important for the early childhood professional. The professional who focuses on meeting the needs of these children and their families should be aware that such terms as *handicapped, exceptional,* and *mainstreamed* have given way to *children with special needs, children at risk,* and *inclusive environments.* Without a doubt, the Americans With Disabilities Act (**ADA** [P.L. 101-336]; see Figure 5.1) and the early intervention movement of the 1990s have created heightened sensitivity and awareness of the importance of using appropriate terms when working with special needs children and their families.

Dangers of Labeling

Educators and parents alike are concerned about the possible harmful and lasting effects of labeling young children with special needs. This concern is reflected in the recent policy initiatives for children with special needs; these do not require categorical labels for the following reasons:

- Young children develop rapidly; thus, their needs also change rapidly.
- Early labeling of young children can lead to long-term restrictions and limits that may not even be relevant.
- Least restrictive services for children encourage inclusion and integration of typically and atypically developing children, and labeling is counterproductive to this policy.

ADA: The Americans with Disabilities Act of 1990 (P.L. 101-336) addresses accessibility issues for individuals with special needs and includes such factors as walks, curbs, ramps, public restrooms, telephones, water fountains, restaurants, emergency procedures and hazards, width of hallways and doors, bathroom facilities, and other related needs.

IDEA: The Individuals with Disabilities Education Act (IDEA), passed as P.L. 101-476 in 1990, shapes what educators and parents can expect and demand for their children who are differently abled. Part H is a grant program for infants and toddlers to assist states in developing early intervention programs; Part B states the extent possible that children with disabilities should receive their special education service in least restrictive environment (LRE).

P.L. 99-457: A public law passed in 1986 by Congress that extends all the rights and protections of P.L. 94-142, the Education for All Handicapped Children Act of 1975, to all handicapped 3- to 5-year-olds by 1990 and that made services available to all 2-year-olds and younger on a discretionary basis.

Figure 5.1   Definitions of P.L. 99-457, the ADA, and IDEA
Source: Marozas and May (1988)

State-level educational reform has focused on families and children at risk. **At-risk children** has been defined as children "with a higher than average probability of problems in development and negative developmental outcomes as viewed as ranging from life threatening or handicapping conditions to school failure" (Safford, 1989, p. 25). The term *at risk* is seen throughout the educational literature. The term is frequently associated with income level, however, and children living in conditions characterized by poverty are considered to be more developmentally at-risk too.

The Law, Special Needs, and the School-Parent Partnership

Children with special needs can be defined from various perspectives: medical, legal, sociological, psychological, and educational. The law defines special needs from the educational perspective, and that is the focus of this chapter. Public laws in the United States determine that *all* children will be educated, special needs or not. These laws determine where, by whom, and with whom special needs children will be educated.

The term **developmental disability** refers to a chronic disability that (a) is attributable to a mental or physical impairment or combination of mental and physical impairments; (b) is manifested before the child reaches age 22; (c) is likely to continue indefinitely; (d) results in substantial limitations in function related to self-care, language (receptive and expressive), learning, mobility, self-direction, capacity for independent living and economic self-sufficiency; and (e) reflects the child's need for a combination and sequence of special interdisci-

The ADA addresses accessibility issues for individuals with special needs.

plinary or generic care, treatment, or other services that are individually planned and coordinated (Safford, 1989; Wiegerink & Pelosi, 1979).

One of the most exciting pieces of recent legislation on behalf of children and families with special needs, P.L. 99-457 (1986) clearly identifies a more basic role for parents of children with special needs. This law not only recognizes and emphasizes the concept of a partnership between parents and professionals but also reinforces the notion that the family shapes the child's life experiences. Thus, the role of schools and professionals is to *support the needs* of families of children with special needs, rather than to supplant them.

As noted in the literature and from our life experiences, parents of exceptional children are impassioned with love and concern for their children's well-being. Ethically and legally, the early childhood professional must work toward provision of least restrictive educational placements; thus, parents should not have to fight for this appropriate educational placement: *It is the right of the family and the child.*

The passage of P.L. 99-457 gave a tremendous boost to the concepts of *early childhood special education* and *early intervention*. Because the law mandated public schools to provide comprehensive educational and developmental services for preschool children with special needs, the need for formal teacher training programs in the areas of early childhood special education and early intervention proliferated. Armed with both legislative and fiscal support, community- and school-based professionals trained to work with young children with special needs increased dramatically.

◊◊ Incidence of Special Needs

Incidence of At-Risk Infants

- Each year, some 425,000 infants are born who will manifest a disability within the first 4 years of life. At the end of 1990, approximately 600,000 children with special needs, from birth through age 5, were receiving intervention services.
- Some 350,000 to 357,000 newborns each year have been prenatally exposed to drugs, including alcohol. Fetal alcohol syndrome is now recognized as the leading known cause of mental retardation in the Western world.
- Each year, more than 400,000 infants are born prematurely.
- The HIV (human immunodeficiency virus) has become the greatest infectious cause of pediatric mental retardation in the United States (Sexton, Snyder, Sharpton, & Stricklin, 1993).

Each year, more than 400,000 infants are born prematurely.

In the United States today, more than one million children of preschool age have special needs, and the range of variations in development is considerable, even in a group of children of the same chronological age, gender, and ethnic group. In some children, the variation is so extreme that identification of a problem is relatively easy. In such cases, a child may clearly fit into a category defined by P.L. 94-142. Younger children, however, require a more flexible definition and should include those children who, prior to their third birthday, have a high probability of manifesting a sensory motor deficit, mental handicap in later childhood that was actually the result of a birth defect, disease process, trauma, or environmental conditions present during the prenatal and/or postnatal period (Dunst et al., 1994; Solit, 1993).

The advantage of a more flexible definition for younger children is that more serious handicaps or delays can be prevented by serving a child early through early intervention (Baker, 1991; Marozas & May, 1988; Solit, 1993). Children from less advantaged environments are overrepresented in special education classes in the public schools, relative to their numbers in the total population. Successful initiatives to prevent more serious delays from developing through early intervention have been reported (Badger, 1981; Baker, 1991; Sexton et al., 1993). Some states have adopted policies that include serving young children outside traditional handicap categories; these children may be identified as "developmentally delayed," "at risk," or "preschool handicapped." Identification of these children at an early age ensures more ready access to early intervention services but, at the same time, does not result in permanent labels being attached to children at such a young age.

◊◊ Psychological and Social Adaptations for the Family of Children with Special Needs

---

VIGNETTE 1

Marie

Marie, who is 4 years old, is deaf. Her parents, who are also deaf, have used American Sign Language with Marie since birth. Marie is bright, friendly, likes to converse, and is sometimes bossy—a relatively typical 4-year-old. She attends a preschool for deaf children 3 days a week. Her parents and teachers think she will benefit from attending a nearby child care center on the other 2 days a week. Her working parents also need child care before and after school, when the deaf children preschool is not open (Solit, 1993, p. 132).

All parents, whether their children have special needs or not, have expectations for their children. Thus, it is difficult to comprehend fully the dynamics of families with young special needs children unless one is, in fact, the parent of an exceptional child (Baker, 1991). Prospective parents who have waited so many months for the birth of their baby may suddenly learn that the newborn does not even approximate their idealized expectations. The amount of stress imposed on the family may depend on how radically the parents' expectations are violated.

The Family as Primary Socialization Agent

In the United States, most young children with special needs live at home with their families; thus, the role of the family in providing a strong, supportive environment for the child is crucial. Recognition of the family's role has only recently been realized and acknowledged formally in legislation based on the convergence of several societal trends: (a) the awareness that the family is actually the first and primary teacher for the young child; (b) the family system's perspective that acknowledges the family unit as a system of interdependent relationships; (c) the philosophy and belief in normalization as a goal for the young child and family; (d) the outcomes of numerous research studies that document the effectiveness of early intervention and early childhood education for long-term societal outcomes; and (e) the legal impact of P.L. 94-142 (the EHA) and P.L. 99-457 (the Education of the Handicapped Act Amendments of 1986).

The Family as Teacher

Through daily interactions with parents and extended family members, young children learn language, cognitive, and social skills as documented in the developmental literature. The family is the primary agent in inducting the child into the complex, rule-based family system that reflects the larger society. Although teaching at home by parents is not as structured and planned as that in the school, the fact is that most language, cognitive, and social skills learned at home by the child are obtained through the daily routines of family life: doing chores, helping with household tasks, playing, viewing television, and other family activities, both at home and within the community. Children also learn important concepts from their families, and these concepts are transferred into larger learning settings as the children mature. Thus, the family should be included in the planning for special needs children because the family plays such a primary role in teaching and socializing young children.

Bronfenbrenner (1974) describes the crucial role of the family unit in support of the developing special needs child:

> The evidence indicates that the family is the most effective and economical system for fostering and sustaining the development of the child. . . . Without

family involvement any effects of intervention, at least in the cognitive sphere, appear to erode rapidly once the program ends. In contrast, the involvement of the parents as partners in the enterprise provides an ongoing system which reinforces the effects of the program while it is in operation and helps to sustain them after the program ends. (p. 55)

Emotional Reactions and Issues for Parents

The impact a child with a disability has on the family is usually a major one. As most people know, the arrival of even a nondisabled child into a family is a stressful, emotional event. Again, the parents' expectations play an important role in the explanation of this stress. Perske (1973) uses the term **superbaby** to describe parents' images of the expected child. Every parent imagines the new child as a future scholar, athlete, beauty queen, and so on. For most families, whose children are typical, these initial dreams change slowly as the reality of the children's development unfolds. These families have time to adjust to their children and for the emerging differences between their children and initial expectations. For families of infants who are identified at birth as having a developmental disability, dreams die quickly and painfully (Baker, 1991; Fallen & Umansky, 1985; Rose & Smith, 1993; Sexton et al., 1993). These parents must deal with deep emotions that include shock, fear, and disappointment. These emotional reactions have been listed by Wolfensberger (1967) and elaborated by Sexton et al. (1993) and Solit (1993), who describe more than 40 reactions, including anger, ambivalence, avoidance, bitterness, disbelief, denial, envy, guilt, helplessness, mourning, sorrow, and shock.

The Grieving Process for the Family

The birth of an atypically developing infant or the diagnosis of a disability or special need in a child sets off a series of emotional reactions for the parents and other family members (Baker, 1991). The psychological process that parents experience is often compared to the grieving process that results at the loss of a loved one. Drotar, Baskiewica, Irwin, Kennell, and Klaus (1975) identified what they believed to be five stages of dealing with the birth of an atypical infant (see Figure 5.2). These stages of grieving are predictable and are observed in today's parent population. Research indicates that the duration and intensity of each stage varies widely among individuals and that rather than pass through these stages in a once-and-for-all sequence, the grieving person usually revisits the stages and reexperiences intense emotions from the initial emotional stage.

It is important to recognize that each family presents a unique profile for coping with this stressor event. For most families, progression through these stages is not an orderly, precise process. Initial feelings of denial and sadness may recur. If new crises occur, new demands for coping also occur. Some families adjust quickly; others require much longer periods of time.

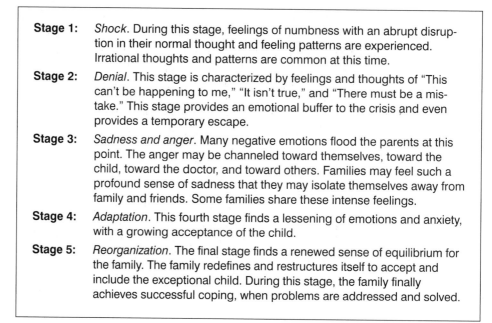

Figure 5.2   Stages of grief: Adjusting to a child with special needs

A family's response to a crisis depends on (a) the stressor event itself, (b) the resources the family has for coping with the stressor, and (c) the specific meaning the family gives to the event.

Normalization as a Goal

The concept of **normalization** centers around the notion that all children are more alike than different and that all children should be educated and served in similar ways. "Normalization" leads to such social policy initiatives as deinstitutionalization, least restrictive environments, inclusive classrooms, and fully integrated learning settings (Fallen & Umansky, 1985; Rose & Smith, 1993; Solit, 1993). As a result of normalization, infants and young children are rarely placed in institutionalized settings, and efforts to support the family are increased so that it can remain the primary agent of education. The notion of normalcy and normalization also plays out in legislation that requires that parents be the primary and first teachers of the child with special needs, so it is indeed a powerful notion.

Parent Advocacy

Parents of children with special needs have become vocal advocates for the rights of their children. Perhaps no other group of parents portrays a higher level of commitment and energy to effective and visible child advocacy. Examples of parent advocacy include the formation of parents into **parent advocacy groups,** such as the Association for Retarded Citizens. Parents' involvement in the legislative process at both federal and state levels has resulted in increased legislative initiatives and mandates, such as the successful passage of P.L. 99-457 in 1986.

In addition, funding avenues at the federal and state levels now must address specifically the role of the family and the need for family support as part of their program implementation and evaluation. Professionals who write grants to obtain funds to serve young children with special needs and maintain these grants successfully now realize that one of the most crucial components of their successful grantsmanship is the inclusion of clearly defined mechanisms of parent involvement. Examples of these mechanisms are (a) assessment of family and parent needs, as well as child needs, (b) ongoing monitoring of family support needs, (c) documentation of provision of collaborative support services for families, and (d) evaluation research that documents successful program outcomes for the child, the parent, and the family.

Parents of children with special needs have become vocal advocates for the rights of their children.

Goals for Family Involvement

Programs and organizations for families of young exceptional children may have multiple purposes. Some of the more common purposes of these programs are (a) emotional, physical, and financial support for the family, (b) parent education, (c) individualized education program participation, and (d) child advocacy (Solit, 1993). *Emotional, physical, and financial support* programs have as their main goal to provide emotional support to individual family members, as well as to the family as a whole. As described above, the family of a child with special needs goes through stages of adjustment. Family resources are necessary to facilitate adaptation to a child born with special needs or in whom special needs have been diagnosed. Researchers in individual and family coping suggest that interpersonal networks are crucial as a source of social and emotional support in times of stress and crisis. Such support is often provided by members of the extended family, friends, coworkers, and clergy. Schools have become important resources for these families because of more isolation from extended family members, greater mobility, and more single-parent households.

Physical and financial resources are also called into action when crisis besets a family. Children with disabilities frequently require increased physical exertion for care through lifting, carrying, and pushing. Other family needs are financial in nature. Having a child with a disability can be very expensive for medical care, adaptive equipment, transportation, speech therapists, occupational therapists, psychologists, and other related services. These demands can drain a family's financial resources. The amount of financial resources available to the family depends on amount and type of insurance coverage, income level of the family, quantity and quality of free community services, and capacity of the local school system to meet the needs of the child with the disability. Obviously, when financial resources are lacking, additional stress is placed on the family. Thus, when ample emotional, physical, and financial resources are present, family coping is made much easier.

Family support programs are available in varying degrees throughout the United States. Parents of children with disabilities frequently seek out parents and families of other children who have similar disabilities. Such families may serve as models, demonstrating the positive strengths that families can obtain and use in coping with the specific situation. Formal family support programs involve training of parents in listening skills, types and causes of childhood disabilities, and other relevant topics, so that they can provide needed support and information as families adjust to the knowledge that their children have disabilities. Another important role of the family support group is to assist parents in dealing with feelings of grief and to provide an opportunity to vent and clarify their feelings and receive support for the legitimacy of these feelings they are expressing.

Importance of Siblings

Siblings are sometimes overlooked when family support programs are planned. Sibling support groups, however, are becoming common. Siblings can actually serve as teachers for their brother or sister with a disability. The research literature documents that siblings of children with disabilities frequently reflect feelings of helplessness or empowerment in the situation similar to those of their parents.

Baker (1991) and Stoneman and Brody (1982) made suggestions for families with a disabled child and nondisabled siblings, including the following:

- Children with disabilities should not be institutionalized for the sake of the sibling. Indeed, siblings may actually benefit from the relationship and life experiences with the child with the disability.
- Siblings should not be given extended caretaking responsibilities for a child with a disability that exceed their own level of maturity. This is particularly true for younger siblings who help care for an older child.
- Parents should make a special effort to spend time with the nondisabled children and to show a special interest in their needs.
- The nondisabled child should not be expected to compensate for parents' expectations for the disabled child. This places an undue burden on the nondisabled child.
- Counseling programs can help normal siblings of children with disabilities share feelings and fears.
- "In-home mainstreaming" can be accomplished by encouraging the child with the disability to model behaviors of the sibling and by encouraging the sibling to involve the child with the disability in the everyday routines and chores of the home.
- Parents' ability to adapt to the child with the disability is reflected in the coping skills of the siblings. Thus, if parents are having difficulty in their adjustment, they should seek professional assistance to alleviate these same maladaptive behaviors and feelings in the siblings (Stoneman & Brody, 1982).

Parent education is a second major goal of family involvement. Parent education can take many forms: strengthening general abilities to parent; modeling for parents in the teaching efforts with their disabled child; providing needed information for parents on a variety of topics such as health and medical issues and community resources; strengthening the parent-parent, parent-child, and sibling-sibling relationships; and teaching communication skills.

Parent education programs exist in public and private school systems, in churches and other community institutions, in public agencies related to social services and welfare, and in private initiatives to provide quality parent education. Parent education programs can focus on nondisabling conditions and parent issues too, but these programs are particularly important for the parent of a special needs child because of the level of stress and anticipated financial, educational, and emotional resources needed.

IEP and IFSP participation is the third goal of family involvement. An **IEP (individualized education program)** is now required for many educational programs that serve children with special needs; an IFSP (individualized family service plan) serves the needs of infants and toddlers. Parents have the right to be active participants in the development of their child's IEP, to read all educational records related to the identification and placement of their child, and to pursue legal process, if needed, to obtain services for which they are entitled.

Parents can be encouraged to participate in the IEP and the IFSP process in various ways. Parents' work schedules should be considered when IEP meetings are being scheduled. Transportation may also have to be provided for parents in need. Parents should be encouraged to keep a log of important events and happenings at home that provide valuable insight and information about their child. Having this log at the IEP and IFSP meeting will facilitate planning for the child, validate the parents' role with the child, and actively involve the parents in the planning process. Parents with higher levels of education may understand the importance of their involvement; parents with lower levels of education should be helped to understand this role and assisted in attending the scheduled meetings. At no time should parents be patronized or "talked down to" during the IEP meeting. Indeed, parents of exceptional children should be encouraged to speak up and assert their concerns, issues, needs, and requests. This is the parents' right, not privilege.

The IFSP is the individualized plan to serve infants and toddlers.

Child advocacy, the fourth goal of family involvement, has grown dramatically in the United States during the 1980s and 1990s (Baker, 1991; Sexton et al., 1993; Vincent, 1992). Examples of the growing awareness of children's issues are seen in the publications and legislative work of the Children's Defense Fund, National Association for the Education of Young Children (NAEYC), Division for Early Childhood (DEC), and other national and state organizations. Parents can be very effective and convincing advocates for their own child and for the rights of other children. Caring and committed parents who clearly understand the needs of their child and who are able to articulate these needs to decision makers are making profound changes in the legislative process on a regular basis. State advocacy offices and advocacy-oriented parents often receive assertiveness training, training in strategies to help make institutional change, and training related to the legal process. Figure 5.3 lists other suggestions for professionals working with parents of children with special needs.

◊◊ Descriptions of Special Needs

This textbook addresses children from a developmental perspective; therefore, descriptions of children who vary from the normal pattern of development are described within the parameters of typically developing children. A brief description of common special needs areas follows.

Mental retardation. The most often used definition of **mental retardation** was developed by the American Association on Mental Deficiency (AAMD): "Mental retardation refers to significantly subaverage general intellectual functioning existing concurrently with deficits in adaptive behavior and manifested during the developmental period" (Grossman, 1972, p. 7). Intellectual functioning has traditionally been assessed by performance on

Figure 5.3 Suggestions for working with parents of children with special needs

Source: Adapted from Gargioulo and Graves (1991).

- Explain terminology, as this may be the parent's first experience with exceptionality.
- Acknowledge and accept the parent's negative feelings.
- Listen effectively and attentively.
- Use a two-step approach in informing parents about their child's special needs and planning for intervention; this allows time for parents to comprehend and deal with their own emotional reactions.
- Keep parents informed and demonstrate respect, concern, and a sincere desire to cooperate.
- Be accountable and follow through.
- Respect the parent's level of involvement.

an intelligence test. Mental retardation characterizes a child with borderline subnormal intellect. Children with mental retardation are those who score less than standard deviations below the mean of 100, an intelligence quotient of less than approximately 70. The levels of retardation are as follows:

Levels of Retardation

Mild or educable mental retardation	55–69 IQ*
Moderate or trainable retardation	40–54 IQ
Severe mental retardation	25–39 IQ
Profound mental retardation	Below 25 IQ

*Note: IQ = Mental age/Chronological age x 100

Few standardized intelligence tests are considered developmentally appropriate and statistically sound and reliable for preschool children. Consequently, other strategies and instrumentation may be employed to measure the intellectual capabilities of these children.

Cerebral palsy.   **Cerebral palsy** is a nonprogressive condition in which voluntary control of involved muscles is impaired as a result of brain injury incurred during the fetal period (prenatally), at the time of birth (perinatally), or during the developmental period (postnatally). The term *cerebral palsy* encompasses a broad range of causes, functional levels, and degrees of intellectual, sensory, motor, and communicative involvement (Baker, 1991; Safford, 1989). The location and extent of the brain lesion determines the extent, nature, and severity of the disability for each child.

Cerebral palsy affects the child's motor functioning, movement, and mobility and with significant variation, depending on the specific form. Use of, or control over, arms and legs is most commonly affected; some children may find it difficult to sit in an upright position, turn their heads from side to side, chew and swallow, or even speak normally. The classroom teacher or the caregiver usually works with an occupational or physical therapist to determine specific child needs, to develop activities for intervention, and to evaluate the child's progress.

Hearing impairments.   A hearing loss may be conductive or sensorineural. *Conductive* hearing losses are caused by interference with the sequence of sound vibrations reaching the auditory nerve. *Sensorineural* losses are caused by defects in the inner ear or in the auditory nerve that transmits the electrical impulses to the brain for interpretation. **Hearing impairments** may result from early infections during prenatal or postnatal periods, from an accident, or from exposure to certain prescription drugs. The severity of the impairment depends on the degree of loss and the age of onset. A hearing loss that occurs before a child's learning language requires greater environmental modifications than a loss that occurs after mastery of language. A child with a normal range of hearing can hear sounds as soft as 0 to 25 decibels (dB) within a frequency range of approximately 40 to 4,000 hertz (Hz). Most conversational speech has an intensity of about 55 dB and a frequency range of 500 to 2,000 Hz. A child with a hearing loss of greater than 40 dB will probably miss a considerable amount of spoken information; a profound hearing loss of greater than 90 dB will severely handicap a child.

Speech and language delays and disorders.   Young children exhibit a wide range of typical development of speech and language; therefore, it is difficult to delineate clearly what is and what is not a disorder. Some clear indicators of **speech and language disorder** are a cleft palate, no use of words at 4 years of age, and language limited to replicating the language of others. Great care must be taken in identifying a child within this category, especially when cultural diversity and environment play such crucial roles in forming a child's speech and language patterns.

Impairments in speech and language may accompany other disabilities. Children with a hearing impairment, with cerebral palsy, with an emotional disturbance, or with mental retardation may show atypical speech and language development (Fallen & Umansky, 1985). Early identification of possible speech and language delays is crucial because so much of a child's later development is dependent on communication with other children and adults.

Autism.   Childhood **autism** is now classified as a chronic health problem (it had previously been viewed as an emotional disorder), and language and communication are the major focus for concern and intervention. Children identified as autistic often do not use language effectively and appropriately as typical children of the same age do (Safford, 1989, p. 217). A child labeled autistic is essentially a child who has a mixture of characteristics that are typical mixed with characteristics that are atypical of most children of comparable age. Effective teachers of autistic children are those who are also effective with other populations of young children.

Flexibility in teaching style is crucial, as well as teaching characteristics such as a nonthreatening manner, good observational skills, use of physical contact and physical prompts, use of modified language, initial use of one-to-one teaching relationship, and a very positive attitude and approach (Grant, 1982, cited in Safford, 1989). Teaching autistic children within naturalistic learning settings and classroom environments is recommended; thus, inclusion is very appropriate for these children.

Emotional disturbance.   The origins of **emotional disturbance** in young children are not very well understood. Environmental factors may be the cause, as well as neurological and chemical factors. Emotional disturbance among younger children is believed to encompass many types of problems, some biologically based and others more environmentally based. Examples of behaviors that characterize a child with emotional disturbance may be quite diverse and include withdrawal, depression, anxiety, aggression, and extreme fears or phobias.

The diagnosis of emotional disturbance is based on the frequency, duration, and intensity of these behaviors. Strategies used to remediate emotional disturbance reflect differing theoretical orientations of the respective programs that serve children and families. Thus, intervention strategies include adjusting the diet and other environmental variables, restructuring the physical environment, and examining relationship dynamics between the child and significant others.

Orthopedic impairments.   This is a very broad category and includes any condition that interferes with the health or normal functioning of bones, joints, or muscles. Defects such as spina bifida, club foot, or cerebral palsy may be present at birth. Other problems may develop later as the child matures, such as muscular dystrophy. Causes of **orthopedic impairment** include hereditary factors, the influence of infection or toxic substances on the mother during very early pregnancy, birth injuries, or diseases or accidents that occur after birth. Many children in this category do not require special education services. Adaptive equipment for some children may help them function more independently in typical settings.

Visual impairments.   Most **visual impairments** in young children are caused by prenatal factors, serious infections such as rubella, and specific hereditary factors that may manifest themselves in blindness at birth or create a likelihood that the child will require special education services. A child is considered blind if visual acuity is poorer than 20/200 in the better eye after correction or if the field of vision is limited to an angle of less than 20°. A child with partial sight has an acuity of less than 20/70 but greater than 20/200; an acuity of 20/200 indicates that the child can see at 20 ft what an individual with normal vision can see at 200 ft. Preschoolers whose vision is too poor for them to benefit from printed materials should begin a program that sensitizes them to tactile learning materials. This provides an introduction to prebraille and braille reading skills.

Giftedness.   In this discussion of children with special needs, it is important to include those children who have special gifts. Often lost in the societal shuffle, these children make up a significant portion of the school population in the United States. These children, like the children described above, also have special educational needs. According to Safford (1989), "In fact, when educators fail to respond to the unique needs of gifted and talented children, these children become handicapped" (p. 240).

Who is the gifted child? Responses to this question vary, depending on the source. Most agree, however, that the gifted child demonstrates some exceptional quality or potential for accomplishment. Determining or assessing **giftedness** has been the source of debate and educational reform. Young children who are very bright are also very heterogeneous. Parents of a gifted child may expect that child to excel in all areas of development or to excel in emotional as well as intellectual development. In fact, gifted children vary widely in their talents and abilities. Children who are gifted are still young children who still need hands-on, developmentally appropriate learning activities. The fact that they are intellectually advanced does not make them more able to complete paper-and-pencil assessments. Parents also need to respect their child's individual interests and to set their expectations accordingly. Individual traits that may be correlated with giftedness include excellent memory, curiosity, sense of humor, perfectionism, rapid learning ability, unusual alertness, long attention span, high activity level, keen sense of observation, and advanced ability to play with manipulative such as puzzles and mazes. Creativity is also associated with giftedness even though the child may not demonstrate measured intellectual advancement. Creativity has to do with a child's ability to problem-solve in multiple dimensions, capacity for organization, use of fantasy for problem solving, and ability to produce new combinations through manipulation (Safford, 1989; Torrance, 1983).

Of special interest is the child who has both giftedness and a disability. This child, because of his or her **handicapping condition**, may be overlooked for giftedness. According to Safford (1989), the "full range of intellectual potential is represented among children with impaired mobility, vision, or hearing or with chronic health problems"(p. 244). Ironically, the gifted child may be identified as a problematic child because his or her high energy level, extreme curiosity, and constant thirst for new knowledge may challenge the teacher, resulting in behavioral or management issues in the classroom. For this reason, the gifted child must be included in the "special needs" category; teachers and caregivers should be on the alert for children who demonstrate these exceptional qualities.

HIV and AIDS. As the second decade of **HIV/AIDS** is well under way, the number of pediatric cases is expected to rise significantly (Savage, Mayfield, & Cook, 1993). With advances in treatment, more infected children

Children learn best through self-initiated, self-chosen activities.

are expected to live longer. Legislation mandates that children with HIV/AIDS not be excluded from educational programs in which typical children participate (Americans With Disabilities Act of 1990). Most children with HIV/AIDS function well within the regular classroom, and they are eligible for special education services unless they are evaluated and meet the stated criteria for specific disabilities. They may, however, qualify for other services, such as Other Health Impaired category, which means "limited strength, vitality, or alertness due to chronic or acute health problems which adversely affect educational performance"(Savage et al., 1993, p. 11). Teachers in early childhood settings should read about HIV/AIDS and attend in-service workshops to stay current with the latest medical information, as well as with appropriate teacher-child-parent needs and issues.

Crack, cocaine, and heroin effects. The use of crack, cocaine, and heroin by pregnant women and the general adult population in the United States has increased dramatically over the past decade. Early childhood teachers and caregivers are reporting increased numbers of young children in their settings that demonstrate **crack/cocaine/heroin effects.** Defining what is developmentally appropriate for this population is challenging, but educators have developed strategies that usually involve higher levels of structure, repetition, and teacher-directed activities. Because these children display difficult interactional patterns from birth, it is important for teachers to be informed about the latest developments in this child population. Children with this background frequently display attachment disorders, asocial behaviors, aggressive or inappropriate peer interactions, and more social difficulties in general (Griffith, 1992). Although these children may not automatically be categorized as having "special needs," they clearly are at risk and should be monitored for assessment and **screening and referral.** In addition, dealing with parents of crack/cocaine/heroin affected children is essential to maintaining consistency between the classroom and home environments.

◊◊ Role of Early Childhood Professionals in Providing Family Support

With the passage of P.L. 94-142 and P.L. 99-457, the role of the public school in the lives of children with special needs and their families increased dramatically. The 1986 passage of P.L. 99–457 signaled the crossing of an important threshold for young children with special needs: The public school is legally responsible for the provision of comprehensive services to these children and their families, beginning at age 36 months, and for infants and toddlers as defined by each state's capacity.

Defining the role of the school and its professional staff is the goal of this section. Included are issues related to creating linkages with the school, identification, assessment, IEP development, program development and delivery, and ongoing child progress and program evaluation.

Creating the School-Family Link

Following is an example of the crucial link between the child with special needs, his or her parents, and the local public school system:

VIGNETTE 2

Mary Kate

Mary Kate Smith, age 3, had been slow to talk and to communicate with her parents and 7-year-old brother, Matt. Mary Kate's mother, Susan, read about the new legislation and its impact on the public school's role in serving special needs children beginning at age 36 months. With this in mind, Susan called her nearby elementary school, Epsworth Elementary School, where her son Matt was in the second grade. She asked to speak with the special education coordinator, Ron Simmons. Susan described Mary Kate's speech patterns, her apparent delay in verbalizing her needs, and her own concern about possible language delay. Mary Kate's language development was clearly behind that of her older brother when he was 3, but Susan really did not know whether there was a delay: "What should I do?" asked Susan. Mr. Simmons made an appointment for Susan to bring Mary Kate to the school for an assessment by the school psychologist.

Defining the School's Role

Even with the force of P.L. 99-457, which defines the public school's role in the provision of services for children with developmental delay or disability or both, the actual availability of services for children and parents varies remarkably, both in quantity and quality. The school is legally responsible for providing services for these children, but how this process evolves for each child and family is dependent on many variables. This section addresses the role of the school from an *ideal* perspective; that is, the processes of identification, assessment, program development, IEP procedures, and child progress and evaluation are described because they constitute a complete set of services for a child with special needs and his or her family.

The ability of a school district to carry out these various services is dependent on the following factors:

- Size of the school and comprehensiveness of programs offered
- Availability of school psychologists, counselors, special education teachers, social workers, and other support personnel
- Financial status of the respective school

- Availability of community agencies, organizations, and other resources to provide collaborative services with the school district
- Philosophy of inclusion of children with special needs in classrooms for typically developing children
- Parent education, parent support, and child advocacy groups within the school system

Even in school systems that lack some of these variables, parents of children with special needs can exert tremendous political and legal pressure on the school to carry through on its responsibilities as mandated through P.L. 99-457.

Identification, Assessment, and IEPs and IFSPs

During the past several decades, educators have become increasingly aware that optimal learning can best be fostered by recognition of, and attention to, individual differences. Individualization of instruction, the development of individual programs for all children in Head Start, and the development of individual education programs for children with special needs can contribute a great deal to meeting individual child needs. Individualization of instruction does not necessarily imply one-to-one instruction, except for possible short periods of time, but rather planning and providing activities and programs appropriate for meeting each child's individual needs.

In many children, a special developmental delay or condition is present and potentially diagnosable at birth. In other children, conditions present at birth may potentially lead to a disabling condition. In still others, no necessarily predisposing factors are present at birth; whether a child acquires a special condition in many instances depends on the circumstances of his or her early care (Safford, 1989). P.L. 94-142 specifically charges the public schools with the responsibility of identifying all children who may have special needs and, therefore, potentially are eligible for preschool special education services. This responsibility includes children not only of school age but also of preschool age. The major means of identifying children in need of special services include the following:

- *Screening procedures* conducted at predetermined and specific times each year by the school district
- *Referral procedures* initiated by anyone, including the child's parent (or other close relative), teacher, pediatrician or family physician, health or other social service agency representative, or concerned other who suspects a problem
- For children who are in school, a *systematic review* of their records, particularly if referred by a school psychologist, social worker, or teacher

Screening.   Screening is a gross means for economically scoring possible "cases" from the general population (Safford, 1989). Screening is not equivalent to diagnosis. Screening procedures vary in their levels of effectiveness, and one major criticism of the screening process is that children with serious problems can "fall through the cracks." Safford (1989) states that familiar screening procedures are those used in public schools, community clinics, and doctors' offices for hearing and vision. Meisels (1986), who has studied the screening strategies used by public schools, states that instruments are frequently used for screening even though that is not their intended purpose. Meisels also cites the Early and Periodic Screening and Developmental Testing (EPSDT) as an example of a screening procedure that frequently fails to identify positively children in need.

Referral.   Most schools have clearly defined procedures for making referrals. Referrals can be made informally, such as when a teacher mentions to a supervisor that a particular child seems to be having great difficulty. Written procedures must be followed, however, to state the reasons for referral. It is important to remember that referral is not the same thing as diagnosis and should be conducted with great caution. An appropriate referral is a descriptive one: a factual statement that describes a child's behavior. Therefore, a classroom teacher simply refers a child for a determination of whether comprehensive assessment is indicated, not for special education. According to Safford (1989), teacher referral is the primary means for in-school identification of students who may be eligible for, and able to benefit from, special education services.

Classroom teacher referral skills.   To make appropriate referrals, the classroom teacher needs certain skills. These include the following:

- Knowledge of the school system's or community-based program's referral policies and procedures
- Some understanding of typical child development
- Awareness of important symptoms or indicators that might be associated with certain problems
- Ability to make objective and documented observations of a child's behavior or development that may be causing concern
- Familiarity with the school's recommended procedures for communication with the child's immediate family or extended family members
- Willingness to follow through and provide support to the child and family as the referral and assessment process unfolds

Making a written referral.   A written referral should include a description of what attempts have been made to provide for the student's needs through such means as (a) conferences with parents; (b) conferences with the child (if appropriate); (c) individual tutorial assistance and effort; (d) attempts to adapt the daily schedule, environment, assignments, and so on for the child; and (e) any special motivational or management procedures that have been used (Safford, 1989, p. 31).

In short, the teacher's role is to initiate a proper referral procedure for a particular child. The referral itself should be viewed as a facilitative and linked effort to obtain possible needed intervention. The purpose of the referral is not diagnosis, and the teacher should refrain from making diagnostic remarks or conclusions, especially to the parents. Self-referrals by children to school personnel are more common in intermediate and secondary schools but less so in elementary schools. Children below the age of 10 usually need assistance in interpreting personal needs. Thus, the school social worker or guidance counselor is another excellent source of child referral.

Multifactored Assessment.   The passage of P.L. 94-142 (the EHA) ensured that the following crucial reforms were mandated in the assessment process:

- No single test can be used as the only basis for placement.
- Each child's need must be analyzed on an individual basis and described in an IEP (individualized education program), along with specifications of how those needs will be met and how stated goals will be evaluated.
- Annual review (at least) of the IEP is required and must be completed by a team of professionals, including the parents, who are working to meet the needs of the child.
- Fully informed parental consent must be obtained before any procedures can be carried out.
- Assessment must be interdisciplinary in nature.
- The major purpose of the assessment procedure is to link instructional strategies with assessment.
- Instruments used for screening, assessment, and diagnosis must be valid and reliable.

The IEP and the IFSP.   The IEP (individualized education program) becomes the ongoing tool for providing, monitoring, and evaluating services for a child. Although each school district establishes its own format for the IEP, the law does set forth basic parameters. The IFSP is the individualized family service plan that is developed to serve infants and toddlers.

The term "individualized education program" means a written statement for each handicapped child in any meeting by a representative of the local education agency (LEA) or an intermediate educational unit who shall be qualified to provide, or supervise the provision of, specially designed instruction to meet the unique needs of handicapped children, the teacher, the parents or guardian of such child, and, whenever appropriate, such child, which statement shall include (A) a statement of the present levels of educational performance of such child, (B) a statement of annual goals, including short-term instructional objectives, (C) a statement of the specific educational services to be provided to such child, and the extent to which such child will be able to participate in regular educational programs, (D) the projected date for initiation and anticipated duration of such services, and appropriate objective criteria and evaluation procedures and schedules for determining, on at least an annual basis, whether instructional objectives are being achieved. (P.L. 94-942, Section 4 [19])

The school system represents the child with special needs and his or her family's best hope for obtaining affordable, accessible, and reliable identification, assessment, and program planning. Because of legislation, the family of a child who is believed to have a developmental delay, disabling condition, emotional need, or some other form of special need is ensured free and ongoing services. The school personnel most involved in this process are the classroom teacher, school psychologist, social worker, school counselor, special education teacher, and immediate administrator.

P.L. 99-457 requires that school systems serve all children who are 36 months of age with special educational services if these services are indicated. The ability of a school district to provide these services varies greatly, but all school districts have the legal responsibility to assist a family within its respective districts to seek out and successfully obtain professional assistance.

◊◊ Community Resources and Collaboration Strategies

Referring again to Bronfenbrenner's ecological model (1975), we turn now to the interrelationships between the family of a child with special needs and the immediate community and its resources. The family with a child with special needs depends greatly on the resources of the school and the community to provide support for a variety of needs: financial, emotional, social services, general family support. We have discussed the specific roles of the school professional in addressing the needs of the child with a disability. Now we turn to the use of community resources and **interagency collaboration** to address family financial and social support needs and resources.

Families Under Stress: A Community-Based Model

The conceptual scaffolding of families under stress depends on three variables: (a) the family, (b) a crisis-provoking event, and (c) the meaning attached to the event. Viewed externally, the family often appears to be a closed corporation, particularly in urban areas where the nuclear group of father, mother, and their children is clearly differentiated from the kinship extensions of maternal and paternal grandparents and other relatives. The closed nature of the family is nevertheless selectively opened for transacting business with other agencies, including kin and professionals. These agencies can be ranked according to their accessibility to the interior of the family: immediate kin highest, family friends and neighbors next, the family physician, the family pastor, the family lawyer, and so on.

Other agencies enter the family with greater difficulty and often through the intermediation of individual family members who act as liaisons for the family: the school, the employer, the health clinic, the casework agency, and other such formal agencies. Viewed historically, the family today is much more dependent on other agencies in society than were families in the past.

Seeking Help from Formal Resources.   Families of children with special needs frequently need to turn to formal community resources to obtain information, help them cope, and make decisions. **Formal community resources** refers to agencies, institutions, governmental programs, local services, and so on, ranging from those using a wide variety of trained professionals to those using few or none at all (Rose & Smith, 1993; Solit, 1993).

The most common types of formal community resources include the following:

Social Security offices

Mental health clinics

Health departments

Social services offices (financial resources)

School district main office and neighborhood sites

Resource and referral agencies

Parent support groups for designated disabilities

Crisis centers and hotlines

Family physicians and pediatricians

Social workers

Human resource offices and departments

Libraries

Hospital social service departments

Community bulletin boards

Churches

Local politicians

These formal community resources can be located in the yellow pages or a special city/county/state governmental listing in the local telephone book, as well as through interagency and network telephone lists and communication systems.

Suggestions for Seeking Resources.   When families need to refer to community resources for assistance, they may feel overwhelmed and intimidated by their lack of understanding of the roles of different agencies, the systems and procedures for gaining access to these community resources, and the organizational structure or hierarchy of the agency. Suggestions for families seeking community resources include the following:

- Use informal resources as much as possible and then turn to formal resources as the next step.
- No one kind of resource is the best. The best resource is one that works for that family, and this will depend on the quality of a particular resource, the individuals within each family are, the needs they have, and what is available in the local area.
- The mystique the surrounds professionalism contributes to a self-perpetuating cycle in which professional help is seen as the only kind of help with any value, and the professional's view of a situation the only valid one.
- Agencies and institutions have a varying degree of social responsibility. All professionals must work to educate ourselves to understand the nature of our society and the problems facing it, and we must work to improve the ways society relates to and supports its members. Hence, some agencies will leave parents feeling more overwhelmed, inadequate, and isolated, whereas others will contribute to a sense of strength and self-sufficiency on the part of the family.
- Some agencies have deficiencies and biases that affect the accessibility and quality of services provided. Fathers, for example, are sometimes made to feel distinctly out of place when they try to function as parents to their children with disabilities. Poor families and minority-group members often feel the sting of scorn or outright exclusion in contacts with institutions. Also, some agencies believe more in treating problems rather than in contributing to the prevention or early intervention of existing, smaller family problems.

Most parents have not been instructed on how to interface effectively with formal resources such as agencies. To empower parents of children with special needs to obtain services effectively, the following suggestions are made:

1. *Identify and State the Problem.*   Parents may want to write out a description of the problem or need to more clearly articulate their needs before going to the agency. Asking for help is the crucial first step and can be very empowering.
2. *Start With What You Already Have.*   Informal networks often provide families with individuals who can gather or provide information related to child care, health care, employment, social security, and other governmental programs and benefits.
3. *Look for Allies.*   Several parents with similar needs may get more action than just one parent alone. *Parent power* should not be overlooked.
4. *Write It Down.*   Often when parents need help, they also feel confused and overwhelmed. Families should be encouraged to maintain a log or

journal in which they identify resources, assistance provided, dates, names of resource persons and agencies, and general comments about services provided.

5. *Make Contact.*   Some agencies are aware of how important the first contact is, and they make sure it is a welcoming one. At other times, families must deal with agency personnel who themselves are over-worked and overwhelmed. Parents should keep trying and not assume that there is nothing for them behind that wall or that no one else in the agency has a genuine commitment to help.

6. *Be Persistent.*   Unfortunately, when families seek formal assistance from community agencies, they are already feeling tired and demoral-ized. Breaking through the barriers of some agencies is challenging. Families should be encouraged to be persistent and *not give up.*

7. *Be Open to New Sources of Information.*   Help can come from places families don't expect. Good sources of information on available local community resources are social workers, local newspapers, libraries, community bulletin boards, hospital social service departments, churches, schools, local mental health centers, hotlines, local politi-cians, and resource and referral centers.

8. *Let Friends Help.*   A good tip for families is to ask a friend or relative to help when they're feeling "stuck." A relative or friend can sit with the parents while they make phone calls, visit a doctor's office, go to a men-tal health clinic or welfare office, or attend a parent-teacher conference.

9. *Ask for Referrals.*   If the community resource cannot provide needed help, families should ask for the names of two or three other commu-nity agencies that can.

10. *Keep the Proper Perspective.*   Sometimes parents may feel a power imbalance between them and the professionals, or they may run up against personal or institutional biases. Encourage parents to keep their perspective: Agencies are run by people, and all people have their own personal needs and conflicts.

11. *Do Not Be Intimidated.*   Remember that it can be a sign of strength to reach out for help, just as it is a sign of strength to give help.

Financial Assistance and Funding Mechanisms.   Financial resources are available for most families of children with special needs. Knowing where these resources are located is a challenge for each professional because resources vary widely from one community to another. To begin with, the family should rely on the school system for this information. The special education director, school counselor, or other authority responsible for implementing services for children with special needs will have a list of community resources. These resources usually consist of the following:

- Financial assistance for medical care (federal and state programs)
- Food stamps, WIC, and other food-related programs
- Federal and state programs that cover all or partial payments for medical equipment, braces, and other developmental needs
- Community programs that provide care and educational support in addition to the school's for the child with special needs
- Insurance available for children with special needs, and special programs that provide for out-patient services

Parent Empowerment and Self-Care

As discussed in this chapter, parenting a child with special needs is a challenging life task. Regardless of the nature or severity of the problem, parents may at first feel overwhelmed with shock at seeing their image of an ordered and ordinary life so abruptly shattered. It is important to remember that as overwhelming a problem as it may seem, as deeply committed as a parent may always be to caring for his or her child, the parent's need to self-care and to separate from the problem should be a goal from the outset. Thus, in supporting parents of children with special needs, encouraging the parents to take good care of themselves is crucial so that feelings

Parents who are involved in child advocacy efforts often feel empowered to deal with their own personal situations.

of isolation, fear, and loneliness do not surround them. Parents need to learn to take care of themselves so that they are able to problem-solve and meet the needs of their child.

◇◇ **Public Laws and Advocacy on Behalf of Families**

In recent years, families of children with special needs have gained advocacy successes and made tremendous legislative gains. This section identifies important pieces of legislation that are contributing to the expanded educational program and service options now available to these families. Also included is information on child and parent advocacy initiatives on behalf of children with disabilities.

Appropriate Education for All Children: P.L. 94-142

The key word regarding teaching exceptional children is not *mainstreaming*, but rather *appropriate* (Mallory & New, 1994; Safford, 1989; Sexton et al., 1993). The major policy document in this area, P.L. 94-142 (the Education for All Handicapped Children Act of 1975), is often referred to as "the main-streaming law." In fact, the word *mainstreaming* never appears in this law, whereas the word *appropriate* appears repeatedly. The central purpose of P.L. 94-142 is to ensure that all children with disabilities are provided a *free appropriate public education* (FAPE). P.L. 94-142 also requires the use of an *individualized education program* (IEP) as the tool to design and implement each child's appropriate education. Another important feature of this law is the requirement of a *least restrictive environment* (**LRE**) for each student's school placement. As part of the IEP, the planning team, including parents, teachers, and other appropriate individuals, must indicate and define the extent to which the child will participate in regular educational programs.

One of the most important pieces of legislation for young children with special needs and their families was P.L. 94-142, which mandates that parents be provided the opportunity to become involved in decisions concerning the education of their exceptional child. Thus, parental involvement in education programs is now a right guaranteed by law.

P.L. 99-457

In 1986, President Reagan signed into law P.L. 99-457 (the Education of the Handicapped Act Amendments of 1986), which mandates further and more specific criteria for identifying and serving children from birth to age 5 with disabilities and developmental delay. The goal of these identification procedures is not to screen out or otherwise segregate young children with special needs as was done in the past, but to locate children in order to provide appropriate services for each child's unique needs. P.L. 99-457 has had a major impact on public schools and other institutions in the United States because it legislates that services for all children with disabilities be provided beginning at age 3. Thus, school districts are now responsible for serving families of children with disabilities in the preschool years.

P.L. 99-457 does not require or emphasize categorical labels for the following reasons:

- Young children's needs are difficult, if not impossible, to categorize with traditional labels.
- Especially during the early years, these needs change rapidly.
- Categorical labels have no utility for young children because categorical programs may not be appropriate.
- Early labeling of children may limit and restrict them because others may respond to these labels in limiting and restricting ways.
- Labels tend to follow the child, even after they are not longer applicable or appropriate. A label is a hard thing to lose!
- Least restrictive services for young children, required by P.L. 99-457, are intended to foster the interaction of children with and without disabilities. Labels tend to impede that interaction (Safford, 1989; Sexton et al., 1993; Solit, 1993).

P.L. 99-457 identifies a more basic role for parents of young children with disabilities than that stipulated in P.L. 94-142. This legislation (a) de-emphasizes disability labeling and categorical placement of children with disabilities; (b) encourages creative partnerships and collaboration between the public schools and other agencies; and (c) requires involvement with nondisabled children. Agencies involved may include both public and private programs, provided that services are appropriate and of high quality and integration is present. Such partnerships may increasingly involve programs that in the past have served mainly nondisabled children, including proprietary, cooperative, and other community nursery schools.

Other Important Legislation

Other examples of important legislation on behalf of children with special needs are the following:

- Handicapped Children's Early Education Act (P.L. 91-230)
- Head Start Handicapped Mandate (P.L. 92-424)
- **Developmental Disabilities Act** (P.L. 95-602)
- **IDEA Legislation** (P.L. 101-476, the Individuals with Disabilities Education Act of 1990)

Developmentally Appropriate Practice: NAEYC

Leaders in early childhood education have responded to the need for *developmentally appropriate practice* **(DAP)** in the education of young children (Bredekamp, 1988). The National Association for the Education of Young Children (NAEYC) has adopted position statements based on key dimensions of developmental appropriateness and include the following dimensions:

- Children learn best through self-initiated, self-directed, and self-chosen activity.
- The teacher facilitates learning by providing a variety of activities and materials and by reflecting with children about their play.
- Different types of activities and materials are appropriate for children of different ages.
- Children learn through play; transformational materials (sand, water, clay, blocks), puzzles, manipulatives, dramatic play props, science equipment, books, records, paper, paint and markers, and so on are all appropriate for early education classrooms.
- All children should be exposed to multicultural activities, materials, and equipment. (Bredekamp, 1987; Mallory & New, 1994)

As Mallory and New (1994) point out, developmentally appropriate practice continues to be redefined and reconstructed, particularly in the areas of inclusion and multiculturalism.

Advocacy Groups and Initiatives in Early Intervention

Mounting evidence indicates that, at least for some infants and preschoolers with special needs, early intervention can have a markedly positive effect on their development. Partly because of the influence of advocacy organizations, such as the National Association for Retarded Citizens, the United Cerebral Palsy Association, the Society for Autistic Children, and the Epilepsy Foundation of America, decision makers have become more responsive to the needs of children with disabilities. In addition, the experiences of agencies offering early intervention programs have contributed to an atmosphere of urgency. They have also revealed such benefits as significant long-term savings in program costs as children's needs for complex and expensive services decrease with time.

Parents of children with special needs should be encouraged to join and participate in advocacy groups relevant to their children's needs. Familiar advocacy groups include the following (see "Sources for Further Information" at the end of the chapter for complete addresses of advocacy groups):

Administration for Children, Youth and Families (ACYF)

Alexander Graham Bell Association for the Deaf

American Association of University Affiliated Programs for the Developmentally Disabled

American Diabetes Association

American Foundation for the Blind

American Occupational Therapy Association (AOTA)

American Physical Therapy Association (APTA)

American Red Cross

American Speech-Language-Hearing Association (ASHA)

Arthritis Foundation

Association for Childhood Education International (ACEI)

Association for Children and Adults with Learning Disabilities (ACLD)

Association for Education of the Visually Handicapped (AEVH)

Association for Retarded Citizens (ARC)

The Association for the Gifted (TAG)

The Association for the Severely Handicapped (TASH)

Asthma and Allergy Foundation of America

Child Development Clinic

Child Welfare League of America, Inc.

Council for Children with Behavioral Disorders (CCBD)

Council for Exceptional Children (CEC)

Cystic Fibrosis Foundation (CF)

Division for Children with Communication Disorders (DCCD)

Division for Children with Learning Disabilities (DCLD)

Division for Early Childhood (DEC)

Division for the Physically Handicapped (DPH)

Division for the Visually Handicapped (DVH)

Division on Mental Retardation (CEC-MR)

ERIC Clearinghouse on Handicapped and Gifted Children

Family Service Association of America, Inc.

Gesell Institute of Human Development

Head Start

John F. Kennedy Institute

Leukemia Society of America

March of Dimes Birth Defects Foundation

Mental Retardation Association of America (MRAA)

Muscular Dystrophy Association (MDA)

National Association for the Education of Young Children (NAEYC)

National Center for Clinical Infants Programs

National Council on Family Relations (NCFR)

National Easter Seal Society

National Federation of the Blind (NFB)

National Hearing Aid Society

National Hemophilia Foundation

National Mental Health Association

National Society for Autistic Children (NSAC)

National Society to Prevent Blindness (NSPB)

National Spinal Cord Injury Foundation

Office for Maternal and Child Health

Parents of Down's Syndrome Children

Spina Bifida Association of America (SBAA)

United Cerebral Palsy Associations, Inc. (UCPA)

Advocacy and Parent Empowerment

Parents involved in child and family advocacy efforts often feel empowered to deal with their own personal situations. There is strength and comfort in numbers; people working together for a common cause can provide a much-needed outlet for parents of children with disabilities. The success of the legislation described above is a result of the ongoing, effective, and persistent efforts of parents advocating for the educational, health, and social programs needed by their children. In no other area of education is the need for parent involvement in advocacy groups so great nor so well-documented.

Summary Statements ◊

- The emerging **inclusion movement** in the United States has brought law and logic together to ensure that families of children with special needs will receive the greatest possible normality in the educational experiences of the children.

- Exceptionality is generally defined through societal consensus and from various perspectives: medical, legal, sociological, psychological, and educational.

- Children with special needs are typically those with mental, communicative,

social-emotional, or physical characteristics requiring some adaptations in the educational program for optimal learning to occur, and an estimated one million children of preschool age with disabilities live in the United States.

- Children from less advantaged environments are overrepresented in special education classes in the public schools, relative to their numbers in the total population.

- The amount of stress imposed on the family with a special needs child may depend on how radically parental expectations are violated; the impact of a child with a disability on a family is major.

- The identification of a child with a disability sets off a process of adjustment for the parents that includes shock, denial, sadness and anger, adaptation, and reorganization.

- Recent legislation on behalf of children with disabilities recognizes the family as the first and primary teacher and emphasizes the role of the family in the support of the child's growth and development.

- The philosophy of normalization has made a major impact on services delivered to exceptional children and their families, and schools serving children with disabilities must now comply with legislative mandates for the least restrictive learning environments for these children.

- Parents' involvement in the legislative process at both the federal and state levels has resulted in increased legislative initiatives and mandates, such as the successful passage of P.L. 99-457 in 1986.

- Family support programs can serve multiple needs: emotional, physical, financial. Advocacy groups also provide many of these support mechanisms.

- The decline of neighborhood networks, the increased mobility of the population, the increase in single-parent families, and the increased distance between members of the extended family have combined to create a situation where many families with children with disabilities feel isolated and alone.

- All members of a family of a child with a disability are in need of support, including siblings and extended family members.

- An IEP or IFSP is now required for many educational programs that serve children with special needs, and parents have the right to be active participants in the development of their child's IEP.

- The school professional provides a crucial link among the family of a child with a disability, the school system, and referral to relevant community resources and agencies.

- Public schools are legally responsible for providing educationally related services for all children beginning at the age of 3, as mandated through P.L. 99-457.

- Screening is a gross means for economically scoring possible cases of disability from the general population and is a first step in the identification process.

- **Multifactored assessment** is required through P.L. 94-142 and P.L. 99-457 and includes individual assessment, annual review, fully informed parental consent, and multidisciplinary assessment.

- The family under stress must somehow adapt to the stressor event, and the resources located in the immediate community provide the next available rung of assistance to families, after immediate and extended family members, friends and neighbors, and pastors and family lawyers.

- Accessing formal community resources can be an intimidating and confusing process for families of children with disabilities; families need support in negotiating the referral process.

- Public laws and advocacy initiatives for children with disabilities increased dramatically during the 1980s and 1990s; parents who become involved in advocacy efforts frequently feel empowered to deal more effectively with their particular situation.

Activities ◊◊◊

1. What evidence indicates that early intervention for children with special needs really makes a long-term difference?
2. P.L. 94-143 is referred to as the All Handicapped Children's Act. Explain your interpretation of this statement.
3. P.L. 99-457 was passed in 1986 and opened the door to younger children with disabilities. Explain what doors were opened and how this legislation has affected public school systems.
4. Identify at least three incidences or examples of how parent involvement in child advocacy efforts has been successful.
5. Define *early labeling* and explain why recent legislation discourages the use of labeling, especially for preschool children.
6. To what does *least restrictive environment* refer, and how is this policy implemented in current school systems in the United States?
7. Accepting a child's disability is a major challenge for a parent; describe the five stages involved in reaching adaptation.
8. Explain Bronfenbrenner's ecological model as a frame for the successful coping of families of children with disabilities. Give two examples.
9. Explain the concept of *normalization* and describe its impact on services delivered to exceptional children and their families.
10. Name at least three advocacy groups related to disability and explain possible ways these groups could assist or support parents and families of children with disabilities.
11. Explain how parents can most effectively access and use formal community resources such as agencies, organizations, and advocacy groups. Name at least five community resources.
12. Explain how the family system, including siblings, is affected by the presence of a child with a disability.
13. Describe the IEP and IFSP processes in a typical school setting.
14. Explain multifactored assessment and its importance in current school policies and practices for children with disabilities.
15. Why are **parent empowerment** and self-care so important? Give examples of how parents can nurture and take care of their own health, emotional, and other needs.
16. Relate NAEYC's developmentally appropriate practice (DAP) to the inclusion movement and the philosophy of least restrictive environment.

Additional Exercises ◊◊◊◊◊◊◊◊◊◊◊◊◊◊◊◊◊◊◊◊◊◊◊◊◊◊◊◊◊◊◊◊◊◊◊◊◊

Exercise 1: Peer Visitor

Children learn about disabilities by interacting with other children who have disabling conditions, retardation, developmental delays, and other types of disabilities. Because the formation of attitudes toward disability occur at a young age, inviting a peer to the classroom to talk about his or her disability can be a very meaningful experience. The child should be included in the classroom routine, such as sharing lunch, recess, or other activities, so that the class learns positive attitudes toward inclusion.

Exercise 2: Integrated Curriculum Activities

Involving children in language arts, science, art, and other curricular activities related to disability can be an effective way to increase their knowledge about disability, as well as affect their attitudes. Children can share their written reports through small groups, oral reports, posters, videotapes, and other strategies.

Exercise 3: Role Playing

Children learn best through hands-on activities. Engaging young children in dramatic play and role playing that includes the challenges and rewards of a child with a disability can be an effective way of integrating the curriculum and increasing their understanding of what it is like to have a disability. Children can use wheelchairs, crutches, seeing eye dogs, and other means to act out the real-life encounters of a child with a disability.

Exercise 4: Resource Persons

Many people in the local community have connections to children and families with disabilities. Invite a mother of a special needs child, a physical therapist, an occupational therapist, a pediatrician, a surgeon, or an animal trainer to class to discuss support for persons who are blind or visually-impaired. Involve the class members in discussion and then assign a follow-up activity for the class. As much as possible, document students' work through photographs, audiotapes, videotapes, and so on.

Sources for Further Information

Council for Administration in Special Education (CASE) of the Council for Exceptional Children, 615 16th Street, N.W., Albuquerque, NM 87104 (505) 243-7622.

Division for Early Childhood (DEC) of the Council for Exceptional Children, 1920 Association Drive, Reston, VA, 22091, (703) 620-3660

National Association of State Directors of Special Education (NASDSE), 1800 Diagonal Road, Suite 320, King Street Station 1, Alexandria, VA 22314 (703) 519-3800

U.S. Office of Special Education, Programs Early Childhood Branch, 400 Maryland Avenue, S.W., Washington, DC 20202 (202) 708-5366

References ◊◊

Badger, E. (1981). *Infant learning program.* Washington, DC: Edufax.

Baker, J. N. (1991, Summer). Beating the handicap rap [Special issue]. *Newsweek,* 36–37.

Bredekamp, S. (1987). *Developmentally appropriate practice in early childhood programs serving children from birth through age eight* (exp. ed.). Washington, DC: National Association for the Education of Young Children.

Bredekamp, S. (1988). NAEYC position statement on developmentally appropriate practice in the primary grades, serving 5- through 8-year-olds. *Young Children, 43*(2), 64–84.

Bronfenbrenner, U. (1974). *Is early intervention effective? A report on longitudinal evaluation of preschool programs* (Vol. 2). Washington, DC: U.S. Department of Health, Education, and Welfare.

Bronfenbrenner, U. (1975). Reality and research in the ecology of human development. *Proceedings of the American Philosophical Association, 119,* 439–469.

Drotar, D., Baskiewica, A., Irwin, N., Kennell, J., & Klaus, M.(1975). The adaptation of parents to the birth of an infant with a congenital malformation: A hypothetical model. *Pediatrics, 56,* 710–717.

Dunst, C. J., Johanson, C., Trivette, C. M., & Hamby, D. (1991). Family-oriented early intervention policies and practices: Family-centered or not? *Exceptional Children, 58,* 115–126.

Fallen, N. H., & Umansky, W. (1985). *Young children with special needs.* New York: Macmillan.

Field, T. (1986). Models for reactivity and chronic depression in infancy. In E. Z. Tronick & T. Field (Eds.), *Maternal depression and infant disturbance.* San Francisco: Jossey-Bass.

Gargiulo, R. M., & Graves, S. B. (1991, Spring). Parental feelings: The forgotten component when working with parents of handicapped preschool children. *Childhood Education, 67,* 176–178.

Griffith, D. R. (1992, September). Prenatal exposure to cocaine and other drugs: Developmental and educational progress. *Phi Delta Kappan,* 30–34.

Grossman, F. K. (1972). Brothers and sisters of retarded children. *Psychology Today, 5,* 82–87.

Mallory, B., & New, R. (1994). *Diversity and developmentally appropriate practices: Challenges for early childhood education.* New York: Teachers College Press.

Marozas, D. S., & May, D. C. (1988). *Issues and practices in special education.* New York: Longman.

Meisels, S. J. (1986). Testing four- and five-year-olds: Response to Salzer and to Shepard and Smith. *Educational Leadership, 44,* 90–92.

Perske, R. (1973). *New directions for parents of persons who are retarded.* Nashville: Abingdon Press.

Rose, D. F., & Smith, B. J. (1993). Preschool mainstreaming: Attitude barriers and strategies for addressing them, *Young Children, 48*(4), 59–62.

Safford, P. (1989). *Integrated teaching in early childhood: Starting in the mainstream.* White Plains, NY: Longman.

Savage, S., Mayfield, P., & Cook, M. (1993, Fall). Questions about serving children with HIV/AIDS. *Day Care and Early Education,* 10–12.

Sexton, D., Snyder, P., Sharpton, W. R., & Stricklin, S. (1993). Infants and toddlers with special needs and their families [Annual theme issue]. *Childhood Education,* 278–286.

Solit, G. (1993, September/October). A place for Marie: Guidelines for the integration process. *Child Care Information Exchange,* 49–54.

Stoneman, Z., & Brody, G. H. (1982). Strengths inherent in sibling interactions involving a retarded child: A functional role theory approach.

Torrance, E. (1983). Preschool creativity. In K. Paget & B. Bracken (Eds.), *Psychoeducational asssessment of preschool children* (pp. 509–520). New York: Grune & Stratton.

Vincent, L. J., (Summer, 1992). Implementing individualized family service planning in urban, culturally diverse early intervention settings. *Osers News,* 29–33.

Wiegerink, R., & Pelosi, J. W. (Eds.). (1979). *Developmental disabilities: The DD movement.* Baltimore, MD: Brookes.

Wolfensberger, W. (1967). Counseling the parents of the retarded. In A. A. Baumeister (Ed.), *Mental retardation.* Chicago: Alpine.

6 Children of Divorced and Blended Families

Meeting the Needs of "New" Families

For all parents, creating and raising a family consist of one adjustment after another. . . . All families worry about making mistakes. Not only are mistakes unavoidable, . . . but parents learn their job through mistakes.

Brazelton, 1989, p. 1

Key Terms

anger inhibition
bibliotherapy
blended family
disruption of attachment
divorced family
instant love
logical consequences
nonresidential home
permeable boundaries
Phoenix concept
pileup

rates of divorce
reconstituted family
teacher self-assessment
stages of divorce adjustment
stepchild
stepfamily myths
stepfather
stepmother
superdad
wicked stepmother

The idealized model of the nuclear family in U.S. society has consisted of an ever-married couple with children, the father being the economic provider and the mother being the homemaker. Only a minority of contemporary U.S. families fit this description, however, and U.S. schools and child care settings provide educational and support services for a changing population of children who are a part of this marital revolution. Projections indicate that over one third of children in the United States can expect that, before their 18th birthdays, their parents will divorce (Strangeland, Pellegreno, & Lundholm, 1989).

Significantly, recent research indicates that divorce can have a major and disruptive effect on the long-term development of an individual's attitudinal and emotional development (Axinn, 1996; Wallerstein & Blakeslee, 1995). Because of the powerful emotional effect of divorce on children (Keith & Finlay, 1988), it is important that teachers be aware of related issues that affect children and their families. Further, research indicates that children in preschool and early elementary settings want their teachers to know and understand about the divorce that is occurring (Frieman, 1993).

Two family forms that continue to increase in numbers are *divorced* and *blended* (remarriage) families, and U.S. school children reflect this growing trend. Although **rates of divorce** have leveled off somewhat during the 1990s, the divorce rate for first marriages is still approximately 50% (Darden & Zimmerman, 1992; Walsh, 1992). The divorce rate for remarriages is even higher. In addition, it has been projected that well over one half of today's youths will become stepdaughters or stepsons by the year 2000 (Glick, 1989; Walsh, 1992). Thus, divorced and blended families have become increasingly normative in U.S. society (Darden & Zimmerman, 1992).

Because research indicates that teachers frequently have negative perceptions of children who are a part of divorced families (Ganong, Coleman, & Maples, 1990), it is important to include information on the impact of divorce and remarriage on children's development. In addition, teachers benefit from understanding the legal differences between, and the rights of, stepparents and biological parents (Fine & Fine, 1992).

This chapter focuses on children from divorced and blended families and makes suggestions for appropriate teacher and caregiver decisions, as well as school and community services and interventions. Topics include the following:

- Definitions and demographics
- Special problems and issues faced by children who are experiencing the divorce process or are a part of blended families or both
- Intervention models and the role of the school or child care center in meeting the needs of these children

Figure 6.1 shows the change of the family system from predivorced state, through the divorce process, and to the establishment of the remarriage system. Solid lines indicate the creation of new subsystems; dashed lines represent subsystems that influence one another. Note the relative complexity of the **divorced family** subsystem (ex-spouse subsystem, single parent-child subsystem, visiting parent-child subsystem, and sibling subsystem) and the new remarriage (**blended family:** couple subsystem, parent-child subsystem, and sibling subsystem).

◇◇ Definitions and Demographics: Divorced and Blended Families in the United States

Divorce is the legal process of two individuals dissolving a marriage relationship or the dissolution of a marriage bond by legal process or by accepted custom (*American Heritage Dictionary*, 1996). A **blended family** is defined as a family in which one or both spouses in a remarriage have a child or children by a former marriage (Walsh, 1992). Other terms used to describe blended families are *reconstituted families, stepfamilies,* and *reorganized-, combined-,* and *remarried-families.* Historically, most terms associated with blended families seem to be surrounded by guilt or some other negative quality (Lindner, Hagan, & Brown, 1992; Smith, 1992; Walsh, 1992).

Divorce in the United States is so common that teachers often report a majority of the children in their classrooms are from homes where divorce is either currently occurring or has already taken place (Brazelton, 1989; Walsh, 1992). This text is written to assist school-based personnel and child care professionals in addressing the changing needs of children in their care. In an effort to bring professionals up to date on divorce and remarriage in the United States, it is important to provide current data on the frequency of divorce and some demographic variables related to divorce.

Figure 6.1 Process of transition to the blended family

Source: Adapted from Poppen and White (1984).

Note: Dashed lines = subsystems influencing one another; solid lines = creation of new subsystems.

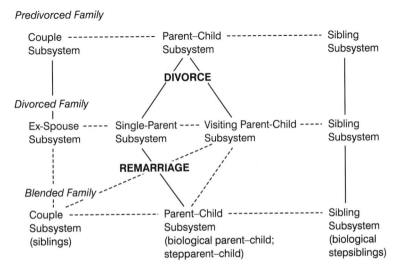

The following list of demographic descriptors will help the professional in understanding the frequency of divorce in the United States and why the divorce process can be potentially very stressful for the child in a school or child care setting.

- Slightly more than half of all couples have children at the time of a divorce, accounting for more than 2 million children whose parents divorce each year.

- More than 1.5 million children under the age of 18 are affected each year by family breakups.

- Seventy-seven percent of children not living with both biological parents are from families with incomes of less than $5,000; only 16% of children not living with both parents are from families with incomes of over $25,000.

- Divorce rates differ dramatically according to race, age, and socioeconomic status: Blacks are more likely than Whites to divorce, but particularly they are more likely to separate and live apart without a legal divorce; younger couples are more likely to divorce than those who marry at a later age; and divorce is much more prevalent among families at the lower end of the economic ladder.

- Divorce is likely to be followed by remarriage, and statistics indicate that five out of six divorced men and three out of four divorced women remarry.

- Remarriage rates among Whites are higher than among Blacks, and 1 child in 10 will undergo two or more family disruptions before the age of 16.

- Today's couples are less likely to remain married for the children's sake.

- Children's ages may affect the parents' decision to divorce, with divorce rates of couples with preschool children being about half of those with children of school age; for couples with school-age children, divorce rates are about equal to the rates for childless couples.

- The number of children in a family is related to the divorce rate: Families with one or two children have considerably lower divorce rates than families with three or more children.

- Divorce rates are higher when a marriage is preceded by a premarital pregnancy or out-of-wedlock birth and when stepchildren are a part of a remarriage.

- About 40% of children living in mother-only households have not seen their fathers in the past year.

- Despite popular views that the rate of paternal custody cases is increasing, about 10 times as many children reside with a single mother as with a single father.

- Older children, particularly older boys, are more likely to live with their fathers than are younger boys.

- The divorce rate is higher for remarriages than for first marriages, about 60%.

- The presence of one's own biological children appears to be a disincentive to divorce in first marriages, whereas the presence of stepchildren is related to an increased likelihood of divorce in remarriage. (Anderson & White, 1986; Diamond, 1985; Galston, 1996; Smith, 1992; Walsh, 1992)

◊◊ Impact of Divorce on Children: How the Schools Can Help

Teachers today report how complex their classrooms are, especially when compared with a decade ago. This complexity is the result of several factors, but the changing family structure is one of the most significant factors. For schools, the issues related to divorce are many. They include the simple, technical aspects, such as keeping track of the child's last name, who has custody, and who the primary responsible adult is. More serious concerns are related to such issues as "entry and exit," the moving back and forth between custodial and noncustodial parents and possible custodial disagreements, which can result in intense parental disputes on the school grounds or even in kidnapping situations (Walsh, 1992). Typically, Mondays and Fridays are most difficult for children of divorce because of the emotional stress of leaving one parent and going to another (Francke, 1983).

Wallerstein and Blakeslee's (1995) research cautions professionals not to take divorce too lightly. Longitudinal outcomes for adult children of divorce suggest that myths about quality of time versus quantity of time lack validity and that children between ages 8 and 10 at the time of their parents' divorce may have more negative long-term outcomes that affect their own personal relationships as adults.

Examples of Children's Responses in the Classroom

According to Frieman (1993), children explicitly state that they want their teacher to know about a separation or divorce so that the teacher will be more tolerant and understanding of their behavior. Examples cited by Frieman include Karen, a first-grader, who says, "I'm thinking about the divorce sometimes in school and not doing my work. I don't want my teacher to think that I don't care about my work." Scott, another first-grader, states, "I want her to know so that when I'm feeling sad, she will know the reason and not yell at me" (Frieman, 1993, p. 86).

For the preoperational child, including infants, toddlers, and preschoolers, reactions can be intense. Separation distress can be observed in toddlers whose parents are separating or divorcing, even after showing no separation distress in the earlier months of life (Godwin, Groves, & Horm-Wingerd, 1993). Separation distress can be observed in infants after 7 months of age and reappear in toddlers 18 to 24 months of age. These typical behaviors are intensified during parental separation or divorce because routines and relationships at home have been disrupted.

Separation distress can be observed in young toddlers whose parents are separating or divorcing.

In general, schools and child centers must deal with the more pervasive, day-to-day emotional struggles that are evident among many young children as they learn to cope with new living arrangements, estranged relationships with noncustodial parents, new financial limitations, and the lack of emotional support from parents who themselves are struggling to cope and redefine their lives (Walsh, 1992). Usually, teachers learn about a child's divorce experience through observation of changes in the child's behavior and then inquiring of parents because of concern. Thus, teachers comment that their roles have taken on new dimensions, such as informally counseling and supporting children, referring parents and children to community agencies for formal intervention, and generally expending more emotional energy themselves on the classroom and teaching processes (Lindner et al., 1992; Walsh, 1992). Children are resilient, however, and 80% to 90% of children recover from the initial shock of divorce in about a year (Jellinek & Klavan, 1988).

Parental Emotions in Divorce

Parents' emotions at the time of separation or divorce range from relief that a bad relationship is over to severe depression (Diamond, 1985; Smith, 1992). Although some parents contact their children's teacher or other school personnel without hesitation, many parents are too emotionally overcome to make this contact. Many parents try to cover up their feelings and to project a strong image to their children's teachers. In fact, a study by Wallerstein and Blakeslee (1995) found that half of the children's teachers did not know about the divorces among the children in their classrooms.

Common emotions and respective verbal expressions of divorcing parents include the following:

Failure: "I couldn't make my marriage work."

Shame: "There's a stigma attached to being divorced; there's a strike against the children."

Guilt: "I'm very sad that I've had to put my children through this. I feel guilty about not having given them the best I could give them."

Insecurity: "I had no identity. When the 'Mrs.' came away, I collapsed."

Sensitivity: "Unsolicited advice is awful." (Diamond, 1985; Walsh, 1992)

So, despite broader acceptance of divorce in U.S. society today, the fact is that divorce imposes tremendous emotional turmoil on families undergoing it. With experience, teachers become more sensitive to parents who are divorcing, and this sensitivity can be a major support mechanism for both children and parents (Walsh, 1992).

Typical Child Responses to Divorce

The nature of a child's reaction to divorce depends on many factors: ego strength, age, gender, relationship with parents, extended family support, communication and understanding about the divorce, and perceived support at school, at church, and within the community. Research reflects, however, that divorce is very painful for just about all children. Teachers should be alert to a variety of possible emotional reactions to divorce, including sadness, depression, denial, embarrassment, anger, guilt, concern about being cared for, regression, maturity, and physical symptoms (Diamond, 1985; Frieman, 1993; Hagan, Hollier, O'Connor, & Eisenberg, 1992; Hayes & Hayes, 1986; Smith, 1992). Table 6.1 lists symptoms of these various emotional states.

◊◊ How Teachers Should Respond

Even if teachers and other school personnel have intense feelings about divorce or the specific dynamics of a child and her or his family (Lindner et al., 1992), they should make every effort not to project those feelings. In general, teachers should remain as neutral as possible. Their focus should continue to be on the child's well-being, not on making judgments about the parents. In the process of objectively listening to a divorcing parent, the teacher can provide emotional support and also collect much-needed information. According to Diamond (1985), pieces of information that should be

Table 6.1   Emotional descriptors of children in divorce

EMOTIONAL STATE	DESCRIPTION
Sadness or Depression	Sadness or depression is a normal reaction that may last for months. Younger children may even say "I feel sad." Children may look fatigued, tired, or sad. Depression is serious and should be anticipated. Eating and sleeping habits may change. Children who are depressed may state that they feel very alone or that no one really cares about them.
Denial	Denial allows the children to shelter themselves from the pain at hand. Children are not aware of this process. Reasons for denial are to escape pain and to hope for some kind of reconciliation on the parents' part.
Embarrassment	Embarrassment is perhaps the most common emotion that teachers will have to deal with. Children do not like being different from their peers even though their peers are also experiencing divorce. Research indicates however, that embarrassment can last for years after a divorce and is very common as a childhood response.
Anger	Intense anger is common among children of divorce, especially for 9- to 12-year-olds. Anger results from a fundamental feeling of collapsing: everything that they have known has now given way. Unless parents contribute to anger, it should subside in time.
Guilt	Guilt is really anger turned inward. Children experience feelings of guilt especially about parent loyalty. They want to show a commitment to both.
Fear of Abandonment	A common reaction for children is to feel abandoned. Basic feelings of "who will take care of me?" are typical and understandable. Even older children report these feelings. Younger children miss the noncustodial parent and fear that if one parent left, maybe the other one will too.
Regression	Teachers especially see evidence of regression. Regression involves the child's freezing at the current point of maturity or moving back to earlier stages. Younger children may whine, cling, and seek attention from the teacher. Older children may also try to befriend the teacher in excessive ways. Children who were once independent may display more dependent behaviors.
Physical Symptoms	Wallerstein's research on divorce reflects that elementary-age children may express more frequent somatic symptoms, such as headaches and stomachaches. School nurses report that all children seem more emotional, tearful, and needy. Mostly, they just need to interact with a caring adult.

gathered from the divorcing family by the school or child care setting include the following:

- When did the separation or divorce occur?
- When did the parents tell the child?
- Has the mother or father left? When? Where did she or he go? Should the school have her or his telephone number? Address?
- Does the mother or father visit regularly?
- Do both parents want to be informed of school events?

- What is the school's responsibility to the noncustodial parent if she or he contacts the school?
- Who should be contacted about emergencies?
- Have any other changes occurred in the home situation?

Individual families will handle the divorce situation differently. All parents, however, seem very sensitive at the outset of the separation and divorce process. Thus, the teacher or other professional should seek information that is comfortable for the parent to share, rather than attempt to elicit a great deal of factual information at one time. The underlying reason for a parent to disclose anything about the divorce is usually for the well-being of the child. The teacher can take into account the stress of the child and adjust classroom expectations, such as saying, "Chris, I know it's difficult to concentrate when you are concerned about your parents' separation. Instead of reading, why don't you write about how you're feeling in your journal?" (Frieman, 1993, p. 87). Encouraging the child to talk about her or his feelings also validates what the child is experiencing. Comments such as "How did that make you feel?"; It's hard, isn't it?"; "That must have made you feel bad"; and "Tell me about how you're feeling" are examples of statements that teachers can make to children experiencing separation or divorce.

Teacher-Parent Responses

Parents simply need support during this time, not advice. The teacher can convey this support and concern by asking for a separate meeting with each of the parents to discuss how their child is doing in class and any issues that seem relevant. Mostly, parents need someone to listen to them. They make take some comfort in knowing that the teacher has dealt with this issue before, because the most pressing emotion during the separation and divorce process is the tremendous feeling of "aloneness" (Diamond, 1985). The teacher can be supportive and empathetic; she or he can state, "Oh, we've dealt with this many times before," or, "Several children in the class have experienced divorce; perhaps that will be helpful for (child's name)".

Teacher Self-Assessment

Teachers need to consider their own feelings and attitudes about divorce. If they are very much against divorce (Lindner et al., 1992) or if they have had very little direct experience with divorce, they especially need to reflect on their own possible reactions to parents undergoing divorce. Parents need an objective, professional response. If teachers are not in touch with their own feelings, they may react very emotionally themselves. Researchers cite situations in which teachers actually cried themselves, took the side of one or the other parent, gave the parents personal advice, scolded them and encouraged them not to divorce, or referred them inappropriately (Diamond, 1985; Lindner et al., 1992). Usually, these reactions are attributable to lack of readiness on the teacher's part to deal with this information and with the emotional intensity expressed by the parents. Parents are very sensitive and insecure during this time, however, and they remember for a long time the reaction of the teacher to their divorce situation. Thus, **teacher self-assessment** is very important for the teacher.

During a self-assessment, teachers should ask themselves the following questions:

- How many times have I been involved in a divorce situation?
- Has anyone close to me gone through a divorce?
- How does my own marital situation affect my attitudes about divorce?
- What are my value judgments about divorce?
- Can I be truly objective with a parent who is divorcing?
- What statements can I say to parents to support them as they announce their divorce?
- Can I separate my own personal feelings about divorce from my actions and attitudes toward the children I teach?
- What appropriate community agencies can I refer parents to for assistance?
- Am I prepared to ask appropriate questions of, and offer emotional support to, the child who is experiencing divorce?
- What developmentally appropriate activities in the classroom encourage the child to express her or his feelings in a safe way (e.g., sensory experiences, open-ended expressions of art, puppets and language arts experiences, opportunities to help children verbalize their feelings)?

The Need for Order and Consistency

Teachers and other professionals working with children undergoing divorce in their families can offer a precious gift: consistency. Because the home situation seems so unstable and even frightening at this time, school can actually serve as a haven and constructive outlet to a child. The teacher should assess each child in the classroom for individual needs; the child of divorce is especially in need of this assessment. The teacher's personal qualities can have a very positive impact on the child; this is especially crucial during the first year after the separation and divorce. According to Robert Weiss, parents experience disorganization, depression, unmanageable restlessness, and a chaotic search for escape from distress immediately after the separation (Lindner et al., 1992; Smith, 1992; Weiss, in Diamond, 1985).

Practical Suggestions for Teachers

By now, it is clear that children undergoing the divorce experience at home are more emotional and sensitive than other children. They are easily embarrassed, and feelings often seem out of proportion. To minimize embarrassment and to facilitate class process, the following suggestions are made for teachers:

- Assume that some of your students are not living with both natural parents, and then identify those students.
- Get the names right.
- Make it easy when written communications or gifts are to be sent home.
- Avoid embarrassing questions.
- Respect confidentiality.
- Recognize that certain class projects may cause embarrassment; then take advantage of opportunities to legitimate differences.
- At Open House and similar events, expect from one to four parents.
- Maintain an open mind regarding the worth of single-parent homes.

A Teacher's Limits

Although a teacher cannot solve the problems of children or families in divorce situations, she or he can help the children and parents cope. Giving the children a chance to feel in control in the classroom will help alleviate the out-of-control feelings they experience related to their families and parents. Relating to parents who are in a conflict is challenging, but the teacher should make an effort to communicate with both parents, rather than just the custodial parent (Frieman, 1993). Staying out of the parents' dispute will help the teacher remain neutral and constructive. There are limits to what a teacher can do during a child's divorce situation, but many valuable classroom interventions will increase the chances for the young child to cope with the transitions and changes until the family is redefined and more stable.

In this section, we have discussed the incidence of divorce for American families and the divorce issues that affect the school or child care center and the teacher. Divorce is usually the beginning of a new and somewhat painful odyssey for children, frequently resulting in the reconstitution of a new family in subsequent months or years. The prevalence of divorce has given rise to another new family form: the blended or reconstituted family, which is discussed next.

◊◊ Demographics of Blended Families

Why should teachers, caregivers, and school personnel be concerned about the needs of children from blended families? Demographers now document the growing numbers of families and children who represent this emerging lifestyle and family form. By the year 2000, the stepfamily will outnumber all other types of families in the United States (Darden & Zimmerman,

1992). Remarriage is becoming increasingly common, and the majority of these remarriages include children. Of all marriages, 30% are a remarriage for at least one partner. Other demographic information on remarriage and blended families follow:

- Almost one in five married-couple families with children have a stepchild living in the household.
- In Black married-couple families, one in four children under age 18 is a stepchild.
- Most stepchildren live with their biological mothers and stepfathers, and prevailing data suggest little conscious effort on the part of divorced parents to collaborate on child care; parallel parenting prevails over coparenting.
- More than six million children, or 9 out of 10 stepchildren in married-couple families, live with their biological mothers and stepfathers. Only 740,000 stepchildren live with their biological fathers and stepmothers.
- Most stepfamilies are at an economic disadvantage as compared with other married-couple families with children, but they are more economically secure than single-parent families.
- Parents in stepfamilies are less well educated than parents in first-marriage families, in general.
- Approximately 13% of American children under age 18 live in families in which one of the two adults is not the biological parent.
- The proportion of children in blended families will increase because 80% of all divorced persons remarry and 60% of these remarriages involve an adult with physical custody of one or more children.
- Annually, one-half million adults become stepparents in the United States. Both girls and boys in stepfamilies demonstrate more behavioral problems than children in nondivorced families (Darden & Zimmerman, 1992; Furstenberg, 1988; Lindner et al., 1992; Smith, 1992).
- Demographers anticipate that, by the turn of the century, nearly one out of every six children under age 18 will be a stepchild, representing 13% of the child population under 18 years of age (Kosinki, 1983; Smith, 1992).

Characteristics of Stepfamilies

Stepfamilies and nuclear families are dissimilar in terms of structure, roles, and boundaries. Stepfamilies are of three basic types: (a) a stepmother with no children and a father and his children; (b) a stepfather with no children and a mother and her children; and (c) a couple, each partner of which is both a parent and a stepparent. Visher and Visher (1983) insist that stepfamilies are structurally the most complex of all families and that the most structurally dissimilar families are stepfamilies and nuclear families.

According to Visher and Visher (1983), the major characteristics or traits of stepfamilies are as follows:

- A biological parent is elsewhere.
- Virtually all family members have sustained a primary relationship loss.
- An adult couple is in the household.
- The relationship between one adult (parent) and child predates the marriage.
- Children are members of more than one household.
- One adult (stepparent) is not legally related to a child (**stepchild**).
- The complexity of stepfamily structure tends to discourage cohesiveness.

The boundaries of blended families are more "permeable" than the boundaries of nuclear families, according to Walsh (1992), Lindner et al. (1992), and Smith (1992), who have analyzed families from the perspective of family boundaries and roles. Several factors promote this permeability. A **reconstituted family** lacks the common household residence of natural parents and the common household locus of parents' authority, and economic subsistence may be shared with the former spouse of one or both adult partners. Children in a blended family find their affection and loyalties divided between two parents' households. Roles are more clearly defined in nuclear, rather than blended, families.

We now turn to more specific information about the blended family, America's newest and fastest growing type of family. Included in the discussion are myths about the roles of stepfamily members, the special needs of children and families who have experienced the blending of a new family, and suggested activities for these families that can be carried out by the child's lead teacher and by other child care and school personnel.

Myths and Roles of Stepfamily Members

Teachers should be aware of how the stepfamily is viewed in order to better understand the child's role (Walsh, 1992). Assuming a new role in a blended or stepfamily is a challenge, and several **stepfamily myths** exist about the roles of stepfamily members. In this section, we address the common problems and issues that surround the roles of stepmother, stepfather, and stepchild. Included in this discussion are common myths associated with each role.

Stepchild's Role.   A child who becomes a "step" child through remarriage of a parent experiences a wide range of emotions (Lindner et al., 1992; Walsh, 1992). Even in the most well adjusted families that are blended, both boys and girls report feelings of loss for their prior family and its unique characteristics. Emotional responses to remarriage depend significantly on how the new relationship has been explained and integrated into the child's living situation. Most stepchildren report feelings of anger, hostility, denial, loss, anxiety, fear, excitement, curiosity, hesitancy, happiness, jealousy, and unrealistic expectations. Because the child has already experienced one major loss (one parent in the prior family), she or he may fear future abandonment by the remaining primary parent and/or the new stepparent (Walsh, 1992). Adjustment to the new reconstituted family takes years. Teachers, caregivers, and other school personnel can facilitate this adjustment period by helping the child recognize and accept the wide array of emotions and set realistic expectations for accepting and adjusting to a new life.

Stepmother's Role.   The role of **stepmother** is a complex one. Stepmothers tend to create unrealistic expectations, and many try to make up to the children for the upset caused by the divorce or death in the original family (Hayes & Hayes, 1986; Kosinki, 1983; Walsh, 1992). A stepchild may resent the stepmother's warmth and love as an attempt to replace the child's biological mother, and her husband may feel left out because of the inordinate amount of attention paid to the children. Also, stepmothers may unrealistically attempt to keep all members of the family happy and content. Expecting that a stepfamily will be equal to an effective nuclear family in cohesiveness, stability, and interpersonal warmth and that it is feasible to please everyone is expecting too much (Visher & Visher, 1983).

Common myths that stepmothers frequently must deal with are the myth of the **wicked stepmother** and the myth of **instant love.** For example, a new stepmother may attempt to be a super-perfect stepparent in order to disprove the wicked-stepmother myth, and she will likely become very frustrated. In addition, "instant love" between stepmother and stepchild is almost never achieved. Thus, if a new stepmother assumes her role with these two myths in mind, she is likely to feel that she has failed. In reality, her expectations are not realistic (Walsh, 1992).

The amount of adjustment required by the stepmother depends on many variables. A remarried mother with no stepchildren has fewer conflicts than other women in stepfamilies. Her husband can relate to her children more like natural children, and there is no competitiveness between her children and his children. A remarried mother with no stepchildren may experience two problems, however. First, she may desire assistance from her new husband in disciplining her children but, at the same time, may become protective or defensive when her husband tries to implement discipline. Second, she may feel guilty because her husband does so much for her children but she has no stepchildren to do things for in return. Stepmothers with no children of their own may have a more difficult time. They are inexperienced, and they also have the more negative image of "stepmother" without enjoying the positive image of "mother." Also, the husband, who has children, will have more need to stay in touch with his ex-spouse. This contact can lead to jealousy on the part of the stepmother.

Stepfather's Role.   A **stepfather** is usually less involved than a step-mother in parenting; therefore, he is less likely to have problems (Lindner et al., 1992; Walsh, 1992). Visher and Visher (1982, 1983) outlined three important psychological tasks for a stepfather: (a) joining a functioning group and establishing a place for himself, (b) working out rules regarding family behavior, and (c) handling unrealistic expectations both on his part and on the part of the new family.

Most stepfathers experience resistance because they are trying to break into a unit of mother and child or children whose bonds predate the relationship between the adults. Also, mothers tend to think that stepfathers discipline too harshly. Children may say, "I don't have to do what he says; he's not my real father." The stepfather is often caught in a bind of trying to become a disciplinarian too soon and of choosing not to become actively involved in discipline, thus isolating himself and appearing to not be interested in the children. Also, the stepfather may feel guilty for having abandoned his own children. He may tend to overcompensate by playing **super-dad** to his natural children when they visit. Because of this guilt, some stepfathers may also withhold themselves from their stepchildren. Conflict may also surface over money and the use of surnames. Stepfathers may have to cope with sexuality issues too. Teenage stepchildren who have not grown up together may be attracted to each other, and stepfathers may be sexually attracted to stepdaughters or vice versa (Kosinki, 1983).

Special Issues for Children in Blended Families

Children in blended families have unique emotional and academic needs that can be addressed by teachers, caregivers, and school personnel. This section describes special issues of stepfamilies and appropriate school programs and interventions. Despite the increasing prevalence of stepsons and stepdaughters, few individuals have been socialized to live in a stepfamily environment. Consequently, many stepfamily members have unrealistic and inappropriate expectations. They have even been surprised at their own emotional reactions to daily stepfamily living, and they may feel alone in their attempts to cope (Coleman & Ganong, 1990). Unexpected feelings, such as embarrassment, ambivalence, and guilt, add to their stress (Lindner et al., 1992; Smith, 1992; Visher & Visher, 1983).

Unfortunately, in traditional early childhood teacher education programs, helping professionals such as educators and caregivers typically are not adequately trained to understand stepfamilies. This lack of professional training and preparation affects the effectiveness and appropriateness of teacher-child interactions, parent-teacher communication, curricular decisions, classroom environment and activities, and selection of books and other learning materials. Intervention strategies appropriate with other families are often not successful with stepfamilies. Counselors note that many conflicts and problems encountered by stepfamilies are not a result of individual psychopathology, but instead are attributable to potentially preventable situations (Stanton, 1986; Visher & Visher, 1988).

What the Teacher and the Caregiver Need to Know

Common issues for students who are members of stepfamilies include (a) embarrassment over divorce and remarriage (Visher & Visher, 1988; Walsh, 1992), (b) social stigma over "step" status that may inhibit the sharing of family experiences with others (Coleman & Ganong, 1990; Lindner et al., 1992), (c) unresolved mourning of the loss of a previous family member that interferes with the formation of a new family unit, and (d) feelings of confusion and "Where do I belong?" that are common for children in the process of family reorganization. This confusion is compounded by the fact that children become members of two households, each with its own style and pattern, and one is not necessarily better or worse than another. Adjusting to the **nonresidential home** is challenging.

Hostility problems are extremely common in stepfamilies (Gardner, 1984; Lindner et al., 1992), and **anger inhibition,** which is the turning inward and suppression of feelings of anger, is understandable for stepchildren. They have already been "abandoned" by a parent, often a father, and they fear that the other parent may also abandon them. Anger inhibition can be serious and may result in childhood depression, particularly for elementary-age children and young adolescents. These children are afraid to express their resentment because they fear that their father will reject them further. Children may be afraid of expressing anger toward their mother because she too might abandon them (Walsh, 1992).

Sibling rivalry between full siblings is fierce, and the rivalry between stepsiblings is even more virulent (Gardner, 1984). Adjustments to new stepbrothers and stepsisters are brought on abruptly, in contrast with the gradual adjustment to a newborn full sibling.

Ambivalent feelings toward new stepparents are common. Development of a loving relationship between a child and a stepparent takes time, and the child often does not realize this. Parents and teachers tend to view girls in stepfamilies as better adjusted than boys in stepfamilies (Lindner et al., 1992).

Loyalty conflicts are almost inevitable in the stepfamily, as children wonder and question their natural parents, "Whom do you love more—your legal spouse or your natural-born children, your own flesh and blood?"(Walsh, 1992). Feelings of hope for a new and better family situation, known as a **Phoenix concept,** are typical. The hope is that the stepfamily can be a reborn family, reborn from the ashes of the old, dead marriage (Gardner, 1984).

Disruption of attachment is normal in the adjustment process, and recovering from this sense of loss may take 2 to 5 years (Lindner et al., 1992; Visher & Visher, 1988). Bringing past family histories with them is common for stepchildren. These histories affect the definition of roles, rights, and responsibilities. The lack of continuity is a source of stress. In a blended family, the spouses have no time to solidify their bond before they attempt to face the demands of parenting. Stepchildren feel this stress and yearn for the continuity and familiarity of their own earlier family.

Discipline and parenting techniques of the new stepparent can be a source of major stress for the stepchild, particularly during the first 1½ to 2 years (Gardner, 1984; Lindner et al., 1992). Financial resources cause additional stress for the stepchild because funds are being stretched now in more directions. Wallerstein and Kelly (1980) report that the standard of living in a blended family is considerably lower than in the predivorce family.

Effects of Cumulative Stress

The concept of **pileup** was introduced by McCubbin and Patterson (1982). This concept simply means that children in stepfamilies may experience the cumulative effects of major changes and stresses, rather than any one factor or situation in isolation. Pileup occurs mostly during the first 1 to 2 years, and the stressors described above are concrete examples of why pileup is likely to occur.

Building Blocks and Assets of Blended Families

Thus far, our discussion has placed the new, blended family in a rather complex, somewhat negative context. Teachers and professionals should

Stepfamilies can have many strengths and assets.

also realize that blended families can bring together many assets and strengths. Interventions with children will certainly be more effective if the positive outcomes and aspects of their new families are emphasized. Teachers can facilitate children's adjustment process by helping them identify and build on specific and positive characteristics and traits of the newly formed family units; suggestions for how teachers can accomplish this are listed below:

- Setting realistic expectations about stepfamily life (Visher & Visher, 1983)
- Recognizing cultural and ethnic differences among blended families
- Identifying special, positive personality traits of the new parent and how these traits and skills can benefit the child
- Identifying mutual interests of the child and the new stepparent and beginning to schedule special times and events with that new parent
- Describing ways the new parent is making the biological parent happier and more content
- Discussing how finances and shared resources may now be greater because of the sharing of the new parents with the children in the stepfamily
- Beginning to make memories through scrapbooks, planned vacations and excursions as a family, photographs, and other ways of building a new sense of family and future

Teachers and caregivers can help members of a blended family cope with the complexities of their situation in three ways: by consulting, by coordinating resources, and by informal support and referral to counseling (Poppen & White, 1984). Research on stepfamilies and the unique intervention needs of stepchildren has only recently emerged in the literature. Professionals in education, child development, psychology, sociology, counseling, and marriage and family therapy all are contributing to the growing understanding of stepfamilies and their adjustment tasks.

Community-based and elementary school counselors can work with teachers and caregivers to facilitate improvement in stepfamily relationships. Froiland and Hozman (1977) have developed a model based on Elisabeth Kübler-Ross' concept of loss that is still applicable to today's families. They state that, for couples and children, a divorce signifies the death of a relationship. The divorce process is conceptualized as similar to the process of facing and coping with death. The model consists of these stages of adjustment: denial, anger, bargaining, depression, and acceptance. The Froiland-Hozman model is useful conceptually because an almost universal characteristic of stepfamilies is mourning the loss of a relationship.

The role of teachers and caregivers is to help children (a) come to terms with these normal feelings of loss, (b) acknowledge their existence and origins, (c) verbalize feelings, and (d) move toward acceptance of their new family situation. Because teachers, caregivers, and school support person-

The role of the teacher or caregiver is to help children come to terms with normal feelings of loss.

nel have consistently large periods of time with the child, they have ample opportunity for observing the children in social and academic settings in the school or center, for intervening on an individual basis with each child, and for becoming familiar with each child's family members and situation.

Actions that teachers can take to facilitate children's feelings of loss include the following:

- Acknowledge to the child her or his feelings of loss
- Validate the child's feelings as being normal and acceptable
- Engage the child in language arts and art activities that promote the expression of feelings
- Share a book about a child who experiences divorce in her or his family
- Talk about the advantages of having two homes
- Encourage the child to talk regularly about new changes in her or his life
- Provide the child with a special place in the classroom for conversations with you or to engage the child in special activities
- Validate the child's identity and sense of self-worth
- Involve the child in caring for a pet in the classroom

Focusing on the child first and then gradually involving the parents can forge an effective intervention that merges the role of the teacher or caregiver with the role of family advocate. Helping a child acknowledge feelings of loss and then facilitating that child as she or he moves through each stage can result in positive outcomes for the child emotionally, academically, and socially.

The teacher should not attempt formal counseling intervention, but rather should learn from these models about the sense of loss experienced through remarriage. The teacher can effectively devise learning activities that encourage the children to express orally, through written work, or through art expression, their feelings of loss. Teaming with a community-based counselor is a good strategy for a teacher dealing with postdivorce and remarriage issues involving students. The counselor will be able to suggest both general and specific strategies for the teacher to implement that will encourage the healthy expression of feelings by the children.

Children in a blended family seem to function more effectively when there is a strong, caring alliance between the couple, along with more **permeable boundaries** than is optimal in intact, nondivorced families (Visher & Visher, 1983). Stepfamilies seem to require boundaries that are more ambiguous and permeable. For example, children need the freedom and independence to move freely back and forth between two different living situations. Thus, stepfamilies may appear to be more disengaged and less cohesive than is considered optimal for intact or nuclear families.

◊◊ Goals for Stepfamily Education

The main purpose of supporting children of divorce in educational settings, especially those in preschool and primary grades, should be to help them cope with the changes of transition until things stabilize. Teachers and caregivers have both advantages and disadvantages in their work with stepchildren. On the one hand, the children are a captive audience 5 to 7 hours (or more) a day, and they can benefit therapeutically without direct cost to parents. On the other hand, parents are often less available to a teacher or caregiver than to a private practitioner (Gardner, 1984). The goals for the teacher or caregiver should be in a supportive role, rather than in a formal counseling role. By spending some time observing the child, identifying needs of the child, and communicating these needs to parents, the teacher or caregiver can facilitate the referral process to a community-based or private practitioner who specializes in family therapy and specific divorce and remarriage issues.

Research outcomes for remarried families are mixed, and recent case study research by Wallerstein and Blakeslee (1995) paints a discouraging picture for adult children of divorce. Remarriage generally makes things better for younger children, but researchers have found that, for about one fourth of children in their study, remarriage was not seen as improving their lives, especially if the children were age 10 or older at the time of remarriage (Lindner et al., 1992; Wallerstein & Blakeslee, 1995; Wallerstein

& Kelly, 1980). In either case, the children's problems were fewer if the original parents and remarried parents were not warring with one another. Thus, teachers and caregivers seem to need a stepfamily education program that attempts to accomplish the following goals:

- Helping stepchildren understand the complexity of stepfamily functioning
- Helping stepchildren and their parents develop positive relationships
- Teaching stepchildren and their parents how to communicate effectively with one another
- Teaching stepparents how to manage their emotions in stepparenting by learning to think rationally and to dispute their irrational beliefs
- Teaching stepparents and stepchildren how to use principles of social learning and logical or natural consequences to solve adult-child conflicts in stepfamilies

A school-based or center-based program for stepfamily education should include two elements: (a) giving participants information about the cultural and structural characteristics of stepfamilies and the roles, expectations, and difficulties of individual stepfamily members and (b) teaching communication and parenting skills to all (Kosinki, 1983).

◊◊ Intervention Approaches for Families

This section describes several recognized models or approaches to effective intervention for children adjusting to a blended family situation, as well as for children experiencing change in their lives generally. These models are derived from the literature on family therapy, school counseling, child psychology, and child development. All models presented in this chapter include a theoretical basis involving parent involvement, family participation, the family systems approach, and child development. These models are now discussed, with suggestions for implementation in a school or child care center learning environment.

Bibliotherapy

The use of shared and mutually-selected or assigned readings, also known as **bibliotherapy,** may be especially useful in educational, preventive programs for stepfamilies (Coleman & Ganong, 1990). Bibliotherapy has been defined as "the use of reading materials for help in solving personal problems or for psychiatric therapy" (Merriam-Webster, 1993, p. 111) and "a family of techniques for structuring an interaction between a facilitator and a participant . . . based on their mutual sharing of literature" (Berry, 1978, p. 187). Through books, readers can escape into new roles and identities and sample lifestyles vicariously. Both fiction and nonfiction can provide children and adults with models to help them handle situations they might encounter. Both types of books can be important aids to educators, caregivers, counselors, and other helping professionals working with stepfamilies.

The goals of bibliotherapy include the following:

- Teaching facts about particular life situations, such as stepfamilies, divorce, death, and remarriage, and the incidence of these situations in society as a whole

- Informing stepchildren and their parents about step relationships and the unique challenges they may encounter

- Obtaining insight or self-understanding as they read about a character who is facing a similar situation to their own

- Helping the children and their parents better understand their own emotional reactions, conflicts, cognitions, motivations, feelings, and thoughts through identification with a central character in an assigned reading

- Stimulating discussion between children and their parents by allowing the family to react to the characters in the reading, thus providing the children and parents with a safe outlet and forum for discussing their own issues

Bibliotherapy provides a variety of books for parents and children to share.

Selecting reading materials for children and parents of stepfamilies is not necessarily an easy task. Several criteria have been identified for selecting stepfamily books: (a) The stepfamily issues should be the main focus, (b) the book should be at an appropriate reading level, (c) the stories should be about modern children and families or have universal appeal, (d) characters should be realistic, and the solutions to problems should be realistic, (e) materials should not offend religious beliefs or values of the reader, (f) problems should be dealt with in a manner consistent with research or prevailing clinical opinion about stepfamily functioning, and (g) good coping strategies should be modeled in the reading (McInnes, 1982).

Books or other reading materials cannot be chosen until the specific stepfamily's situation is known. Thus, structural characteristics of the family, such as the number of siblings, stepsiblings, and half-siblings, the cause of the dissolution of the parents' marriage (death or divorce), and the extent of contact with the nonresidential parent, are considered part of the family situation. The presenting problem or central issue for child and parents should also be included in the selected reading (Coleman & Ganong, 1990).

Choosing self-help books designed for children, teachers, and parents is relatively easy, compared with selecting fictional books. The main reason for this ease is that few books exist in this domain. Selecting a self-help book depends on the age of the child, the child's reading ability, the nature of the issues and problems being presented by the child, a positive perspective on stepfamilies, and the concreteness of advice and suggestions. Other important considerations include the use of appropriate illustrations, reference lists, appendixes, and the overall visual appeal of the book (Coleman & Ganong, 1990).

Using bibliotherapy with children and their parents from blended families involves three steps:

1. *Planning:*   Includes identification of the individual's needs and selection of appropriate material. Planning demands that the helper know at least some information about the family and the reading material.

2. *Motivating:*   Involves introducing and presenting the reading materials to the child or parents or both in a way that immediately connects them to the reading. Comments such as, "You know, a boy in this book had a family situation pretty much like yours. It might be interesting for you to read this, just to see how he handled it. We could talk about it afterward and think of ways the story could have been different," might serve as motivation (Coleman & Ganong, 1990).

3. *Follow-up:*   A critical step that can involve a discussion based on previously prepared questions, or it can take whatever format has been decided on. This is a time to clarify any information presented in the books, to review concepts, to evaluate the story or characters in the story, and to explore feelings. Some readers may need assistance in summarizing and evaluating reading materials; others may need help

in exploring their own attitudes and feelings. *Whatever the follow-up activity entails, it is important that the teacher, caregiver, or school counselor respond in a nonjudgmental way to readers' comments.*

Focused Individual and Family Intervention

The teacher or caregiver can provide and facilitate intervention for children who are experiencing divorce and remarriage by working with the school counselor or a community-based counselor. In this case, the teacher is a facilitator of intervention. The counselor can help members of the blended family cope with the complexities of their situation in three ways: by consulting, by coordinating resources, and most important, by counseling. Providing effective counseling intervention with children or parents or both in a stepfamily situation can become quite complex. Nonetheless, joint counseling can prove to be the most effective and efficient way to provide intervention.

Important tasks of the counselor in either individual or group counseling are (a) to help children assess how well and in what ways they are coping with the transition to remarriage; children often report feeling responsible for what happens in the family, feeling unworthy, and feeling helpless about what is happening to them; (b) to recognize the fears that are common among client members of stepfamily situations; children experience a wide range of emotions; (c) to assist in identifying the roots of those feelings, verbalizing existing fears and anxieties, and assisting in learning to communicate effectively with new stepparents; and (d) to alleviate fears of parents, as parents too may be afraid to become involved in a counseling situation; one primary fear of parents is that the counseling experience will reunite former partners. Thus, the main purpose of counseling children, especially those in early childhood and early elementary settings, should be to help them cope with the changes of transition until things stabilize (Lindner et al., 1992; Visher & Visher, 1982).

The school counselor's role in this intervention process depends on several factors: (a) the level of formal training of the school counselor; (b) adequate time for direct intervention with schoolchildren and their parents; (c) the space and facilities available for counseling services; (d) the willingness of the administration to support this effort; (e) the willingness of the parents to become involved at this level in the educational setting; and (f) the willingness of the parents to disclose details about their personal lives; they may fear negative consequences within the school setting.

One of the most difficult goals for counselors working with stepfamilies is the attempt to achieve cooperation between the adults (stepparents and natural parents) in each of a child's households (Lindner et al., 1992). This outlook is especially important if both natural parents play an active part in their child's lives. Interpreting and explaining difficult issues to children, such as visitation rights and financial support, are examples of tasks for the school counselor. In addition, counselors should make it difficult for children to manipulate their natural parents or stepparents on these issues. If cooperation cannot be achieved, then the task for the counselor is to help the child get enough distance and independence, so that she or he can function effectively despite the continued conflicts between the adults. Visher and Visher (1983) maintain that, in many cases, couples education or a few individual therapy sessions for an adult or child can assist a stepfamily in improving relationships and becoming less dysfunctional.

It is absolutely necessary to understand the complexity of stepfamily functioning to be an effective counselor because a counselor cannot evaluate the stepfamily by using the same criteria as those used to evaluate an intact or nuclear family. Stepfamily therapy must take into consideration the complex nature of stepfamilies. The task of therapy is to move from individual family members or subsystems to helping the family view itself as a total interactional unit. The ultimate goal of stepfamily therapy is to effect good or functional stepfamily reorganization, keeping in mind, of course, the somewhat idiosyncratic nature of this objective.

Counseling strategies or approaches used should match the formal training level and skills of the professional, as well as the unique needs of each child and family. Thus, one counselor might use a family systems approach, whereas another might use a client-centered approach. It is important for counselors to have modest goals in the treatment of stepfamilies. The relationships between stepparents and stepchildren are traditionally tenuous. Even when they claim deep feelings and love for one another, stepparents and stepchildren may still not be ready to use these terms legitimately. To help a child, the counselor must also work with the involved adults. Joint counseling is usually essential to a satisfactory counseling experience with students from blended families.

Self-Help Parent Education Model

The literature on parent education programs available for children in school and child care settings is limited. Sheehy (1980) has proposed an educational model for working with stepfamilies and has helped design a self-help parent education program for stepparents (Sheehy & Fisher, 1980). He emphasizes two critical mistakes that stepparents make. The first is the tendency for the stepparent to rush in and assume a role as disciplinarian before a good parental subsystem has been established. The second is using the withdrawal of affection to punish children for misbehavior. In stepfamilies, punishment and withdrawal of love are counterproductive; stepchildren are likely to resent being punished by a stepparent who has not been integrated into the family and are not likely to be influenced positively by the withdrawal of love by that stepparent (Hagan et al., 1992; Walsh, 1992). Thus, Sheehy advocates the use of natural or **logical consequences** (Dreikurs & Grey, 1968) as a principal method of discipline. Stepparents need to be taught how to use natural or logical consequences, to support each other, and to differentiate between the age and characteristics of each child when administering discipline.

◇◇ **Role of the School or Center**

Programs and interventions designed for stepfamily members are most effective if they are surrounded by administrators and organizations that understand the usefulness of these programs. Schools and child care centers play an important role in recognizing, assessing, addressing, and evaluating the educational and emotional needs of children in stepfamilies.

Institutional support for intervention initiatives and programs for stepchildren and their parents include encouraging teachers and other school professionals to view the needs of reconstituted families and students as a unique part of their support roles. For example, administrators can provide adequate space for teachers, caregivers, and other collaborative professional personnel to meet on an individual basis with students and their parents. This space should be private and reflect sensitivity to the need for confidentiality. In addition, financial resources should be provided for purchasing current educational, self-help materials for parents and for reimbursing community resource professionals to assist the teacher, school

Administrators can facilitate programs for students and their parents from blended families.

counselor, school social worker, or other personnel in conducting workshops, parent education programs, and other types of informal educational initiatives in the school setting. Administrators can be more supportive of these efforts if they are well-read themselves on issues related to child development; the impact of divorce on children, parents, and family systems; and the most current research literature on effective intervention programs for reconstituted families. Finally, encouraging school personnel to collaborate in their interventions for children of divorced and remarried families will result in the most comprehensive and effective services for these children.

◊◊ Summary

Projections for the next decade are for divorced and blended families to continue to increase in numbers (Walsh, 1992; Smith, 1992). Societal trends are always reflected in the settings where young children are present—schools and child care settings. Although the numbers of children and families affected by divorce and remarriage have escalated, the recognition of their unique needs and the availability of support and intervention programs for these families are inadequate. Perhaps no other area of intervention is in such tremendous need of "catch up" as is the provision of services for children from blended families.

Meeting the needs of these children requires a commitment on the part of teachers and caregivers and their respective administrators. This chapter addressed the unique emotional needs of children who are experiencing divorce, who are becoming part of blended families, the common issues and problems of these children and their parents, and effective intervention strategies and approaches that have proved successful. Together, early childhood educational professionals can strengthen the umbrella of support available for young children who find themselves with "new" mommies and daddies and the complexities of these family situations.

Summary Statements ◊

- Divorce among first marriages in the United States is around 50%; for remarriages, the divorce rate is higher.
- Divorce is related to the age, socioeconomic status, educational levels of parents, and race, with Black parents having a slightly higher divorce and separation rate than other races.

- Teachers bring to the classroom their own values and attitudes toward divorce; self-assessment of these attitudes is necessary for teachers to meet constructively the needs of the children in their classrooms.
- Emotional reactions vary greatly, but distinct stages of emotional adjustment

are reflected in the research. Teachers should become familiar with these stages and with the intense emotional states that are often displayed by young and elementary-age children.

- Effective strategies for communication between the teacher and the divorcing parent are available. These strategies allow the child to cope with the stress of divorce, ensure that school-family communications will be appropriate, and provide legal protection for the child, parent, and school or child care center.

- Recovery from the divorce experience is long and sometimes very difficult. Research by Wallerstein indicates that adult children of divorce are still recovering in various ways. Teacher should be aware of the depth of emotional distress and pain usually associated with divorce and divorce recovery.

- Most divorced adults remarry; thus, children of these adults usually have several **stages of divorce adjustment—** from predivorce to postdivorce and the creation of a new, blended family.

- By the year 2000, well over one half of today's youth will become stepsons or stepdaughters.

- Several terms are used interchangeably to describe stepfamilies: *blended, reconstituted, reorganized, combined,* and *remarried.*

- Stepfamilies are structurally the most complex of all families and the most unlike nuclear families.

- Assuming a new role in a blended family is very challenging, and several myths exist for stepmothers, stepfathers, and stepchildren.

- Stepchildren have unique emotional, social, and academic needs, yet most teachers, caregivers, and school professionals have very limited formal training in working with stepfamilies.

- Specific intervention approaches are very effective with stepchildren and stepfamilies. The goal of stepfamily education is to ease the transition and roles of the reconstituted family.

- Institutions such as schools and child care centers can provide much-needed administrative and organizational support for teachers, caregivers, and other professionals.

Resources for Teachers, Caregivers, Parents, and Children ◇ ◇ ◇ ◇ ◇ ◇ ◇ ◇

Classic Books for Younger Children

Arnold, W. (1980). *When your parents divorce.* Philadelphia: Westminster.

Brown, M. (1986). *Dinosaur's divorce.* Boston: Little, Brown.

Danziger, P. (1982). *The divorce express.* New York: Delacorte.

Glass, S. M. (1980). *A divorce dictionary: A book for you and your children.* New York: Four Winds.

Helmering, D. (1981) *I have two families.* Nashville, TN: Abington.

Rofes, E. (1981). *The kids' book of divorce: By, for, and about kids.* Lexington, MA: Vintage.

Sharmat, M. (1980). *Sometimes Mama and Papa fight.* New York: HarperCollins.

Simon, N. (1983). *I wish I had my father.* Niles, IL: Whitman.

Classic Books for Elementary Children

Gardner, R. (1977). *The boys and girls book about divorce.* New York: Bantam Books.

Jackson, M., & Jackson, M. (1981). *Your father's not coming home anymore.* New York: Richard Marek.

Makris, K. (1995). *Crosstown.* New York: Avon.

Books for Parents

Berman, C. (1986). *Making it as a stepparent: New roles, new rules* (ERIC No: ED403041).

Bienenfield, F. (1987). *Helping your child succeed after divorce.* Claremont, CA: Hunter House.

Chambers, D. (1997). *Solo parenting: Raising strong and happy families* (ERIC No. ED 403392).

Cohen, M. G. (1991). *The joint custody handbook.* Philadelphia: Running Press.

Enger, A., & Kluneness, L. (1995). *The complete single mother.* Holbrook, MA: Adams Media.

Fassel, D. (1991). *Growing up divorced: A road to healing for adult children of divorce.* New York: Pocket Books.

Francke, L. B. (1983). *Growing up divorced.* New York: Linden Press.

Friedman, J. (1982). *The divorce handbook.* New York: Random House.

Hill, G. A. (1989). *Divorced father: Coping with problems, creating solutions.* White Hall, VA: Betterway.

Kalter, N. (1990). *Growing up with divorce.* New York: Free Press.

Lansky, V. (1989). *Divorce book for parents.* New York: Penguin Books.

Marta, S. Y. (1996). *When death or divorce occur: Helping children cope with loss* (ERIC No. ED 402023).

Morgan, E. (1985). *Custody.* Boston: Little, Brown.

Wallerstein, J. S., & Kelly, J. B. (1980). *Surviving the breakup.* New York: Basic Books.

Books and Articles for Teachers

Bernstein, J. E. (1983). *Books to help children cope with separation and loss* (2nd ed.). New York: Bowker.

Caughey, C. (1991). Becoming the child's ally: Observations in a classroom for children who have been abused. *Young Children, 46*(4), 22–28.

Dreyer, S. S. (1981). *The bookfinder* (Vol. 2). Circle Pines, MN: American Guidance Service.

Francke, L. B. (1983). *Growing up divorced.* New York: Linden Press.

Frieman, B. B. (1997). Two parents—two homes. *Educational Leadership, 54*(7), 23–25.

Jewett, C. (1982). *Helping children cope with separation and loss.* Cambridge, MA: Harvard University Press.

Mack, C. (1991). *Separation and loss: A handbook for early childhood professionals.* Pittsburgh, PA: Center for Social and Urban Research.

McCracken, J. B. (1986). *Reducing stress in young children's lives.* Washington, DC: National Association for the Education of Young Children.

Metcalf, L. (1995). *Counseling toward solutions: A practical solution-focused program for working with students, teachers, and parents* (ERIC No. ED 403505).

Miller, K. (1996). *The crisis manual for early childhood teachers: How to handle the really difficult problems* (ERIC No. ED 41005).

Wallach, L. B. (1993). Helping children cope with violence. *Young Children, 48*(4), 4–11.

Videos and Films

Kimmons, L., & Gaston, J. A. (1986). Single parenting: A filmography. *Family Relations, 35*, 205–211.

Whitely, J. M. (1980). *Stepparenting* [Film]. Alexandria, VA: American Association for Counseling and Development. (This 20-minute film defines problems that occur in remarriage when children are involved. Useful for the general public or for adults or children going through the experience).

Professional Journals

Journal of Divorce. Haworth Press, 174 Fifth Avenue, New York, NY 10010.

The Single Parent. The Journal of Parents Without Partners, Inc., International Headquarters, 7910 Woodmont Avenue, Bethesda, MD 2001.

Agencies and Organizations Supporting Divorced and Blended Families

Sources for Help: Children

National Runaway Switchboard, (800) 621-4000

National runaway hotline; number for runaways to call free to contact relatives. Call to leave a message for friends or relatives.

International Youth Council (IYC)

A division of Parents Without Partners. Offers help for teens who have a single parent.

Stepfamily Organizations

The Stepfamily Association of America, Inc., 900 Welch Road, Suite 400, Palo Alto, CA 94304. Offers educational material, stepfamily survival courses, referral services, newsletter.

Remarrieds, Inc., Box 742, Santa Ana, CA 92701. Offers educational and social programs.

Remarried Parents, Inc., c/o Temple Beth Sholom, 1782 Second Street, Northern Boulevard, Flushing, NY 11358. Monthly meetings, lectures, weekly support groups, socials.

Parents' Groups

Parents Anonymous, 2810 Artesia Boulevard, Suite F, Redondo Beach, CA 90278. Help for parents of abused children.

Divorce Anonymous, P.O. Box 5313, Chicago, IL 60680. Regular meetings for the divorced.

Mothers Without Custody, Inc., P.O. Box 602, Greenbelt, MD 20770.

Parents Without Partners, 7910 Woodmont Avenue, Washington, DC 20014.

Sisterhood of Single Black Mothers, 1360 Fulton Street, Brooklyn, NY.

Local Agencies and Community Resources

Local health department

Mental health/mental retardation department

Marriage & Family Therapists Association

Private counseling centers and professionals

Pastoral counseling—individuals and associations

University training centers for counseling, social work and marriage and family therapy

Regional and local public libraries

Education, psychology, and human development departments and libraries in community college and university settings

Videos from educational catalogs, institutes, and video stores

United Way agencies

Family counseling agencies

Additional Exercises ◇◇◇◇◇◇◇◇◇◇◇◇◇◇◇◇◇◇◇◇◇◇◇◇◇◇◇◇◇◇◇◇◇

Exercise 1: Peer Resource Person

Invite an older child, perhaps a teenager, who has experienced the divorce of parents to come to your classroom or school site to talk with a child or small group of children about this important transition. It is important that this peer resource person be sufficiently mature to verbalize and reflect on her or his personal experience in such a way that the younger child can identify and relate in a positive way.

Exercise 2: Language Arts Activities

Numerous books on divorce, remarriage, and blended and reconstituted families are appropriate to share with small groups of children. Group discussion and sharing can take place as a follow-up activity, which gives the child experiencing this life event a chance to listen to peers' ideas, relate personal experience, and perhaps verbalize needs that she or he is experiencing. Follow-up activities such as the writing of a narrative, personal diary, story, play, or an art activity that integrates the reading experience with the use of paint, chalk, sculpting, or some other art form are all appropriate.

Exercise 3: Video or Television Program

The teacher, counselor, caregiver, or other school professional can show a video or television program, such as *The Brady Bunch* or *Step by Step,* that depicts routine life events in stepfamilies. Although these programs are often humorous, they also provide a good context for discussing unique issues and problems encountered by children growing up in blended families.

Exercise 4: Role Playing

Children who are part of blended families can work collaboratively on projects that encourage and safely allow them a chance to talk about, face, and work through their personal issues. For example, a small group of children from blended families could be assigned to write a script for a television show, radio program, or play. At least some of the main characters should be involved in blended family situations. These projects provide an integrated learning experience for the student participants that can include writing, editing, videotaping, audiotaping, musical production or recording, script writing, publishing, and so on. In addition, these projects provide a constructive avenue for stepchildren to share their common experiences, to find commonalities with their peers, and to experience feelings of success in an academic special assignment.

Exercise 5: Community Resource Person

Invite a family therapist, counselor, pastor, or other community professional to talk with the class as a whole or with a smaller group of children about her or his experience in working with stepfamilies. Encourage this resource person to bring a video to show and to relate to the children how common divorce and remarriage is within their own community. As a language arts activity, children can complete a follow-up assignment, such as writing a review or description of the resource person.

References ◇◇◇

American Heritage Dictionary (3rd ed.). (1996). Boston: Houghton Mifflin.

Anderson, T. Z., & White, G. D. (1986). An empirical investigation of interactions and relation patterns in functional and dysfunctional nuclear families and stepfamilies. *Family Process, 17,* 407–422.

Axinn, W. G. (1996). The influences of parents' marital dissolutions on children's attitudes toward family formation. *Demography, 33,* 66–81.

Berry, J. (1978). *Contemporary bibliotherapy: Systematizing the field.* In E. J. Rulim (Ed.), *Bibliotherapy* (pp. 185–190). Phoenix, AZ: Orene Press.

Brazelton, T. B. (1989). *Families: Crisis and caring.* New York: Ballantine Books.

Coleman, M., & Ganong, L. (1990). The uses of juvenile fiction and self-help books with stepfamilies. *Journal of Counseling & Development, 68,* 327–331.

Darden, E., & Zimmerman, T. (1992). Blended families: A decade review, 1979 to 1990. *Family Therapy, 19,* 25–31.

Diamond, S. A. (1985). *Helping children of divorce.* New York: Schocken Books.

Dreikurs, R., & Grey, L. (1968). *Logical consequences.* New York: Hawthorn.

Emery, R. E. (1988). *Marriage, divorce, and children's adjustment.* Newbury Park, CA: Sage.

Fine, M. A., & Fine, D. R. (1992). Recent changes in laws affecting stepfamilies: Suggestions for legal reform. *Family Relations, 41,* 334–340.

Francke, L. B. (1983). *Growing up divorced.* New York: Linden Press.

Frieman, B. B. (1993). Separation and divorce: Children want their teachers to know. *Young Children, 48*(6), 58–63.

Froiland, D. J., & Hozman, T. L. (1977). Counseling for constructive divorce. *Personnel & Guidance Journal, 55,* 525–529.

Furstenberg, F. L., Jr. (1988). Child care, divorce, and remarriage. In E. M. Hetherington, E. Mavis, & J. D. Arasteh (Eds.), *Impacts of divorce, single parenting, and stepparenting on children.* Mahwah, NJ: Erlbaum.

Galston, W. A. (1996, Summer). Divorce American style. *Public Interest, 124,* 12–26.

Ganong, L., Coleman, M., & Maples, D. (1990). A meta-analytic review of family structure stereotypes. *Journal of Marriage and the Family, 52,* 287–297.

Gardner, R. (1984). Counseling children in stepfamilies. *Elementary School Guidance & Counseling, 14,* 40–49.

Glick, P. C. (1989). Remarriage: Some recent changes and variations. *Journal of Family Issues, 4,* 455–478.

Godwin, L. J., Groves, M. M., & Horm-Wingerd, D. M. (1993, Spring). Separation distress in infants, toddlers, and parents. *Day Care and Early Education,* 13–17.

Hagan, M. S., Hollier, E. A., O'Connor, T. G., & Eisenberg, M. (1992). Parent-child relationships in nondivorced, divorced single-mother, and remarried families. *Monographs of the Society for Research in Child Development, 57*(2–3), 94–148.

Hayes, R. L., & Hayes, B. A. (1986). Remarriage families: Counseling parents, stepparents, and their children. *Counseling and Human Development, 18,* 1–8.

Jellinek, M., & Klavan, E. (1988, September). The single parent. *Good Housekeeping,* p. 126.

Keith, V. M., & Finlay, B. (1988). The impact of parental divorce on children's educational attainment, marital timing, and likelihood of divorce. *Journal of Marriage and the Family, 50*(4), 798–809.

Kosinki, F. (1983). Improving relationships in stepfamilies. *Elementary School Guidance & Counseling, 13,* 200–207.

Lindner, M. S., Hagan, M. S., & Brown, J. C. (1992). The adjustment of children in nondivorced, divorced, single-mother, and remarried families. *Monographs for Research in Child Development, 57*(2–3), 35–72.

McCubbin, H. I., & Patterson, J. M. (1982). *Family adaptation to crisis.* In H. I. McCubbin & J. M. Patterson (Eds.), *Family stress, coping, and social support* (pp. 26–47). Springfield, IL: Charles C. Thomas.

McInnes, K. (1982). Bibliotherapy: Adjunct to traditional counseling with children of stepfamilies. *Child Welfare, 61,* 153–160.

Merriam-Webster's New Collegiate Dictionary (10th ed.). (1993). Springfield, MA: Merriam-Webster.

Poppen, W., & White, P. (1984). Transition to the blended family. *Elementary School Guidance & Counseling, 14,* 50–61.

Sheehy, P. (1980). Family enrichment for stepfamilies: An empirical study. *Dissertation Abstracts International, 42,* 2317A.

Sheehy, P., & Fisher, B. (1980). *Stepping together: A self-help program for stepfamilies.* Unpublished manuscript.

Smith, R. (1992). *Stressor affecting children of African American stepfamilies* (ERIC Document ED 358 389 C 024879).

Stanton, G. (1986). Preventive intervention with stepfamilies. *Social Work, 31,* 201–206.

Strangeland, C. S., Pellegreno, D. C., & Lundholm, J. (1989). Children of divorced parents: A perceptual comparison. *Elementary School Guidance & Counseling, 23*(2), 167–174.

Visher, E. B., & Visher, J. S. (1982). *How to win as a stepfamily.* New York: Dembner Books.

Visher, E., & Visher, J. (1988). *Stepfamilies: Old loyalties, new ties.* New York: Brunner/Mazel.

Visher, E. B., & Visher, J. S. (1983). Stepparenting: Blending families. In H. I. McCubbin & C. R. Figley (Eds.), *Stress and the family: Coping with normative transitions* (Vol. 1). New York: Brunner/Mazel.

Wallerstein, J. S., & Blakeslee, S. (1995). *The good marriage: How and why love lasts.* Boston: Houghton Mifflin.

Wallerstein, J. S., & Kelly, J. B. (1980). *Surviving the break-up: How children and parents cope with divorce.* New York: Basic Books.

Walsh, W. M. (1992). Twenty major issues in remarriage families. *Journal of Counseling & Development, 70,* 709–715.

7 "Chosen" Children
Building Partnerships with Adoptive Families

Once upon a time there lived a man and woman named James and Martha Brown. They had been married for a long time and were very happy together. Only one thing was missing in their lives. They had no babies of their own, and they had always wanted children to share their home. One day James and Martha said to each other, "Let's adopt a baby to bring up as our very own."

Wasson, 1939/1977

Key Terms

adoption
autonomy versus doubt and shame
cultural heritage
ego identity versus identity
   confusion
ego integrity versus despair
foster care
generativity versus stagnation
grief
industry versus inferiority
initiative versus guilt

international adoption
intimacy versus isolation
physical self
psychological self
psychosocial task
single-parent adoption
social self
special needs adoption
transracial adoption
trust versus mistrust

Wasson's classic *The Chosen Baby*, first published in 1939, depicts the warmth and love that adults and children can bring to each other as a family is created through adoption. It also represents the traditional form of adoption people may have grown accustomed to expect. "In the first half of this century, adoption typically involved the placement of an infant with a childless, infertile couple of the same race (and often the same religious background)" (Brodzinsky & Schechter, 1990, p. xi). Today, adoption is a more complex issue as (a) family compositions and the lifestyles of individuals desiring to adopt children become more varied; (b) the number of children available for adoption decreases with the greater availability and acceptance of abortion; (c) the geographic origins of the infants and children being adopted broaden as do the political complexities; (d) the number of individuals, including attorneys and physicians, and agencies, both public and private, involved in child procurement and placements increases; (e) the laws designed to protect birthparents, adoptive parents, and children become more restrictive; and (f) the strategies that prospective parents employ to locate and legally secure a child become more diverse and aggressive.

The parenting journey is an emotional one filled with love, joy, compassion, delight, fear, frustration, and many unknowns. Healthy parents want their child to be happy and secure in their love and will work very hard to ensure that the child's environment protects and nurtures those feelings. Nevertheless, parents cannot control every aspect of their child's life, be it a genetic predisposition or an environmental influence. An adoptive parent faces even more unknowns about a child's genetic history, prior experiences, how the child will make adjustments to being adopted throughout life, and the child's connection with his or her family of origin.

VIGNETTE 3

Thomas

Thomas was 11 when he casually told his adoptive mother one day that he wanted to meet his birthmother. He had known since he was a very young child that he was adopted, but he had never expressed any interest in knowing more about his birthmother. Surprised by the fear that rose to her throat, Thomas' mother told him she would help him find his birthmother when he reached 18. Later, when she reflected on the conversation, she realized she was trying to prolong the possibility that Thomas would somehow be "lost" to her and that she would need to deal with her fears in meeting the very natural desires of her son to know more about his heritage.

While providing a wonderful opportunity for sharing love with a child, the journey that begins for both child and adult as their lives become intertwined

is a path marked by changes in the child's cognitive and emotional understanding of the adoption process and search for self and the adult's emotional
taking in and letting go of the child, conceived by and born of another, but
seen as one's "own." As experienced by Thomas's mother and by the parents
of many children who are adopted, it is a journey of love and joy, fears of the
unknown, and acceptance. When professionals teach and care for young children, they become a part of the network of individuals who will nourish,
guide, and protect those children. The network components, though sometimes changing, are interrelated, and professionals must share what happens
to each child at school with his or her family and be willing to engage the parents in communication that will help build understanding of their goals and
concerns for their child and their own needs as parents.

VIGNETTE 4

Jason

Jason was a wonderful participant in the 3-year-old nursery. He
painted with flourishing strokes at the easel and built bridges and
roads in the block corner. His only difficulty seemed to be separating
from his mother each morning. He happily appeared each morning
at the door with mother in tow. The teacher encouraged him to hang
up his coat and to say good-bye, which he did. The mother stood at
the door with some last-minute reminders: "Mommy will be back in
3 hours, Jason!" "Don't be upset when Mommy leaves, Jason."
"Mommy loves you, Jason." With each comment, Jason became a little less certain of his willingness to move into the room.

The teachers who watched this display were somewhat annoyed at this over-
protective mother. After a few weeks, a parent conference was scheduled, and
the teacher and Jason's mother talked. The teacher shared that she wanted to
help Jason separate more easily each morning and so asked his mother for her
perspective. During the conversation, Jason's mother shared that Jason was
her only child and that she and her husband had waited years to adopt a baby.
Their first attempt at adoption had resulted with the child being given back to
the birthmother, who had changed her mind about the adoption. It was a heart-
breaking story, but the teacher understood a great deal more about the separation dilemma. During the next few weeks, the mother and the teacher worked
together to transition Jason into school and to alleviate the mother's fears.

Educators and caregivers working with families who have adopted children or are raising children not their own by birth need some knowledge of
the challenges faced by these families. As a part of that education, it is also
of interest to explore the history and changes that have occurred in the

adoption process. To our effort to further these goals, this chapter covers the following topics:

- The history of adoption
- Types of adoptions and strategies for adopting
- The emotional journey that adults undertake in their quest to adopt children
- Psychosocial stages depicting the adoptee's adjustment across the lifespan
- Role of the teacher in building relationships with adoptive families
- Considerations for children with disabilities who are adopted and their families
- Considerations for children who are a part of transracial and intercountry adoptions
- Challenges to adults serving as foster parents

◊◊ History of Adoption

In the history of children, the primary goal of the adoption process has not always been the building of loving families. Prior to the 20th century, **adoption,** rarely formalized, was characterized by matching children who were homeless or whose families could not financially support them with labor. Until the early part of the 20th century, children might be placed in situations where they could be used as cheap labor, as indentured servants, or as apprentices to tradespeople in return for food, shelter, and perhaps a skill. This practice was particularly common in America during colonization. There was little reason to legalize adoptions during this time because inheritance was "determined solely by blood lineage" (Sokoloff, 1993, p. 17). One well-known example of matching family and labor in the United States was the "orphan trains." In 1853, Reverend Charles Loring Brace founded the Children's Aid Society in New York City so that children could be placed with families "settling" the rural sections of America. Between 1854 and 1929, some 100,000 children were placed on trains and transported to communities where they were shown for selection by local residents. In some cases, siblings and family groups were separated. Most of these adoptions were not formalized (Hollinger, 1993).

Understandably, the humaneness of this type of "adoption" has been debated. Some hailed Brace as a visionary in child welfare because he recognized the need to move children from institutions at the earliest age possible. Others thought the Children's Aid Society did not screen prospective families or make certain that children placed did not, in fact, have living relatives (Sokoloff, 1993).

The 20th century has been characterized by the onset and continued revision of laws designed to protect the rights of children and adults involved in the adoption process. **Adoption** severs the legal relationship

Adoption is one method in which individuals "build" families.

between a child and the child's biological family and establishes the adoptive parents as the child's legal parents. Legal adoption was not generally recognized before the 1850s (Hollinger, 1993, p. 43). The 20th century has been characterized by a shift from the "taking in" of older children to a desire by prospective parents to adopt infants. This shift in attitudes has resulted from the decrease in infant mortality because of advances in prenatal and infant care, the development of successful formulas for feeding infants, research that has highlighted the child's environment as a major factor in growth and development, and a growing acceptance of building families with children who are not "our own" by virtue of blood.

◊◊ Characteristics of Families with Adopted Children

"Half or more of all adoptions (in this country) are by stepparents or other relatives" (Hollinger, 1993, p. 44). This figure correlates with the increased rates of divorce and subsequent remarriages that characterize American families and the growing number of stepparents adopting children of their spouses.

Today, an estimated one million individuals make up the growing list of potential parents (Harnack, 1995) who attempt to adopt children (primarily infants) in this country each year. Who are these individuals? Many are men and women, married and unmarried, faced with fertility issues. Despite advances in modern medical technology, including fertility drugs, in vitro fertilization, and specialized surgeries, some individuals remain unable to become biological parents or choose not to seek such treatment for economic or religious reasons. Some individuals do choose to explore and use surrogate mothers and sperm donors via artificial insemination.

The number of single men and single women who desire to have families as single parents is also increasing. These individuals may have had life experiences that prompt them to avoid traditional marriage, or they may simply have not found partners with whom they can parent. **Single-parent adoption,** artificial insemination, and surrogate mothers are options for these single, prospective parents.

The number of gay and lesbian couples seeking to have families has also increased. It is estimated that about 10% the U.S. population is homosexual, roughly 25 million Americans. It is estimated that the number of gay and lesbian parents is well over 2 million and that the number of children raised by them may be as high as 6 million (Collum, 1995). Children in many of these families originated from marriages and relationships that occurred during a previous heterosexual lifestyle. Acceptance of the gay and lesbian lifestyle in the United States has increased, as is indicated by Briggs's (1994) report that the percentage of Americans who preferred not to have homosexuals as friends declined from 54% to 41% between 1979 and 1993. Individuals responding were generally female, more highly educated, or residents in urban areas. Blue-collar workers showed a decrease in tolerance. Resistance to same-sex marriages and other legal arrangements that recognize the couples as legal partners is still great. Consequently, gay and lesbian couples and individuals seeking to adopt children legally meet with resistance and may resort to alternative strategies to build families; these include using sperm donors, artificial insemination, and surrogate mothers. Issues such as health insurance, rights of the coparent, and custody are still controversial and continue to be tested in the judicial arena.

Although most adoptive parents continue to want a newborn (generally White), the number of prospective parents is far greater than the number of newborns available in the United States for adoption. Legalized abortion, improved and more accessible methods of birth control, and a heightened acceptance of unmarried mothers parenting their own children have all contributed to reduced numbers of healthy infants available for adoption. In the 1950s and 1960s, 90% of all adoptions were of children born to unmarried mothers (Solinger, 1992). These young women were sent to homes for unwed mothers or to live with relatives and friends in other communities. Today, these same young women might choose abortions or to raise their own children with the help of school-based child care centers and family members.

◊◊ Finding Children to Adopt

Since 1975, the federal government has not provided a system for collecting comprehensive adoption data, including the number of adoptions formalized each year or categories of those adoptions, including nonrelated and related, special needs, transracial, intercountry, and infants versus older children. "By most estimates, there are more than a half-million children eligible for adoption within the United States. From this population, Americans adopt more than 100,000 children annually" (Harnack. 1995, p. 13). The remaining numbers generally represent children who "are older, are children of color, are members of sibling groups, and may have emotional, physical or mental disabilities—children with 'special needs'" (Schulman, 1993, p. 5). These children remain in foster care and residential facilities.

How do adults wishing to adopt find children? Historically, couples registered with state government affiliated adoption agencies or private agencies. In some cases, aunts, uncles, and other relatives "adopted" the children of young, unmarried relatives or friends. Many of these adoptions were secret, and adoptees might never be told of their true biological heritage. "During the first half of the twentieth century, secrecy, anonymity, and the sealing of records became statutorily required and standard adoption practice"(Sokoloff, 1993, p. 21). Proponents of laws such as the Minnesota Act of 1917 were concerned about keeping adoption proceedings from public scrutiny. Social workers were particularly concerned about protecting the adopted children from the stigma of illegitimacy (Sokoloff, 1993).

As the number of people attempting to adopt infants has increased and the number of healthy infants available for adoption has decreased, state adoption waiting lists have become longer, and years may pass before a waiting couple is called. Available figures indicate that the number of women who seek to adopt exceeds the number of unrelated adoptions formalized annually by a ratio of 3.3 to 1 and that the waiting period is 2 or more years to adopt healthy, White infants (Stolley, 1993, p. 37). Consequently, alternative strategies for matching children and families have evolved. According to the *Adoption Factbook* of the National Committee for Adoption (1989), 104,088 domestic adoptions took place in 1986. Of those adoptions, 52,931 were related, and 51,157 were not related, to the adoptive family. Of unrelated placements, 20,064 children were placed by public agencies, 15,063 children were placed by private agencies, and 16,040 adoptions were individually arranged.

As the number of children available for adoption decreases and the complexity of locating and having a child placed in one's family increases, many prospective parents are looking for alternative opportunities, including international adoptions, adoptions of children with special needs and challenges, and transracial adoptions. These adoptions require that individuals be resourceful and prepared to deal with financial, political, and social issues that surround the adoption process.

Adopting Children of Other Countries and Races

In her book *Family Bonds: Adoption and the Politics of Parenting* (1993), Elizabeth Bartholet provides the reader with important insights into the

international adoption experience. The Harvard law professor details her experiences in separate journeys to Peru to adopt each of her two sons as a single mother. Her stays in Peru, where her care for each child was scrutinized and where she negotiated the legal and social systems, language, economics, and culture and customs, required both wisdom and tenacity. The fear that she would not be able to return to the United States with the child so precious to her was pervasive throughout the adoption process. She witnessed prospective parents being given a child, only to have it taken away, and birthmothers both reluctantly and obediently handing over their children for adoption. Her insights into the political nature of international adoptions reflect both joys and hardships.

International adoptions become more prevalent following periods of war in countries where children are left without parents and homes. One such example followed the period of the Korean War (1950–53), when Harry Holt, an American farmer, worked to place Korean children in homes. Today, the Holt agency represents the largest international adoption agency and places children throughout the developed world (Silverman, 1993). During the 1980s, more that 40,000 children from Korea alone were adopted by North Americans.

Over the years, I (author) have watched a number of families—friends and neighbors and families of children with whom I have worked—adopt children from Korea through the Holt agency. Perhaps, the fondest memory is of the young couple living next door who had waited patiently for their baby to arrive. The call came at the Christmas holidays, and they drove to a city some 4 hours away to pick up their baby girl arriving on a plane from Korea. I recall feeling such anticipation as we waited for them to return! In our community, families adopting children from Korea through Holt gather on a regular basis to provide time for sharing their experiences and for the children to play and talk with other children of similar experience. Families discuss the same issues that all parents of young children discuss, as well as ideas for helping children acquire information about and maintain aspects of their cultural heritage. The support that families bring to each other is invaluable.

Of the estimated 15,000 to 20,000 international adoptions completed each year, approximately 10,000 children come into the United States. These children make up one fifth to one sixth of all nonrelative adoptions in this country and a somewhat larger proportion of all infant adoptions (Bartholet, 1995, p. 180).These placements are complicated by the laws of various governments, changing political situations that affect the release of children from other countries, and cultural practices that often determine who will be allowed to receive a child.

Proponents of international adoptions cite the blessings that surround taking a child from a situation of poverty and aloneness to a home where the child will be "safe" physically, economically, and emotionally. Those who oppose such adoptions view this as exploitation by the privileged classes in the industrialized nations of the children in the least privileged groups in the poorest nations, the adoption by whites of black- and brown-skinned children from various Third World nations, and the separation of children not only from their birthparents, but from their racial, cultural, and national communities as well. (Bartholet, 1993, p. 180)

Families of children adopted from other races and cultures and teachers and caregivers who work with and love these children are, indeed, faced with the challenges of building each child's awareness of cultural customs and traditions so that each child's heritage is preserved. "These are families whose members must learn to appreciate one another's differences, in terms of racial and cultural heritage, while at the same time experiencing their common humanity" (Bartholet, 1993, p. 180).

Americans have engaged in **transracial adoption**—that is, adopting children of a race not one's own—for a long time, including Asian children from Korea and Hispanic children from South and Central America. Most transracial adoptions that have occurred in the United States have involved the placement of African American children with White parents. This movement became increasingly popular during the 1960s and continued into the 1970s. Such adoptions leveled off, however, following a resolution adopted by the National Association of Black Social Workers (NABSW) during their first annual conference in 1972 that vehemently opposed transracial adoption out of concern for maintaining the **cultural heritage** of the African American child (Silverman, 1993). The NABSW reaffirmed this position during the 1994 conference with a declaration that "It is the right of a child to be raised in a permanent, loving home which reflects the same ethnic or racial group" (Russell, 1995, p. 188). Proponents of transracial adoption stress that the positive effects of being placed in a loving environment outweigh the negative effects of not being placed with a same-race family. This position is supported by resolutions presented at the 1992 conference of the NAACP (Simon, Altstein, & Melli, 1995). The placement of African American children with non-Black families is, once again, becoming a more accepted practice in this country.

Recently, students in a practicum class shared their questions about an African American child adopted by White parents. One student, also African American, was somewhat uncomfortable that the mother had asked her questions about how best to care for the child's hair. It was a wonderful opportunity to address our self-consciousness about discussing our differences. It was also a wonderful opportunity to acknowledge the student's success in building a relationship with the parent that made the parent so comfortable as to be able to ask for help.

Similar concerns surround the adoption of Native American children by White families, and in 1978 the Indian Child Welfare Act placed responsibility for child custody matters, including adoption, under the jurisdiction of the tribe to which the child was born. Adoption of Native American children by families who are not Native American remains very low (Silverman, 1993).

Parenting Adoptive and Foster Children with Special Needs and Challenges

Adoptive parents are also exploring **special needs adoption**. "Special needs adoption refers to the adoption of children who are particularly difficult to place in permanent homes" (McKenzie, 1993, p. 62). These children are generally thought of as children with specific disabilities—physical, cognitive, and/or emotional. However, they may also be children at risk for, or testing positive for, HIV, children who have been sexually abused, children whose mothers were addicted to chemicals (alcohol or drugs) during pregnancy, children of color, and/or children who have been moved for years though the foster care system and exhibit behaviors that naturally result from feelings of abandonment, anger, shame, hopelessness, and lack of attachment.

It is estimated that more than 400,000 children live in **foster care** in the United States (Children's Defense Fund, 1993). Generally, existing nuclear families, rather than childless couples, become foster families (Barbour & Barbour, 1997). Most arrangements involve reimbursement from state agencies for the care of the children. Children may remain in foster care for several weeks or many years, and they may experience more than a single foster home.

Although adoptive families of children with special needs are a diverse group, "the single most dominant feature of the special needs adoptive family is that the vast majority of them have been foster parents first" (McKenzie, 1993, p. 68). Extended family members; recruited, prepared special needs adoptive families, including single- and two-parent families; and infertile couples make up the remaining groups that typically adopt children in the category of special needs.

During an interview regarding a pending adoption, the attorney asked Mr. and Mrs. Jackson if they would accept a child with disabilities. It was a difficult question, but both parents agreed they would be able to work with a child with mild to moderate disabilities. Their son, Jason, was a beautiful and peaceful child with no apparent disabilities. After a few months, his adoptive mother knew there were developmental issues. Jason was verbal but could not walk independently until he was 20 months old. Later, it was discovered that Jason had severe hearing loss in one ear, attention deficit disorder, and learning disabilities in math. Although nothing was known about the father, the prenatal history of the mother did not indicate possible complications for the infant. In middle childhood, he is bright, an avid reader, and a joy to the adults who share his young wisdom about life. His accomplishments, however, have not come without struggles and commitment from him and from those caring for him.

It should also be noted that some children who are not identified with special needs at birth may, in fact, have special needs identified later, such as learning disabilities, anxiety and obsessive-compulsive disorders, and attention deficit problems.

In their comprehensive work with children who are adopted, Brodzinsky, Schechter, and Henig (1992) note that these children are about four times as likely to be diagnosed as learning disabled than children who are not adopted. Perhaps this is a result of the nature of the pregnancy with poor nutrition or chemical abuse or both present. Perhaps it is a result of the emotional state of the birthmother or simply a genetic issue. Certainly, a portion of those labeled as learning disabled are perceived as such by adults by the very nature of their being adopted.

◊◊ The Search for Self

VIGNETTE 5

Michael

When Michael was 4, he asked, "Mommy, was I the most beautiful of all my brothers?" Confused, his mother asked him to explain. "Did you and Daddy pick me because I was the most beautiful of all my brothers at the hospital?" Finally, his mother understood. Michael seemed to have the notion that his adoptive parents came to the hospital and chose him from his "brothers." His mother reassured him that even though he was quite beautiful, he had no brothers remaining at the hospital from whom he was chosen.

Michael's question is one indication that, even as young as 4 years old, he had begun the complicated psychological search for self. This concept of *self* evolves from birth through our experiences in relating to the people and events in our immediate worlds. It encompasses our awareness of our

Physical self: Perceptions and feelings about how we look in terms of our physical traits in relation to others

Psychological self: Perceptions and feelings about our own intelligence and personality traits

Social self: Perceptions and feelings about how others see us and whether they "like" us

The evaluative component of the self is "self-esteem." "Self esteem is the value an individual places on himself or herself" (Barrett, Kallio, McBride, Moore, &

Wilson, 1995, p. 391). This value or sense of self-worth derives from a blending of our reactions to experiences with those who serve as our "mirrors" in life—birthparents, adoptive parents, stepparents, grandparents, teachers, caregivers, siblings, friends, coworkers, and children—and the genetic predispositions we have to behave in certain ways or to exhibit certain personality traits.

As with nonadopted individuals, children and adults who are adopted will engage in the life-long search for self—that is, who they are. This journey of self-discovery "begins at birth and continues through old age, with many ups and downs along the way to resolution" (Brodzinsky et al., 1992, p. 3). As we will see, the issue is complicated by coping with the sense of loss and the process of grief that each adopted individual must face. As one would expect, although some patterns that guide the knowledge we have about adjustment to life as an adopted child are universal, each individual copes in unique ways dependent on his or her life experiences, genetic predispositions, and development with respect to cognitive and psychosocial skills.

In *Being Adopted: The Lifelong Search for Self* (1992), Brodzinsky et al. explored the developmental process that characterizes the adoptee's search for self. They noted: "The experience of adoption—like any other experience—is not static. It changes with time as the forces of development shape and reshape the way we think, feel, relate, and grow" (p. 2).

The focus on understanding the developmental changes that humans experience should not be limited simply to the early childhood period, because we are, in early childhood, dealing with issues that lay the groundwork for the lifespan.

◊ ◊ Developmental Issues for Individuals in Coping with Their Adoption

VIGNETTE 6

Thomas

Thomas began to talk with his family about wanting to meet his birthmother when he was 11. One afternoon, his adoptive mother heard him talking with his 9-year-old brother, Ben. Apparently, he had been telling Ben that he wanted to meet his birthmother. Ben, who was not adopted, shared his viewpoint that the birthmother might feel "bad" if contacted because she had, after all, given Thomas away. Later, Thomas shared the conversation with his mother and told her he guessed he would wait because he did not want to upset his birthmother. Thomas's experience at 11 is an example of the emotional and cognitive struggles children experience as they come to terms with various aspects of their adoption.

To better understand the developmental changes that adoptees experience over time and with changing cognitive and psychosocial understandings, Brodzinsky et al. (1992) used Erik Erikson's (1950) model of psychosocial tasks. Erikson, a Danish-born psychoanalyst, developed an 8-stage model noting universal **psychosocial tasks** that individuals experience as they move through the lifespan. According to Erikson, each stage in life finds the individual experiencing a two-dimensional conflict (e.g., trust vs. mistrust) during the period of infancy. As conflicts are resolved, individuals move to the next stage. Conflicts of each stage can be "revisited" throughout life, however. "We are forever struggling with the issues we seem to have resolved at an earlier period of life" (Brodzinsky et al., 1992, p. 15). Let's consider each of these stages and how the resolution of their respective conflicts relates specifically to the psychosocial development of the adoptee.

Infancy

The first of Erikson's (1950) stages involves the infant's acquisition of a sense of **trust versus mistrust**. During this time, the infant is forming important attachments to primary caregivers. As noted by Brodzinsky et al. (1992),

> a true attachment to a primary caregiver, the kind that lasts a lifetime, doesn't happen in utero or in the first moments after delivery. It is something that grows slowly, over weeks, months, and even years of loving interaction, and it can grow just as well between a parent and infant who are not biologically connected as between a parent and infant who are. (p. 32)

A sense of trust is acquired when the infant's primary needs (e.g., food, clothing, shelter) and needs for nurturing and love are consistently met by those with whom attachments are forming and when the infant knows he or she can depend on personal behavior for comfort. Mistrust occurs when the infant comes to know that he or she cannot depend on primary caregivers or self for nurturing and comfort.

With mistrust comes a flawed sense of self-worth and limits on the individual's abilities to trust those encountered throughout life. These issues will be revisited at varying stages of the lifespan. This stage has added implications for the adopted child particularly with respect to the age at which the child is brought into the adoptive home, the frequency with which the child is moved from one caregiving situation to another, and the quality of the caregiving environments.

As noted earlier, the quality of attachment between adoptive mothers and children can be like that of biological mothers and children. Differences can be noted, however, when children are adopted after 6 months of age because "these babies have usually already formed an attachment with their

*Children who are adopted
will experience a variety of
stages across the lifespan
as they come to terms with
the loss of their families of
origin and the building of
their new families.*

biological or foster parents," and "they come to the adoptive parents follow-ing a sense of disruption of a previous relationship, which often leads to a sense of loss and emotional or behavior disorganization" (Brodzinsky et al., 1992, p. 36). During the first 6 months, the greatest amount of stress can be seen when children change placements during the period from 4 to 12 weeks. Distress takes the form of difficulty in eating and sleeping and irri-tability. At this age, infants can attune to all new stimuli but have difficulty closing it out when it becomes too much. When placement occurs during the second 6 months of life, babies grieve for the loss of their primary care-givers by exhibiting searching behaviors, withdrawing, engaging in uncon-trollable crying, clinging, and experiencing frequent illnesses (Call, 1974).

This adjustment to new parents can also be affected by the child's person-ality and the match of that personality to the personalities of the adoptive par-ents. Each individual has a unique personality based on certain genetic pre-dispositions, as well as features that result from life experiences. High-risk pregnancies involving such factors as drugs or alcohol, teenage mothers, and poor prenatal care may alter the child's personality to one that is tempera-mental, quite active, and generally difficult for some adults to manage.

Regardless of the obstacles that adoptive families face in helping children transition from one home to another, children are quite resilient and will generally adjust to the new home situation. This is, of course, dependent on the quality and availability of the consistent nurturing that is required of

Caring adults assist children in feeling secure that they are loved and will not be abandoned.

adoptive families and on the infrequency of moves and adjustments a child is expected to make.

Toddlerhood

Toddlerhood, or the period from 1½ to 3 years of age, encompasses the psychosocial task of **autonomy versus doubt and shame.** Those who spend time with toddlers will witness the growing sense of self as statements such as "mine," "me want," and "me go" punctuate their rapidly expanding language. As toddlers "set their boundaries" with adults, peers, and siblings, their independence and separateness, so necessary for growth, become mightily apparent. Adults foster this growth by providing opportunities for children to engage in developmentally appropriate self-care and play routines and by encouraging their competence while continuing to provide a loving "home base." This home base also includes a set of reasonable limits for behaviors that all children need in order to provide a sense of structure in their lives and some beginning understanding of right and wrong.

During this period, many adoptive families focus on telling the adoption story to their children. Young children love the warmth and affection that accompanies reading stories about adoption and hearing their parents tell about their adoption. These events become particularly important when families engage in various forms of open adoption wherein the birthparents may be in some way remain involved in their children's lives. Adults must be aware, however, that during this age, children cannot cognitively comprehend the complexities of how they were born and adopted. In fact, they may be just at the beginnings of understanding something about birth, given the opportunity to witness people and other living creatures in pregnancy. Children brought from another country will not comprehend that Korea, for example, is another country in another part of the world. They are at the beginnings of their awareness of this abstract concept. (I am reminded of the preschool classroom where 3-year-old Daniel asks how Jipu, a child from China, traveled to school each morning. This teacher, who shared the globe with the children, pointing out Jipu's homeland, told Daniel that Jipu rode a bicycle with his mother each morning. Given his age, Daniel's response was not surprising: "Jipu sure has a long way to ride!")

At this age, adults are building stepping stones in the child's growing awareness of the meaning of adoption. These stones must be laid with realistic expectations of the child's cognitive capabilities. As adoption researchers (Brodzinsky et al., 1992) explain:

> The advice of most adoption experts is to start talking to children about being adopted during toddlerhood, before they have a chance to develop their own ideas about adoption. Most parents dutifully follow this advice. But our research suggests that most children haven't the foggiest idea what Mom and Dad are talking about. (p. 50)

Preschool

The preschool years, from ages 3 through 5, are characterized as a period of egocentricity with respect to the child's thinking. According to cognitive theorist Jean Piaget (1929), this is a period of preoperational thinking in which children begin to understand cause-and-effect relationships but as yet are unable to engage in the mental operations required for logical thought. Most children do not begin to understand the meaning of being adopted until 5 to 7 years of age, and even during this time their understanding is limited (Brodzinsky, Singer, & Braff, 1984). The preschool child may be able to describe the events leading to being adopted, but this is based on the repeated stories provided by their adoptive parents. The warm and loving, shared storytellings and cognitive limitations characteristic of the preschool child provide assurance that the young child will view the adoption in a positive light (Brodzinsky & Schechter, 1990).

What psychosocial tasks are to be accomplished during the preschool years? According to Erikson (1950), preschool children are engaged in establishing a sense of **initiative versus guilt.** During this period, children continue to build their competence and autonomy in all aspects of their development—social, emotional, physical, cognitive, and aesthetic. Adults nurture this aspect of growth by providing opportunities for children to engage in developmentally appropriate experiences in play with materials and other children. Guidance strategies that focus on reinforcing the positive behaviors that children exhibit and on helping children understand the logical consequences of their actions also foster the children's increasing sense of competence and initiative. Primary caregivers who have a positive sense of their own competence and self-worth are much more able to foster such growth in a healthy way than adults who do not possess these characteristics.

With increasing cognitive capabilities and social experiences, preschool children become more aware of the physical and social differences in the individuals in their lives. Gender identity and racial identity appear with the child recognizing that he or she is a boy or a girl and of a particular skin color. Not until the child is at the upper end of the preschool age-group, however, does he or she begin to understand that gender and race do not change as one becomes older (Edwards, 1986). This awareness of physical differences is necessary for the child to define self and relationships with others.

During this time, children adopted across racial lines begin to feel that they look different from the other members of their families. Adults sometimes expect children to understand cognitively the nature of the adoption when they, again, have limited cognitive and social capabilities in doing so.

Adoptive parents may rationalize their children's questions as evidence that they fully understand the meaning of being adopted. But generally this

Adults who model respect for the uniqueness of each child assist young children in understanding the diversity of the families of their friends.

is not true. A preschooler may recognize that Mommy is White and he is Black, but this is a far cry from understanding how this difference came to be or what it means to have another mommy who is Black. As we shall see, the cognitive foundation for this type of understanding usually does not develop until the elementary school years (Brodzinsky et al., 1992, p. 60).

Preschoolers define family as people who live together. Families who adopt children during the preschool years will need to be prepared for the possibility of dealing with the children's **grief** at losing their previous caregiving placements regardless of the nature of those situations. Children mourn the loss of their "families" and, in cases where another language was spoken, their mother tongue. Children adopted during this time need adoptive parents to accept their need to talk about their prior families and to grieve. This grief can be eased when adoptive parents and caregivers are aware of the children's routines, schedules, and habits and the names of the children's previous caregivers. This type of loving acceptance and continuity is critical for easing children's grief and adjustment to their new families and surroundings (Brodzinsky et al., 1992).

Middle Childhood

Erikson (1950) defined the psychosocial task of middle childhood, ages 6 to 12, as **industry versus inferiority.** Although there are great differences between the child at age 6 and the child at age 12, it is generally a time when children seek to broaden their relationships with peers and to be accepted. Also during this time, each child formulates a sense of self or self-image. Self-esteem is based on how they see themselves in relation to others. At a time when being different is not perceived as "good" by many children of this age, adopted children may be faced with being not only physically different from family members but also different from their peer group. Middle childhood is often the time when being adopted is seen by children as being a problem (Brodzinsky et al., 1992).

The response to physical differences and other adoption concerns occurs in accordance with an increasing level of social and cognitive sophistication. According to Piaget (1929), the elementary-age child's thinking is characterized as the period of concrete operations. Children are now capable of more logical and reflective thought processes. Not only do they recognize the physical differences among members of the family, but they also understand that no biological relationship exists between them and their adoptive parents. "As children mature cognitively . . . their capacity for understanding logical reciprocity leads them to a profound insight—to be adopted, one must first be relinquished or surrendered" (Brodzinsky, 1990, p. 13). The sense of loss that comes with understanding that birthparents "gave them up" before they came into an adoptive family can take the form of emotional and behavioral changes. These changes are associated with the different ways children deal with the grieving process as they move though and

Adults must be open to listening to the concerns of children as they experience growth and be willing to help the children deal with those concerns.

revisit shock, denial, despair, recovery, and reintegration. Adoption is a more pervasive loss than death or divorce of parents because children may have little or no connection to the birthparents. Society does little to validate the adopted child's grief (Brodzinsky et al., 1992).

During the period of middle childhood, we "begin to see a rise in psychological, behavioral, and academic problems that are more common in adoptees" (Brodzinsky et al., 1992, p. 69). As difficult as it may be, family members will need to be accepting of the child's feelings in discussions of the child's adoption. It is natural for adoptive parents to feel somewhat threatened when a child expresses grief over losing a birthparent or a desire to find a birthparent. It is also natural for adoptive parents to feel threatened and angry when the child rejects them. Many of these expressions, however, are a part of the child's experience in dealing with feelings of grief and also guilt in wanting to know more about the birthfamily at the emotional expense of the adoptive family. All of this occurs at a time of increased cognitive understanding and heightened social pressure.

As done historically, some parents want to keep the adoption a secret. Although citing protection of the child, keeping the secret is often done to protect the adults in the family from the discomfort of sharing such information with the child, family members, and other adults. Such secrets are detrimental to the child's sense of trust in those who care for him or her. Denying the child's feelings and discouraging the child from expressing those feelings in open discussion also protects the adult from discomfort but denies the child the right to express grief that may be a part of accepting the loss of a birthfamily and an identity with a biological family. Providing a supportive and nurturing environment is essential in helping a child move through and revisit stages of grief.

Adolescence

Although the focus of this text is the period of early childhood, it is important to reflect on the human way of coping with adoption throughout the lifespan. According to Erikson (1950), adolescents experience **ego identity versus identity confusion.** Teenagers often resist the authority of parents and become part of cliques as peer relationships and approval become increasingly important. As teenagers move toward independence, adoptive parents may become easy targets and biological parents idealized. Adoptive families may worry that the teenagers will become like the biological parents, and the teenagers may attempt to take on characteristics of the birthparents. It often becomes more and more important to acquire information about the birthparents. For many young people, acquisition of this information is a relief (Brodzinsky et al., 1992).

Young Adulthood

Intimacy versus isolation describes the period of young adulthood. This is often a time when couples date and marry and when children are born. Adoptees often worry about the genetic background they bring to a newborn. They may also revisit feelings of grief because they are unable to share the joys of childbirth and grandchildren with their birthparents. Life situations such as this often increase an adoptee's interest in searching for birthparents.

Midlife

In midlife, adults experience a stage Erikson (1950) described as **generativity versus stagnation.** For many individuals, this is a busy time of life when aging adoptive parents may need care and when children may continue to need adult support. Adoptees recognize that the time to search is becoming limited as birthparents are also aging.

Late Adulthood

Finally, in late adulthood, individuals are sharing the wisdom gained through their life experiences with their children and grandchildren. During this period of **ego integrity versus despair,** those who remain in good physical and mental health may share the knowledge of their heritage and continue to pass on those values and beliefs they have come to hold as important. Even though their birthparents may no longer be living, they may still search for knowledge about their birthright, siblings, and other family members as they resolve their personal conflicts about being adopted.

In addition to understanding the developmental changes that occur throughout the life of the adoptee, it is important to realize that some individuals are more resilient than others to stressful life events such as adoption or being raised in foster homes of varying quality. Wolin and Wolin (1993) identified seven characteristics that help human beings endure and overcome stressful life events: (a) a willingness to take initiative in engaging in appropriate experiences, (b) insight into the realities of the family situation, (c) healthy independence, (d) seeking relationships with healthy people, (e) finding outlets for creativity such as play, art, and writing, (f) humor, and (g) a sense of morality.

As teachers, caregivers, and administrators, it is important for us to see each child as an individual in the role that he or she plays in the adoption process. Although there are common challenges and joys, as well as reactions to those challenges and joys, each individual brings unique characteristics and needs to the building of families through adoption. Teachers will need some understanding of this as they select appropriate strategies for building bridges with families.

◊◊ Strategies for Teachers and Caregivers

Chapter 3 provides strategies, such as home visits and parent conferences, that are useful in communicating and building "bridges" with families. What situation specifics do teachers and caregivers need to consider when cooperating with adoptive families, foster families, and grandparents (or other individuals) caring for young children? The following insights from parents are quite useful to us in this discussion.

Insight 1: The "Real" Child

I have two children. The older is adopted; the younger is not. Both are boys. The older is quite a bit smaller than the younger, and they really do not resemble each other. A recent experience in the grocery store represents a type of incident that happens many times. At the checkout, the clerk asked, "Are both of these boys yours? Why don't they look alike? Why did you adopt him?" All of these questions were asked in the presence of my sons. Since they were small, people have asked, "Which one is yours?"

The comments described above are hurtful and will likely prompt families to close communication. In a warm environment, families will generally share information about the family composition. Get to know the family situation. This can be done through conferences, home visits, and informal conversations. Determine with whom will you be responsible for establishing a "parent-teacher" bond. Recognize that children who are adopted are "real" children and "real" sons and daughters whether or not they were born to the adoptive parents. Find out what the children know about their adoptive or foster situations and what the legal guardians think should be shared in the classroom setting. Respect the privacy of each family. Trust is built between families and teachers when parents or legal guardians see that teachers and caregivers act in an ethical manner and protect the family's right to privacy.

Insight 2: Take This Home to Mommy

My sister was unable to care for her young daughter, Janie. Janie came to live with me, her aunt, for a year. One day, she came home from school crying because the teacher had asked her to bring home a note to "Mommy." All of my niece's feelings about not living with her mom and not "fitting in" were triggered. I had had several talks with the teacher, and she knew Janie's family living arrangements.

Be aware of the language and activities you use in the classroom. When a child is being raised by a grandparent or a series of foster parents, it is discouraging to be directed repeatedly to take a note to "Mom" or to ask "Dad." Children often feel "less than" and "not a part of" the group. Similarly, teas for "moms" and "daddy" nights are also difficult for children who do not have moms and dads readily available. Building "family trees" can also foster a variety of emotions in children who may have been abandoned.

Insight 3: What Does Adopted Mean?

As I looked around my son's classroom, I saw several children who I knew had been adopted. Some were from other countries. I could not help but think what a wonderful opportunity it would be for children to learn about the different ways families come together to love and care for each other. It seemed, however, that the subject of adoption made the adults uncomfortable and I didn't pursue the idea.

Include opportunities in your curriculum for adopted children to share the uniqueness of their situation. Adoptive parents of children from other countries may find this a wonderful opportunity to share something about the culture of that child's family of origin. Similarly, a grandparent or foster parent might become a special visitor to the classroom, sharing an experience or skill or reading books to the children. Use children's books to foster discussion about adoption and the many ways families are formed. Such books include the following:

Books for Young Children About Adoption

Banish, R., & Jordan-Wong, J. (1992). *A forever family.* New York: Harper-Collins.

An 8-year-old girl describes living in many foster families before she was adopted at age 8.

Caines, J. (1973). *Abby.* New York: HarperCollins.

Abby is adopted by an African American family living in a city apartment. She loves to hear how she was adopted and to be reassured by her older brother that he loves her.

Girard, L. W. (1986). *Adoption is for always.* Morton Grove, IL: Albert Whitman.

A little girl deals with her feelings of anger and frustration at being adopted, with the help of her adoptive family.

Girard, L. W. (1989). *We adopted you, Benjamin Koo.* Morton Grove, IL: Albert Whitman.

A 9-year-old Korean boy details what it is like to be adopted from another culture.

Livingston, C. (1978). *Why was I adopted? The facts of adoption with love and illustration.* New York: Carol.

Questions are answered in a fun manner through the use of cartoonlike characters and illustrations.

Stinson, K. (1992). *Steven's baseball mitt: A book about being adopted.* North York, Ontario: Firefly.

During a search for his baseball mitt, Steven wonders about his birth-mother and what she might be like.

Turner, A. (1990). *Through the moon and stars and night skies.* New York: HarperCollins.

A little boy travels by plane to his new family in this story about an inter-country adoption. He shares his fears and his need for a momma and poppa of his own.

Insight 4: I Need Someone Like Me

When my daughter reached third grade, she began to talk about her birthmother. We had always been honest about her being adopted. She had really shown no interest, however, until she was 8 or 9 years old. I thought she was happy.

Even the most secure parents can become disconcerted when their children want to find out more about their heritage. Parents need information and support from those who can acknowledge their feelings and who understand the developmental shifts that children experience. Offer workshops, reading materials, and parent-teacher discussions that will assist the child's guardian understand the developmental shifts that children experience in their growth and as they relate to an adoption experience. Build a resource file of community service offerings for families and children. Provide opportunities for support groups for families and children to form within the school setting. Understand the complex journey that many parents and children have taken to become families. Be proactive in keeping open the line of communication between the school and the families. Be responsive to parents' needs for sharing and receiving information.

Insight 5: My Child Is Special

I have a beautiful son adopted at birth. He is a loving and wonderful child whose life is challenged by a hearing impairment, attention deficit, and learning disability. When I go to school, I am overwhelmed by the number of people with whom I have to deal and the extent to which I have to advocate to get services that are appropriate for my child.

Parents with children who are adopted and who have special needs have unique challenges. Assist these parents by collaborating with other teachers, guidance specialists, social workers, and family members in building your knowledge about appropriate methods for introducing and addressing the issues arising from adoption and foster parenting.

As with the children to whom we give birth, the children we adopt as "our own" bring joys, love, and a myriad of other emotions. Added complexities, however, have to be considered at the time of adoption and throughout the life of the individual. This chapter has provided some insights into those complexities and some strategies that you can begin to employ as you create partnerships with these and other families.

Summary Statements ◊

- Adoption is a complex issue because of the varied compositions of families seeking to adopt children, the declining number of children available for adoption, the varied geographic origins of children to be adopted, more comprehensive adoption laws, and more aggressive strategies employed by prospective parents to build families through adoption.

- More than 400,000 children in the United States live in foster homes. Many of these are termed "special needs" or "hard-to-place" by virtue of age, disability, skin color, and emotional issues.

- Stepparents constitute the highest percentage of adoptive parents.

- An increasing number of single men and single women are seeking to adopt children.

- It is important to assist children adopted from other races and cultures to maintain their cultural heritage.

- Each individual who is adopted goes through a series of psychosocial stages in coping with his or her adoption over the course of a lifetime.

- Teachers and parents must respect the cognitive characteristics of the age and the individual in explaining the process of adoption to children who are adopted.

- All individuals who are adopted search in some way for their biological families and experience grief in their search.

- It is important that all adults working with an adopted child communicate relative to the process of sharing information about the adoption with the child.

- It is important that an adoptive family does not "cover up" the adoption in an effort to protect the child.

- Some human beings may be more resilient than others in dealing with issues such as adoption and placement in foster care. Resilient features include initiative, insight, independence, relationships, creativity, humor, and morality.

- Teachers and caregivers must be sensitive to the language and activities they plan in the classroom so that children with legal guardians other than birthparents are not excluded.

Activities ◇◇◇

1. You are observing the 3-year-olds in your classroom during an independent choice time of day. Three children are engaged in pretend play in the housekeeping area of the classroom. Soledad is rocking a baby doll, and Jason and Julia are dressing up in the pretend clothes. Julia tells Soledad and Jason with some pride that her mom will soon have a new baby. In response, Soledad announces, "I'm adopted." Jason asks what she means, to which she replies, "My mom and dad chose me!" Jason looks puzzled and asks Soledad what she means, to which she responds, "I was so special, they adopted me." Rick and Jamal enter the area and distract Jason and Soledad from their conversation. You know that Soledad is adopted by the information sheet submitted by the family. After hearing the conversation among the children, what should your role in the situation be relative to the family, classroom activities, and Soledad?

2. You and your staff have recently engaged in a self-study involving all aspects of your program, including curriculum, relationships with families, and guidance of the children. From your work, it appears that the multicultural component of the classroom needs enhancing. In staff meetings designed to plan resolution of this situation, one teacher notes that two of the children in her classroom are Korean and were adopted by a local family as infants. As a teacher, should you pursue building aspects of the Korean culture of these children into the curriculum? If so, what would be the considerations, and how might this be accomplished?

3. Four-year-old Sara is African American. She was adopted at 6 months of age by Mark and Patty. During a family conference, Mark and Patty (both are White) ask your advice on how to assist Sara in maintaining her African American heritage and how to prepare her for the issues she will face as a member of a transracial family. What might your response be to Mark and Patty?

4. The after-school program where you work serves children ages 5 to 12. Con-

sequently, you have some brothers and sisters coming to the program from the local elementary school. Two of the children are brothers—the older adopted. The older child, Robert, is very small. The younger child, Adam, is very tall. These children are quite different, not only in size but also in facial characteristics and personalities. During a recent rainy afternoon, the brothers were building an indoor "fort" with several other boys. Ten-year-old Martin commented, "How can you be brothers? You don't even look alike! How can you be older? He's taller than you?" Later, Robert came to stand by you and said, "I wish I wasn't so different." What do you think would be the best way to assist Robert in dealing with his feelings?

5. As a kindergarten teacher, you often experience the excitement of the birth of new siblings in the classroom. Children become excited, sometimes insecure, and sometimes regress temporarily. This year, you have a somewhat different experience. Alli's mother and father are adopting a new baby. They are waiting for the birthmother to deliver the child and to make a final decision to give the baby for adoption. The adoption is open, and the adoptive parents meet and talk with the birthmother. The adoptive mother plans to be present at the delivery. Alli has been told that she will have a new brother or sister that her family will adopt from a mommy who will not be able to take care of her baby and will need help from Alli and her mother and father. Preparations are made at home for the baby's new room and clothes. Alli's mother attends the delivery. The baby's mother decides, after she sees her baby, that she will not give him for adoption. As a teacher, what might you do to

assist Alli in understanding the situation and in dealing with her grief?

6. You are the director of a hospital-funded day care center serving infants through school-age children. Most children enroll as infants or toddlers and remain in the program until they are old enough to care for themselves. You have a waiting list for infants and are frequently visited by prospective parents desiring to put newborns on the list. Recently, you were visited by a single mother-to-be who disclosed that she had become pregnant through artificial insemination using a sperm donor. What thoughts do you have about this method of building a family, and what issues do you think you might need to discuss with the parent?

7. You are teaching kindergarten in a suburban public school. You often collaborate with a first-grade class to provide both groups with opportunities to engage in learning experiences in multi-age groupings. Several children in your class have siblings in the first grade. One child, Bennett, has a sibling in the first grade who is adopted and has apparent disabilities. Several kindergartners have continued to ask, "Is that really your brother? What's wrong with him, anyway?" Your kindergartner becomes frustrated and asks you, "Why did my parents have to adopt him, anyway?" What do you think would be an appropriate response on your part to this situation?

8. You are a day care provider working with school-age children. Each day, you supervise a homework period during a portion of your program. Josef is 8 years old and has a history of "losing" his homework and procrastinating until it is too late in the evening to complete his homework at home. His parents

have asked that you supervise his homework after school, which you do. Josef becomes angry and tells you that he knows his real mother and father would not make him do homework after school. What do you do?

Resources ◊◊◊◊◊◊◊◊◊◊◊◊◊◊◊◊◊◊◊◊◊◊◊◊◊◊◊◊◊◊◊◊◊◊◊◊◊◊◊

Books

Gilman, L. (1992). *The adoption resource book.* New York: HarperCollins.

Keck. G. C., & Kupecky, R. M. (1995). *Adopting the hurt child: Hope for families with special needs.* Colorado Springs, CO: Pinion Press.

Melina, L. R. (1986). *Raising adopted children: A manual for adoptive parents.* New York: HarperCollins.

Melina, L. R. (1989). *Making sense of adoption.* New York: HarperCollins.

Melina, L. R., & Rosia, S. K. (1993). *The open adoption experience.* New York: HarperCollins.

Sweet, O. R., & Bryan, P. (1996). *Adopt international: Everything you need to know to adopt a child from abroad.* New York: Farrar, Straus, & Giroux.

Wirth, E. M., & Worden, J. (1993). *How to adopt a child from another country.* Nashville: Abingdon Press.

Organizations

Child Welfare League of America, 440 First Street, NW, Suite 310, Washington, DC 20001

National Adoption Center, 1500 Walnut Street, Suite 701, Philadelphia, PA 19102

National Adoption Information Clearinghouse, 11426 Rockville Pike, Rockville, MD 20852

National Council for Adoption, 1930 17th Street, NW, Washington, DC 20009-6207

Resolve, Inc., 1310 Broadway, Somerville, MA 02244-1731

References ◊◊◊

Barbour, C., & Barbour, N. H.(1997). *Families, schools, and communities.* Upper Saddle River, NJ: Merrill/Prentice Hall.

Barrett, K. C., Kallio, K, D., McBride, R. M., Moore, C. M., & Wilson, M. A. (1995). *Child development.* New York: Glencoe.

Bartholet, E. (1993). *Family bonds: Adoption and the politics of parenting.* New York: Houghton Mifflin.

Bartholet, E. (1995). Foreign adoptions should be encouraged. In A. Harnack (Ed.), *Adoption: Opposing viewpoints.* San Diego, CA: Greenhaven Press.

Briggs, J. R. (1994). *A Yankelovich monitor perspective on gays/lesbians.* Norwalk, CT: Yankelovich Partners.

Brodzinsky, D. M. (1990). A stress and coping model of adoption adjustment. In D. M. Brodzinsky & M. D. Schechter (Eds.), *The psychology of adoption.* New York: Oxford University Press.

Brodzinsky, D. M., & Schechter, M. D. (Eds.). (1990). *The psychology of adoption.* New York: Oxford University Press.

Brodzinsky, D. M., Schechter, M. D., & Henig, R. M. (1992). *Being adopted: The lifelong search for self.* Garden City, NY: Doubleday.

Brodzinsky, D. M., Singer, L. M., & Braff, A. M. (1984). Children's understanding of adoption. *Child Development, 55,* 869–878.

Call, J. (1974). Helping infants cope with change. *Early Child Development and Care, 3*, 229–247.

Children's Defense Fund. (1993). *The nation's investment in children: An analysis of the president's FY 1993 budget proposals.* Washington, DC: Author.

Collum, C. (1995). Gays and lesbians should have the right to adopt children. In A. Harnack (Ed.), *Adoption: Opposing viewpoints.* San Diego, CA: Greenhaven Press.

Edwards, C. P. (1986). *Promoting social and moral development in young children: Creative approaches for the classroom.* New York: Teachers College Press.

Erikson, E. H. (1950). *Childhood and society.* New York: Norton.

Harnack, A. (1995). *Adoption: Opposing viewpoints.* San Diego, CA: Greenhaven Press.

Hollinger, J. H. (1993). Adoption law. In R. E. Behrman (Ed.), *The future of children: Adoption* (pp. 43–61). Los Altos, CA: Center for the Future of Children.

McKenzie, J. K. (1993). Adoption of children with special needs. In R. E. Behrman (Ed.), *The future of children: Adoption* (pp. 62–76). Los Altos, CA: Center for the Future of Children.

National Committee for Adoption. (1989). *1989 adoption factbook.* Washington, DC: Author.

Piaget, J. J. (1929). *The child's conception of the world.* New York: Harcourt Brace.

Russell, A. T. (1995). Transracial adoptions should be forbidden. In A. Harmack (Ed.), *Adoption: Opposing viewpoints.* San Diego, CA: Greenhaven.

Schulman, I. (1993). Adoption: Overview and major recommendations. In R. E. Behrman (Ed.), *The future of children: Adoption* (pp. 17–25). Los Altos, CA: Center for the Future of Children.

Silverman, A. R. (1993). Outcomes of transracial adoption. In R. E. Behrman (Ed.), *The future of children: Adoption* (pp. 104–118). Los Altos, CA: Center for the Future of Children.

Simon, R. J., Alstein, H., & Melli, M. S. (1995). Transracial adoptions should be encouraged. In A. Harnack (Ed.), *Adoption: Opposing viewpoints.* San Diego, CA: Greenhaven.

Sokoloff, B. Z. (1993). Antecedents of American adoption. In R. E. Behrman (Ed.), *The future of children: Adoption* (pp. 17–25). Los Altos, CA: Center for the Future of Children.

Solinger, R. (1992). *Wake-up little Susie: Single pregnancy and race before Roe v. Wade.* New York: Routledge.

Stolley, K. S. (1993). Adoption: Overview and major recommendations. In R. E. Behrman (Ed.), *The future of children: Adoption* (pp. 26–42). Los Altos, CA: Center for the Future of Children.

Wasson, V. P. (1977). *The chosen baby.* Philadelphia: J. B. Lippencott. (Original work published 1939)

Wolin, S. J., & Wolin, S. (1993). *The resilient self: How survivors of troubled families rise above adversity.* New York: Villard.

8 Alternative and Future Family Forms

A family is " . . . a group of persons who share common resources and a commitment to each other over time." . . . While understanding a family format requires objectivity, it does not require you to adopt it personally.

Hildebrand, Phenice, Gray, & Hines, 1996, p. 298

Key Terms

bisexual	identity
donor insemination	lesbian
gay	lesbian-headed family
gay-headed family	prejudice
heterosexism	self-concept
heterosexuality	surrogate mother
homophobia	two dads
homosexuality	two moms

Several years ago, my sons were participating in a weeklong day camp. I had heard positive things about this camp and was surprised that neither child seemed to be enjoying this experience. Finally, my 8-year-old opened doors to a new world for me. "Mom, the camp counselor (who was about 14) asked me if I was gay." "Why?" was the best I could manage. "I don't know, Mom. He just said, `What's the matter with you? Are you gay?'" Further talk revealed that this was the young counselor's way of chastising his "wards" when they did not listen to his directions. To say I was surprised is mild. This was, after all, a religious sponsored camp! Did they not monitor the expressions of prejudice of their adolescents? Furthermore, was I really ready for the question that came with this experience? "Mom, what does it mean to be gay?"

As my sons have moved through the elementary grades, I have witnessed the increasing use of such words as *stupid, retarded,* and, yes, *gay* among the group. We have discussed the implications of these remarks in terms of the feelings of others and in terms of the prejudices they express both wittingly and unwittingly. (During these discussions, I wonder at the changes in remarks designed to rebuff, to hurt, to "set territory" used by children today as compared with when I was a child.) At the basis of our talks has been, "Do you understand what you are saying?" and "Do you know how these words affect others?"

The latter question brought my thoughts to another group of children whom we often overlook—those whose parents or other family members are gay, lesbian, or bisexual. These children are subjected to the same prejudices and stereotypes as children of heterosexual parents and other family members. Pennington (1987) shares an anecdote of such a situation in which a young girl accepts her mother's lesbian lifestyle until she encounters stereotypes at school:

> When I was around five, my mom and Lois told me they were lesbians. I said good, and thought I want to be just like my mom. Well, when I reached about the fifth grade . . . I heard kids calling someone a faggot as a swear word, and I thought, "My God, they're talking about my mom." (p. 67)

Helping my sons filter out the prejudicial remarks they hear and understand the meaning of these words for them and for others has, like many of my experiences in parenting, brought me to deal with my own ideas and knowledge about the alternative lifestyles of families. It has brought me to take a closer look at the sources and prevalence of **homophobia.**

> Homophobia refers to an irrational and distorted view of homosexuality or homosexual persons. Among heterosexual persons, homophobia is most commonly manifested as prejudice or general discomfort with homosexuality. The intensity of these feelings is modulated by a number of factors, including personal history, contact with homosexual individuals and individual psychological make-up. (Gonsiorek, 1993, p. 471)

How does a child feel when she or he is exposed to such **prejudice** while being raised by those most loved—her or his parents—who are gay or lesbian? How can schools address the needs of these children and their families? This chapter is designed to address such questions, including the following:

- How do people become or decide that they are gay or lesbian?
- How do individuals who are gay and lesbian create families?
- How many families with gay or lesbian parents are represented in the population?
- What issues do gay and lesbian families face in creating and raising families?
- How do children come to understand the sexual preferences of their parents?
- How does the child adjust to the presence of the parental partner's children?
- How does a young child comprehend this world in relation to the world of other families that she or he encounters?
- What are specific concerns of children growing up in families with gay or lesbian parents?
- What is the role of the teacher in building partnerships with these families? What are unique concerns?

◊◊ The Meaning of "Homosexuality"

Many family members spend a good deal of time searching for answers to why their child, grandchild, or husband or wife is gay. Were they always gay or lesbian, or is this something they "chose"? Seeking answers for these and other questions becomes a factor in the relationships among and between family members.

The question whether individuals are born as homosexuals or become homosexuals through the course of sociocultural experiences has been debated for decades. The question has become of extreme public interest as a result of (a) the political actions of the lesbian and gay liberation movement to obtain equal rights for gays and lesbians and (b) the human immunodeficiency virus (HIV) and its association with homosexuality (DeCecco & Parker, 1995, p. 2).

In addition to the heightened awareness of issues facing gay and lesbian individuals is the ever-increasing effort to locate the biological roots of **homosexuality.** In a review of recent biological research conducted relative to the determinants of homosexuality, DeCecco and Parker (1995) note that, thus far, investigation has occurred in three major areas: hormonal, genetic, and brain research (p. 5). These authors note that, in the late 1980s, the focus shifted from an emphasis on hormones to genetic research. Studies published by Pillard and Weinrich (1986) and, later, by Bailey and Pillard (1991) suggesting the inheritability of homosexuality lend examples of such research.

the contact with other homosexuals becomes an important factor that leads to different forms of behavior depending on whether the contact is perceived as positive or negative" (Cass, 1984, p 151). Individuals maintain a public heterosexual image and a private homosexual image.

4. *Stage 4: Identity Acceptance.* According to Cass (1984), this stage is a relatively peaceful time because the individual has come to terms with who she or he is and where she or he belongs. Friends and relatives may be told, but the heterosexual image is maintained at times where negative reactions would be forthcoming. If the individual accepts the idea of homosexuality as negative and can maintain a heterosexual image to avoid confrontation, development does not proceed.

5. *Stage 5: Identity Pride.* The individual who has accepted homosexuality as a positive image expresses loyalty to homosexuals as a group and a sense of pride in one's homosexuality. Anger may be expressed at the view of heterosexuals toward the gay community. Where confrontations are seen as consistently negative, identity foreclosure takes place.

6. *Stage 6: Identity Synthesis.* "A homosexual identity is no longer seen as overwhelming the identity by which an individual can be characterized. Individuals come to see themselves as people having many sides to their character, only one part of which is related to homosexuality" (Cass, 1984, p. 152). The positive experiences that individuals have with some heterosexuals lead them to drop a good deal of their anger toward heterosexuals. A lifestyle in which one's homosexuality is no longer hidden is developed. One's view of self and the views believed to be held by others of self become integrated, and the public and private aspects of life are united. Again, according to Cass (1984), this process of integrated identity gives rise to a sense of peace and stability, and the process of identity formation is completed.

Although this proposed continuum may seem rather straightforward, many issues affect an individual's progress in development toward identity formation as a homosexual.

> Prior to acquiring a gay or lesbian identity, one has a racial or ethnic identity, which is part of the core of childhood identity. Moreover, racial and ethnic groups experience prejudice and discrimination based on their minority status, which may place constraints on various life options. (Garnets & Kimmel, 1993, p. 331)

Furthermore, the fact that individuals have sexual orientation in common does not mean they have a great deal in common. Cohen (1991) sees a need for a model of sexual orientation based on multiplicity, not sameness, that examines overlapping identities and statuses of gender, race/ethnicity, and sexuality.

In their review of the literature relative to developing an understanding of cultural influences on the lesbian and gay male identity, Garnets and Kimmel (1993) note several themes deserving of reflection and study:

1. *Religion* within the context of culture plays a significant role in the disclosure of a homosexual lifestyle. For example, African American gays and lesbians cannot be comfortable as a part of the religious community if their homosexuality is known. Also, Catholicism plays an important role in many Latino communities and purports homosexuality to be a sin (Garnets & Kimmel, 1993).

2. *Gender roles*, which may be made very specific in given cultures, "increase the difficulty for gay men and lesbians to carve out a nontraditional or androgynous role" (Garnets & Kimmel, 1993, p. 332). This appears to be true for Latino and Asian cultures, which see lesbianism as violating gender role expectations for women to be passive and to rely on and defer to men (Hildago, 1984; Shon & Ja, 1982).

3. The *role of the family within the community* is another theme that bears study. The family may be seen as the primary vehicle for social support and an important tie to one's ethnic community. "The expectations of the group are often paramount over individual desires" (Garnets & Kimmel, 1993, p. 332). Furthermore, "a gay or lesbian identity may be perceived as a betrayal of one's own people, a loss of connection with one's own heritage, a public statement about something that reflects badly on one's culture or religion, a violation of gender role expectations of the culture, or a sign of assimilation into White mainstream culture" (Garnets & Kimmel, 1993, p. 333). In some groups, including African American, a homosexual lifestyle is seen as negative in that individuals are not promoting survival of the group through propagation of the race (Icard, 1985/86). Rates of disclosure to families appear to be relatively low among Asian, African American, and Latino gays and lesbians (Garnets & Kimmel, 1993).

4. "A fourth theme that centers on the *process of reconciling one's ethnicity, gender, and sexual orientation* has been referred to as forming a dual or triple identity (e.g., Latina, lesbian, and female)" (Garnets & Kimmel, 1993, p. 333). Multiple identity integration requires that individuals establish priorities among distinct communities, including racial/ethnic, gay/lesbian, and society at large. These groups may have conflicting value systems.

5. The *degree of the individual's interaction with, and integration into, the White majority culture*—in particular, the Anglo gay and lesbian culture and community—is an additional theme proposed for study by Garnets and Kimmel (1993). "If gay men and lesbians rely on groups and networks outside of their family and culture in which their sexual identity is more accepted, they may lose support for their racial or ethnic identity" (Garnets & Kimmel, 1993, p. 334). Lesbians and gays of color may not receive the same types of psychological support from the gay community that their White counterparts receive and often are faced with issues of racism in addition to issues about sex.

As with heterosexuals, the development of self-identity in homosexuals is affected not only by their biological origins but also by the sociocultural realities of their worlds. In addition to personal self-doubts relative to recognizing and accepting their sexual orientation, issues of prejudice, fear, and misunderstanding are still prevalent and vary across cultures and communities.

◊◊ Families Headed by Gay or Lesbian Adults

It is difficult to acquire exact estimates of the number of same-sex partners cohabiting in the United States today. This difficulty is attributable, in part, to the fear of reprisal in terms of loss of a job, loss of status as an individual within the community, or loss of custody of children sharing the household. Even though the increased acceptability of the gay and lesbian lifestyle and advocacy for rights for gays, lesbians, and their families has been accompanied by more information about the number of gays and lesbians cohabiting in the United States, numbers provided are still broad estimates. The *New York Times* ("The 21st Century Family," 1990) declared that 2 million fathers and mothers in this country were living a gay or lesbian lifestyle.

Formation of Families

For many individuals, the terms *parenthood* and *homosexuality* are seen as contradictory. "This contradiction, however, is of social not biological origin" (Sears, 1994, p. 140). **Gay-headed families** and **lesbian-headed families** are created in a variety of ways. Women leading a lesbian lifestyle may have formerly been in heterosexual married or unmarried relationships in which children were conceived. They may also conceive through **donor insemination,** or they may adopt children. "The 'lesbian baby boom' and the increasing visibility of lesbians who become mothers through donor insemination or adoption constitute the most dramatic and provocative challenge to traditional notions both of the family and of the nonprocreative nature of homosexuality" (Lewin, 1993, p. 19). Men leading a gay lifestyle may have been in married or unmarried heterosexual relationships through which children were born. Gays are also seeking to become parents after "coming out" (Bozett, 1989). They do this through adoption or foster care of biologically nonrelated children or through donor insemination or sexual intercourse with women who may be lesbian or heterosexual. In such a case, the woman may be seen as a coparent to the child, or a same-sex partner may be seen as the coparent (Patterson, 1992).

Whatever the source of children, in this situation the term *family* is used

> to denote a cohabitive living arrangement involving two same-sex adults and their children, biological, adopted or conceived through artificial insemination, from previous heterosexual relationships, marital or commonlaw. The relationship is characterized by mutual commitment, property sharing, and sexual

intimacies similar to that found among cohabiting heterosexuals with children. (Baptiste, 1987, p. 224)

As with heterosexual single parents, it seems important to stress that the single parent who is gay or lesbian living alone with a child or children also constitutes a "family."

Challenges to and About Families Headed by Gays and Lesbians

Many challenges accompany the increasing complexity of family forms. These challenges face researchers in areas of individual and family development, officials of the government and the courts, businesses, schools, and more important, the families themselves. Those of us working with young children and their families are interested in studies of the effects of growing up in alternative family structures on the human being as she or he moves through the lifespan.

> Given the multiplicity of new kinds of families among gay men and lesbians, and in view of their apparent vitality, child development researchers today are faced with remarkable opportunities to study the formation, growth, and impact of new family forms. (Patterson, 1992, p. 1027)

Situations surrounding these new kinds of families remain clouded with myths, stereotypes, and prejudices about the individuals who head these families (e.g., lesbians, gays). These attitudes and stereotypes must be explored, as should the effects of such prejudices on the children who grow up amid them.

In addition, although there continues to be more openness in recognizing alternative family forms, there is still limited recognition of gay and lesbian partnerships by formal religions and in legal situations. Legislatures and judicial bodies are being called on to "define, redefine, and clarify the concept of family" (Wisensale & Heckart, 1993, p. 199). Churches are being challenged to sanctify the partnership as a marriage recognized by the church and its community.

The traditional family—that is, a family headed by a mother and a father living in the same household with their children—has had more rights than the nontraditional family (Wisensale & Heckart, 1993). Examples include the rights to insurance and death benefits, to inherit, and to authorize emergency medical care. As definitions of who constitutes a family change, members of nontraditional family forms are challenging the withholding of rights for partners and children. Wisensale and Heckart (1993) cite several cases, including *Marvin vs. Marvin* (1976), *Renshaw v. Heckler* (1986), and *Watts v. Watts* (1987), in which the rights of unmarried partners are supported. These authors also note cases that have been historic for the gay and lesbian community. The decisions in *Baker v. Nelson* (1971) and *Jones v. Hallahan* (1973) clearly denounced same-sex marriages, but the decision in *Braschi v. Stahl Associates Co.* (1989) found that a gay couple's relationship went beyond that of roommates and that the individual who survived his partner's death of acquired immune deficiency syndrome (AIDS) was considered family under New York City's rent control regulations. The surviving partner was, therefore, able to maintain the rent-controlled apartment they had shared.

In response to the growing numbers of partnerships, local governments and some corporations are adopting domestic partnership laws and arrangements. These laws and arrangements allow unmarried partners benefits traditionally deemed for spouses. Wisensale and Heckart (1993) surveyed 14 cities with domestic partnership laws: the California cities of Los Angeles, Berkeley, West Hollywood, Santa Cruz, San Francisco, and Laguna Beach; Takoma Park, Maryland; Madison, Wisconsin; Seattle, Washington; New York and Ithaca, New York; Ann Arbor, Michigan; Minneapolis, Minnesota; and West Palm Beach, Florida. Thirteen of the 14 communities passed city ordinances that recognized domestic partnerships. Seven of the 14 communities required the domestic partners to register. Five of the 14 communities included medical benefits. Thirteen of the 14 allowed for bereavement leave.

Wisensale and Heckart (1993) also surveyed corporations and found that 14 corporations or nonprofits offered domestic partnership benefits to employees when surveyed in 1992. Individuals were required to register their domestic partnerships with their employers.

It does seem reasonable that, as in heterosexual marriages, employers require employees to register or name their domestic partners for the purposes of accountability in providing benefit packages. For male-female partnerships, this may not pose a problem. It may not pose a problem for same-gender partners. For partners who are gay or lesbian *and* parents, however, this disclosure may bring some discomfort. As stated by Sears (1994), two of the greatest challenges for families with gay, lesbian, or **bisexual** parents are securing and maintaining custody of children and disclosing the nature of their lifestyle to their children. These challenges are, in part, a result of heterosexism in our society. **Heterosexism** refers to

> the presumption of superiority and exclusiveness of heterosexual relationships—(it) is evidenced in the assumption that parents of all children are heterosexual or that a heterosexual adult will *prima facie* be a better parent than one who is homosexual. (p. 148)

Baptiste (1987) addresses specific fears held by parents who are gay or homosexual that their children will be taken away from the family by grandparents, ex-spouses, or others forces. These fears force some families into secrecy about the sexual orientation of the adults and into isolation from those who might reveal their homosexuality.

Although both families headed by gays and by lesbians face disapproval of their lifestyle by those they encounter in the course of daily living, gays face even greater burdens in this area because two men living together raising children are seen by many as more suspect and unacceptable than two women living together in the same situation. Both types of families face societal concerns that children raised in these families will be gay, will be exposed to illicit sexual behaviors, and will be at risk for AIDS.

Many of these concerns are grounded in the myths and misconceptions that seem to surround the gay and lesbian lifestyle. In an effort to explore and "bring light" to these notions, Garnets and Kimmel (1993) engaged in extensive reviews of literature and provided the following summary statements that typify stereotypic attitudes:

1. *Myth 1:* Homosexuals don't want enduring relationships—and can't achieve them anyway . . .
2. *Myth 2:* Gay relationships are unhappy, abnormal, dysfunctional, and deviant . . .
3. *Myth 3:* "Husband" and "wife" roles are universal in intimate relationships . . .
4. *Myth 4:* Gays and lesbians have impoverished social support networks (pp. 397–403)

Although the above concerns seem universal for both gay and lesbian individuals and their families, other concerns are specific to gays and to lesbians. These issues relate to coming out and to parenting.

Challenges to Men Who Are Both Gay and Fathers

As was discussed, men who are gay may become fathers through adoption from a nonrelated source or through a **surrogate mother** using the gay father's sperm. The majority of gay fathers, however, were engaged in heterosexual relationships that generally included marriage prior to adopting a gay lifestyle. Many of these individuals remained in the heterosexual marriage even though they perceived themselves as gay in order to maintain their relationships with their children. A major move in their lives involved divorcing their wives and a heterosexual way of life, risking a relationship with their children, and adopting a gay lifestyle.

Achieving an identity as a gay male and as a father follows a progression:

> By participating over time in both the father world and the gay world, the gay father progresses from being attached primarily to the heterosexual world to a primary connection with the gay world. This progression is achieved by means of disclosing his gay identity to nongays and his father identity to gays and receiving mostly positive sanctions, which have an integrative effect. (Bozett, 1993, p. 439)

This progression leads to *integration,* which Bozett (1993) defines as "a state in which the gay and father identities are congruent, and are appropriately overtly manifested; both identities are accepted by both the father himself and other in his proximate social worlds as nondichotomous" (p. 439).

identity as a woman, and therefore do not experience the role conflict that gay men do" (p. 257).

Regardless of their comfort in the roles of mother and lesbian, women face similar societal and judicial prejudices and concerns in their attempts to parent their children as do fathers who are gay. Falk (1993) notes that, with respect to child custody issues, "Legal decision makers often focus on the mother's homosexuality without even attempting to establish a causal relationship between the mother's sexual orientation and the child's welfare" (p. 422). Concerns include the amount of time the parent will spend with the child as compared with pursuing her relationship with another woman, the possibility that the child will become homosexual or be exposed to sexual behaviors considered deviant, or that the child will suffer the social stigma of having a lesbian parent.

While women who are lesbian are becoming more open about their lifestyle, issues with child custody often prompt many who are mothers to remain closeted. According to Coleman (1985), disclosure of a wife's homosexuality or bisexuality almost always leads to divorce. Male partners appear generally to react in an angry manner, and disclosure to a male spouse is often avoided. A husband may view his wife's homosexual feelings as a kind of infidelity and, in keeping with the double standard between men and women, view this as worse than a man's infidelity (Coleman, 1985). This may be a source of the husband's anger and the ongoing legal battles for child custody that often ensue (Hanscombe & Forster, 1982). Those lesbian mothers who were married when their children were born experience two kinds of transitions on leaving their heterosexual life: (a) They "came out" to themselves and perhaps to others and (b) they left their husbands. In addition to these transitions, lesbian mothers experience similar issues as do single, heterosexual mothers—leaving a marriage, getting a divorce, and dealing with its legal, economic, and emotional ramifications (Lewin, 1993, p. 20). In her interviews with women who have gone through this experience, Lewin (1993) notes a common theme that seems to emerge in which women talk of finally feeling comfortable and "at home" with themselves. (As noted earlier, lesbian mothers are more likely to disclose their lifestyle to their children themselves and at an earlier time than fathers who are gay.)

A woman's choice to disclose her homosexual identity is affected by many factors. We have already discussed fear of losing custody of children and reprisals by the spouse in custody matters. We must also be reminded that given cultures may view this revelation with openness or with anger and denial. Oliva Espin's (1993) observation of the Latino community is used as an example:

> Although emotional and physical closeness among women is encouraged by Latin culture, overt acknowledgement of lesbianism is even more restricted than in mainstream American society. . . . Because of the importance placed on family and community by most Hispanics, the threat of possible rejection and stigmatization by the Latin community becomes more of a psychological burden for the Hispanic lesbian. (p. 353)

Loiacano (1993) details similar findings in the African American community and further notes that support groups for lesbians often do not provide the kind of affirmation that Anglo members receive. Such support is needed as "Lesbianism is largely considered incompatible with the role expectations of the women in the Black community" (p. 365).

In her study of Asian American lesbians and gays, Chan (1993) found that these individuals identified more with their lesbian and gay organizations than with their Asian American identities. Their desire was to be accepted by both groups. In the Asian American community, however, being lesbian might be seen as a rejection of one's primary role and obligation to a family, particularly to one's responsibility to carry on the family through marriage and the bearing of children. Such behavior would be seen not only as the rejection of the mother-child role but also as an indication that the parents had failed in their role of raising their daughter.

Children of Gay and Lesbian Parents

"Central to the problems faced by children of lesbian and gay parents is the heterosexism and homophobia rampant in today's society" (Sears, 1994, p. 148). Surrounding this problem is the reluctance of society to recognize households headed by gay and lesbian individuals as "families."

Studies have been conducted in the last 15 years to determine the effects of being raised by gay or lesbian parents. Some of these studies have evolved from the homophobic world of proving that this type of lifestyle is detrimental to the children. Others are designed to disprove the homophobic view by determining that children raised by parents who are gay or lesbian are as healthy and happy as those raised in heterosexual families. Regardless of the acknowledged or unacknowledged viewpoint of the researcher, much remains to be studied about children raised in alternative family forms, particularly with respect to the diversity of the individuals and their strengths and needs within the family and to the response of the broader community, including schools and child care providers.

Patterson (1992) conducted a comprehensive review of existing studies of children with respect to their own sexual identities (gender identity, gender role behavior, sexual orientation); aspects of personal development (separation-individuation, psychiatric evaluations, assessments of behavior problems, self-concept, personality, locus of control, moral judgment, and intelligence); and social relationships. In her review of studies conducted on 300 children across 12 samples, Patterson concluded that no evidence has been found for "significant disturbances of any kind in the development of sexual identity among these individuals" (p. 1032). Patterson also concluded that existing work reveals no empirical support that children of gay and lesbian parents suffer in the area of personal development, including intellectual and moral development. Existing work also supports the notion that children of gay and lesbian parents are able to form and maintain positive social relationships with both peers and adults.

These studies appear to indicate no differences in the psychological health of children growing up in families headed by heterosexuals or by homosexuals. "Common sense tells us, however, that growing up with two mothers or two fathers is different from growing up with a mother and a father, or with a single parent, for that matter" (Casper, Schultz, & Wickens, 1992, p. 113). Children may be learning to live in blended families, with adoptive parents, with **two moms,** between households headed by hetero-sexual parents and households headed by homosexual parents, and with children who are siblings and those who are not. These are complex issues for both adults and children.

In his work with educators attempting to respond to the needs of families headed by gay, lesbian, or bisexual parents, Sears (1994) summarizes research into statements that may be helpful to teachers/child care providers:

- Children are less accepting when a same-sex parent "comes out" than when a parent of the other gender discloses sexual identity.
- Children of a lesbian or gay parent are no more likely to define themselves as homosexual than children of heterosexual parents, nor are they any more likely to display atypical sex role preferences.
- Lesbian, gay, and bisexual parents often seek to provide their children with a variety of gender role models.
- The earlier the disclosure to the child, the fewer problems in the parent-child relationship.
- Children of a lesbian or gay parent follow typical developmental patterns of acquiring sex role concepts and sex-typed behaviors.
- Children of homosexual parents who have experienced marital turmoil face similar difficulties common to children of divorce.
- Gay fathers may have a more difficult time disclosing their sexuality to their children than lesbian mothers; children of gay fathers are less likely than those of lesbian mothers to know of their parents' sexual identities; and the coming out process is more difficult for men who are gay fathers with children at home.
- Sons are less accepting than daughters when learning a parent is gay.
- As children enter adolescence, the likelihood increases that they will experience peer harassment about their parents' sexual identities and engage in a variety of self-protective mechanisms.
- Gay fathers are more likely than lesbian mothers to report their children experiencing difficulty with peer harassment because of the parent's homosexuality (pp. 151–152).

As we have discussed, it is difficult for many people to consider the household headed by one or more parents who are gay or lesbian a family.

It is also difficult for many people to recognize that such families face many of the dilemmas as do stepfamilies or blended families. Consider the mother who leaves a heterosexual marriage and forms a partnership with another lesbian as one example. Baptiste (1987) has addressed issues that face children raised in stepfamilies. In addition to those issues that are common to children growing up in heterosexual stepfamilies, children growing up in gay and lesbian stepfamilies have unique concerns. "The primary complaint of children living in gay stepfamilies is feeling isolated from peers and their community" (p. 229). There is also a lack of identification with parents who, by and large, grew up in heterosexual families and cannot relate their own experiences as children to those of their offspring. Baptiste further notes that even though children know about their parents' homosexuality, the need to keep it quiet or secret from others becomes wearing on the children and, in a sense, creates a closeted effect. Additional problems may arise with parents' desires to create stepsibling relationships with the children of partners. Because children may not know the adults are partners and because the relationship has no legal sanctions, children may become confused as to the nature of these relationships and will not be heavily vested in building and maintaining such relationships.

◊◊ Implications for Teachers Working with Children with Gay and Lesbian Parents

Although schools have given attention to addressing the needs of gay and lesbian students in a nondiscriminatory manner, little attention has been given to addressing the needs of children who come from alternative family structures. "If we are to truly serve all of our students, then educators must become more aware of the challenges facing lesbian, gay, and bisexual parents and their children" (Sears, 1994, p. 140).

The school serves as a social institution that represents the values of a dominant culture and socializes children into mainstream cultural norms (Casper et al., 1992):

> Young children with gay parents who enter school for the first time, and who previously held an unquestioning acceptance of the naturalness of their family, are suddenly confronted with countless situations in which totally different family configurations are the norm. These children must contend with the frequent representation of *their* family configuration as deviant or, perhaps most common, with the fact that it is not represented at all. (p. 115)

A day care director recently shared her concerns about several staff members who avoided greeting and talking with a child's lesbian parents. Our focus should always remain on providing a loving and developmentally appropriate environment for the child. Doing so requires that we first acknowledge the adult's role as the child's parent and show respect for the child's family in this context. We should regard this aspect of the adult's life before we regard her or his career, ethnic origin, economic situation, or **heterosexuality** or homosexuality.

Such acceptance may require that we examine our attitudes about alternative lifestyles and how those attitudes affect our work with children and their families. Many of these attitudes are present in the behaviors we exhibit. Consider the following questions:

- Do you avoid greeting a mother because you are uncomfortable with her arrangement with a female partner?
- Have you asked a child not to engage in play about two moms in the dramatic play area?
- Have you made efforts to find out about the lifestyle of a dad who you suspect is gay even though he has not disclosed this information to you?
- Do you continue to represent a family as composed of a mother and a father in daily activities with children?
- Have you labeled a child as emotionally traumatized because of her family situation even though she seems happy and interacts well with other children?

Many of these behaviors are based in our own fears about that which is different and unknown and about that which threatens us in some way. Our prejudices, of which we may or may not be aware, stem from our fears. "A generation ago, negative biases on the part of school personnel, neighbors, and often even relatives made it hard for heterosexual mothers who divorced. The problem of prejudice against nonstereotypic families is not new" (Clay, 1990, p. 33).

As teachers, administrators, and caregivers, we must be willing to look at, and deal with, our own fears as they relate to the topic of homosexuality so that we can demonstrate to children and their families that we value them. We must also be willing to learn more about the sociocultural aspects of homosexuality to alleviate the myths and misconceptions that may exist in our minds.

> When the teacher is not gay but the parents are, the cultural values and meanings carried within a lesbian and gay identity have to be added to class, racial, ethnic, and other cultural differences that create rich contexts for one's life, but not be easily understood by an outsider. (Casper et al., 1992, p. 121)

Just as we consider the uniqueness of each child, we consider the uniqueness of the family. Guidelines for working with families headed by gays and lesbians must be considered and implemented in the light of the particular needs of each family. Possible guidelines (Baptiste, 1987; Sears, 1994) may be adapted for children during the early childhood years and are as follows:

- In written materials designed for adults (e.g., policy manuals, handbooks), use such terms as *parent*, rather than *mother* or *father*.
- Provide visual representations of family/cultural diversity in classroom displays and children's books.

- Use language that shows you value and recognize the diversity of cultures and families within your classroom.
- Avoid "quizzing" a child to determine the lifestyle of parents who have not chosen to disclose this to you.
- View a parent as a child's father or mother, not as the child's gay father or lesbian mother.
- Respect and honor the rights of parents to maintain silence about their homosexuality.
- If a parent chooses to disclose her or his homosexuality with you, avoid prejudicial remarks or behaviors.
- Realize that the parent is the most important person to the child and that this relationship should be nurtured by the child's teacher/caregiver.
- Be knowledgeable about homosexuality as a lifestyle.
- Be alert to any situations in which a child might be teased because of a parent's lifestyle. Alert parents should such problems occur.
- Become familiar with organizations and support groups for families within your community.
- Be aware of other issues that are a part of a child's life, including being adopted, being a part of a stepfamily, or experiencing the divorce of parents.

Depending on the nature of the school organization, parents may also be involved in decision making relative to the inclusion of materials depicting gay/lesbian lifestyles within classrooms. For more information about this process, you may want to read about Jennifer Lackey's (1997) experience in doing so in an Oregon Preschool Cooperative. As a board member and parent, Ms. Lackey offers a unique and thorough look at this democratic process.

Granted, some individuals will have a difficult time dealing with "two moms" or "**two dads**," not to mention a parent who is bisexual. Their concerns stem from religious beliefs, personal values, and fears. As professionals, we cannot disregard their feelings. We can, however, keep our focus on the children—their joys and triumphs, their smiles and personalities, their successes and challenges. We can remember that parents are parents first. This is our task.

Summary Statements ◊

- Homophobia refers to an irrational and distorted view of homosexuality or homosexual persons.
- Self-concept refers to people's mental images of themselves: what they think they are like as people.

- Identity refers to perceptions of self that are thought to represent the self definitively in specific social settings.
- Homosexual identity is one of several identities incorporated into a person's self-concept. The homosexual identity

may function as a self-identity, perceived identity, presented identity, or all three.

- Coming out refers to the developmental process that is characteristic of achieving a homosexual identity.

- Disclosure is the disclosing of one's homosexuality to others.

- The fact that individuals have sexual orientation in common does not mean that the individuals are alike.

- The development of self-identity in homosexuals is affected not only by their biological origins but also by the sociocultural realities of their worlds.

- Heterosexism refers to the presumption of superiority and exclusiveness of heterosexual relationships. It assumes that parents of all children are, or that a heterosexual adult will be, a better parent than one who is homosexual.

- Because of fears of losing children in custody battles, many gay and lesbian parents do not disclose their homosexual identities.

- The majority of children living in gay- or lesbian-headed households are children born to these individuals during prior heterosexual marriages.

- Lesbian couples are seeking to have children through donor insemination and through adoption.

- Gay couples are opting to have children through surrogate mothers and through adoptions.

- It is easier for mothers to disclose their homosexuality to their children than for fathers to disclose their homosexuality to their children.

- Children raised in situations where both parental partners bring offspring must deal with the same issues as children in stepfamilies. The lack of legal recognition of these partnerships, however, makes the nature of these relationships unclear to the children.

- A review of studies conducted with children growing up in homes headed by gays and lesbians reveals no differences with respect to the gender choices or sexual preferences of children, their intelligence, or ability to make moral judgments.

- Children raised in households headed by gays and lesbians may experience a sense of isolation prompted by their inability to relate to a child raised in a heterosexual household and to the family's choice to maintain the secrecy of the living arrangement among the adults.

- Teachers can exhibit respect for the diversity of families through classroom displays, materials, and books that depict different cultures and gender roles.

- In working with children of families who have gay or lesbian heads, teachers will need to examine their personal attitudes, prejudices, and behaviors and to practice behaviors that show regard for the role of the adult as first being a parent.

Activities ◇◇

1. Investigate the types of advocacy and support groups available in your community and state for individuals who are gay or lesbian and their families.

What are the specific objectives of these organizations? What issues do they address? What types of support do they actually provide to families?

2. Interview an early childhood teacher relative to her or his experiences in serving the children of families who are headed by gay or lesbian adults. Without identifying those families, discuss issues that may have arisen specific to the family's lifestyle. How did the teacher respond to these issues?

3. Investigate the legal rights of partners of gay or lesbian individuals within your state and at the local level. Consider health benefits, death benefits, rights to inherit, and so on.

4. Read the article "The Attitudes of Undergraduate College Students Toward Gay Parenting" by Crawford and Solliday (see "Resources" for citation). As a class, gather some consensus about your responses to the situation involving the adoption of a child. Do you and your peers feel the same way as those college students in the study, or do you vary in attitudes expressed? If so, explain.

5. Consider the following situation. You are a preschool teacher with a mixed age-group of 3- and 4-year-old children. You are observing two girls playing in the dramatic play area with dolls. One child says, "I have two moms. You can be a mom, and I'll be a mom. The other child asks her to explain. Seeming confused, she looks at you and asks you to explain. What is your response?

6. A mother brings her 5-year-old son to school one morning and asks to speak with you, his teacher. She indicates she has "found out" that another child's father is gay and living with another man. She expresses her concern for the boy of the father who is gay and also concern that her son will get the "wrong idea." How might you handle this situation?

7. An 8-year-old child comes to you in tears because another child has teased her about her father, who is gay and living with his partner. How can you help this child? Should you discuss this incident with her father?

8. Organize a list of children's books that deal with the topic of children in families with gay or lesbian adults. (*Daddy's Roommate* by Michael Wilhoite is one example.) Discuss aspects of the book that should be considered with respect to what is developmentally appropriate for children of ages 3 through 8.

Resources ◊

Alpert, H. (1988). *We are everywhere: Writings by and about lesbian parents.* Freedom, CA: Crossing Press.

Baringa, M. (1991). Is homosexuality biological? *Science, 253,* 956–957.

Belcastro, P. A., Gramlich, T., Nicholson, T., Price, J., & Wilson, R. (1993). A review of data-based studies addressing the effects of homosexual parenting on children's sexual and social functioning. *Journal of Divorce and Remarriage, 20,* 105–122.

Benkov, L. (1994). *Reinventing the family.* New York: Crown.

Briggs, J. R. (1994). *A Yankelovich monitor perspective on gays/lesbians.* Norwalk, CT: Yankelovich Partners.

Card, C. (1992). Lesbianism and choice. *Journal of Homosexuality, 23*(3), 39–52.

Cramer, D. (1986). Gay parents and their children: A review of research and practical implications. *Journal of Counseling and Development, 64,* 504–507.

Crawford, I., & Solliday, E. (1996). The attitudes of undergraduate college students toward gay parenting. *Journal of Homosexuality, 30,* 63–77.

Gibbons, A. (1991). The brain as "sexual organ." *Science, 253,* 957–959.

Hare, J., & Richards, L. (1993). Children raised by lesbian couples: Does context of birth affect father and partner involvement? *Family Relations, 42,* 249–253.

Koepke, L., Hare, J., & Moran, P. (1992). Relationship quality in a sample of lesbian couples with children and child-free lesbian couples. *Family Relations, 42,* 224–229.

Rafkin, L. (1990). *Different mothers: Sons and daughters of lesbians talk about their lives.* Pittsburgh, PA: Cleis.

Schulenburg, J. (1985). *Gay parenting: A complete guide for gay men and lesbians with children.* Garden City, NY: Anchor.

Weston, K. (1992). The politics of gay families. In B. Thorne (Ed.), *Rethinking the family: Some feminist questions* (pp. 119–139). Boston: Northeastern University Press.

Wickens, E. (1993). Penny's question: "I will have a child in my class with two moms—What do you know about this?" *Young Children, 48,* 25–28.

Organizations and Support Groups

Center Kids, 208 West 13th Street, New York, NY 10011

Gay and Lesbian Parents Coalition International, P.O. Box 50360, Washington, DC 20091

Federation of Parents and Friends of Lesbians and Gays, Inc. (P-FLAG), P.O. Box 27605, Washington, DC 20038-7605

References ◇◇

Allen, L. S., & Gorski, R. A. (1992). Sexual orientation and the size of the anterior commissure in the human brain. *Proceedings of the National Academy of Science, 89,* 7199–7202.

Bailey, J. M., & Pillard, R. C. (1991). A genetic study of male sexual orientation. *Archives of General Psychiatry, 48,* 1089–1096.

Baker v. Nelson. (1971). Supreme Court of Minnesota, 291 Minn. 310, 191 N.W. 2d 185, *appeal dismissed* 409 U.S. 810, 93 S. Ct. 37, 34 L. Ed. 2d 65.

Baptiste, D. A. (1987). Psychotherapy with gay/lesbian couples and their children in "stepfamilies": A challenge for marriage and family therapists. *Journal of Homosexuality, 14,* 223–238.

Bozett, F. W. (1989). Gay fathers: A review of the literature. In F. W. Bozett (Ed.), *Homosexuality and the family* (pp. 137–162). New York: Harrington Park.

Bozett, F. W. (1993). Gay fathers: A review of the literature. In L. D. Garnets & D. C. Kimmel (Eds.), *Psychological perspectives on gay and lesbian male experiences* (pp. 437–458). New York: Columbia University Press.

Braschi v. Stahl Associates Co. (1989). New York Court of Appeals, W. L. 73109.

Calfia, P. (1979). Lesbian sexuality. *Journal of Homosexuality, 4,* 255–266.

Casper, V., Schultz, S., & Wickens, E. (1992). Breaking the silences: Lesbian and gay parents and the schools. *Teachers College Record, 94,* 109–137.

Cass, V. C. (1983/84). Homosexual identity: A concept in need of definition. *Journal of Homosexuality, 9,* 105–26.

Cass, V. C. (1984). Homosexual identity formation: Testing a theoretical model. *Journal of Sex Research, 20,* 143–167.

Chan, C. (1993). Issues of identity development among Asian American lesbians and gay men. In L. D. Garnets & D. C. Kimmel (Eds.), *Psychological perspectives on gay and lesbian male experiences* (pp. 376–387). New York: Columbia University Press.

Clay, J. W. (1990). Working with lesbian and gay parents and their children. *Young Children, 45*, 31–35.

Cohen, E. (1991). Who are "we"? Gay "identity" as political (e)motion (a theoretical rumination). In D. Fuss (Ed.), *Inside/out: Lesbian theories, gay theories* (pp. 71–92). New York: Routledge.

Coleman, E. (1985). Bisexual women in marriages. *Journal of Homosexuality, 11*, 87–99.

DeCecco, J. P., & Parker, D. A. (1995). The biology of homosexuality: Sexual orientation or sexual preference? *Journal of Homosexuality, 28*, 1–27.

Espin, O. M. (1993). Issues of identity in the psychology of Latina lesbians. In L. D. Garnets & D. C. Kimmel (Eds.), *Psychological perspectives on gay and lesbian male experiences* (pp. 348–363). New York: Columbia University Press.

Falk, P. (1993). Lesbian mothers: Psychosocial assumptions in family law. In L. D. Garnets & D. C. Kimmel (Eds.), *Psychological perspectives on gay and lesbian male experiences* (pp. 420–436). New York: Columbia University Press.

Garnets, L. D., & Kimmel, D. C. (Eds.). (1993). *Psychological perspectives on gay and lesbian male experiences*. New York: Columbia University Press.

Gonsiorek, J. C. (1993). Mental health issues of gay and lesbian adolescents. In L. D. Garnets & D. C. Kimmel (Eds.), *Psychological perspectives on gay and lesbian male experiences* (pp. 469–485). New York: Columbia University Press.

Gorman, C. (1991, September 9). Are gay men born that way? *Time*, pp. 60–61.

Hanscombe, G., & Forster, J. (1982). *Rocking the cradle*. Boston: Alyson.

Harris, M. B., & Turner, P. H. (1986). Gay and lesbian parents. *Journal of Homosexuality, 12*, 101–113.

Hildebrand, V., Phenice, L. A., Gray, M. M., & Hines, R. P. (1996). *Knowing and serving diverse families*. Upper Saddle River, NJ: Merrill/Prentice Hall.

Icard, L. (1985/86). Black gay men and conflicting social identities: Sexual orientation versus racial identity. *Journal of Social Work and Human Sexuality, 4*, 82–92.

Jones v. Hallahan. (1973). Kentucky Court of Appeals, 73, KY.

Lackey, J. (1997). Teachers and parents define diversity in an Oregon preschool cooperative: Democracy at work. *Young Children, 52*, 20–28.

LeVay, S. (1991). A difference in hypothalamic structure between heterosexual and homosexual men. *Science, 253*, 1034–1037.

Lewin, E. (1993). *Lesbian mothers: Accounts of gender in American culture*. Ithaca, NY: Cornell University Press.

Loiacano, D. K. (1993). Gay identity issues among Black Americans: Racism, homophobia, and the need for validation. In L. D. Garnets & D. C. Kimmel (Eds.), *Psychological perspectives on gay and lesbian male experiences* (pp. 364–375). New York: Columbia University Press.

Marvin v. Marvin. (1976). Supreme Court of California, 18 Cal. 3d 660, 134 Cal Reptr. 815, 557 P.2d 106.

Miller, B. (1978). Adult sexual resocialization: Adjustments toward a stigmatized identity. *Alternative Lifestyles, 1*, 207–234.

Miller, B. (1979) Gay fathers and their children. *Family Coordinator, 28*, 544–552.

Miller, B. (1983). *Identity conflict and resolution: A social psychological model of gay family men's adaptations*. Doctoral dissertation, University of Alberta, Edmonton.

Miller, B. (1986). Identity resocialization in moral careers of gay husbands and fathers. In A. Davis (Ed.), *Papers in honor of Gordon Hirabayashi* (pp. 197–216). Edmonton, Canada: University of Alberta Press.

Patterson, C. (1992). Children of lesbian and gay parents. *Child Development, 63*, 1025–1042.

Pennington, S. (1987). Children of lesbian mothers. In F. Bozett (Ed.), *Gay and lesbian parents* (pp. 58–70). New York: Praeger.

Pillard, R. C., & Weinrich, J. D. (1986). Evidence of familial nature of male homosexual-

9 Assessing and Evaluating Parent-School Involvement

Issues and Strategies

Parents must make room in their hearts and then in their house and then in their schedule for their children. No poor parent is too poor to do that, and no middle-class parent is too busy.

Jesse Jackson

Key Terms

assessment
authentic assessment
consumer-oriented evaluation
developmentally appropriate
  assessment
evaluation
family portfolio
formal evaluation
formative evaluation
informal evaluation
naturalistic, participant-oriented
  evaluation
needs assessment

objectives-oriented evaluation
  approach
objective versus subjective
  evaluation
parent wall
performance-based
phenomenology
portfolio assessment
program evaluation
responsive evaluation model
stakeholders
summative evaluation

with some kind of parent education or parent involvement program, academic gains by a child, effectiveness of some type of new teaching strategy or approach used by the teacher, and comparative measures of one class's performance with other classes or with some standardized measures.

According to Payne (1994), evaluation has three broad functions:

1. *Improvement of the program during the development phase,* also known as *formative evaluation.* Strengths and weaknesses of the program can be identified and enhanced or strengthened. This process involves repetition of trying, evaluating, redesigning, trying, and so on.

2. *Facilitation of rational comparison of competing programs.* Although differing objectives pose a large problem, the descriptions and comparisons of alternative programs can contribute to rational decision making.

3. *Contribution to the general body of knowledge about effective program design,* in which the teacher or evaluator is able to use liberty to search out principles relating to the interaction of learner, learning, and the environment. (p. 8)

Brophy, Grotelueschen, and Gooler (1974) describe three major reasons for conducting evaluations: (a) planning procedures, programs, and/or products; (b) improving existing procedures and/or products; and (c) justifying (or not justifying) existing or planned procedures, programs, and/or products. It may be helpful to point out that evaluation is not the same as research, although they may have similarities. *Evaluation* is usually undertaken to solve some specific practical problem at the local level, whereas *research* is usually conducted for generalizing to a large population. Control of influential variables is generally quite restricted in evaluation studies. Research is concerned with the systematic gathering of data aimed at testing specific hypotheses and contributing to a homogenous body of knowledge (Payne, 1994; Worthen & Sanders, 1987).

Objectives-Oriented Evaluation Approach

One evaluation model that has been used extensively and influenced the educational field dramatically is the **objectives-oriented evaluation approach,** elaborated by Taba (1962). In this model, a logical process is followed by the teacher/educator that includes the following steps:

1. Diagnosis of needs (needs assessment)
2. Formulation of objectives
3. Selection of content
4. Organization of content
5. Selection of learning experiences
6. Organization of learning experiences
7. Determining the "what" and "how of evaluation" (p. 12)

Although educators have altered this process slightly over the years, this basic model continues to provide a good blueprint for evaluation for many early childhood teachers.

The objectives of educational evaluation (Worthen & Sanders, 1987, p. 8) can include the following:

- Student development and performance
- Educator qualifications and performance
- Curriculum design and process
- School organizational structure
- Textbooks and other curriculum materials and products
- Any aspect of school operations (transportation, food services, health services)
- Facilities, media and libraries, equipment
- School-community relations
- Parent education and involvement programs in schools
- School climate
- Ideas, plans, and objectives

Formative and Summative Evaluation

In educational settings, two types of evaluation are commonly described and used: **formative evaluation** and **summative evaluation.** The goal of evaluation is always the same: to determine the worth and value of something (Scriven, 1967, cited in Worthen & Sanders, 1987). The "something" may be an object, an educational program, a curriculum unit, or almost any other entity in the educational setting (Payne, 1994). Depending on the role the value judgments are to play, evaluation data may be used developmentally or in a summary way. In the case of an overall decision, the role of evaluation is summative in nature. In contrast, formative evaluation is aimed at improving an educational program or experience during its developmental phases. Feedback is provided to the teacher or evaluator on a continuous basis so that adjustments and improvements can be made to better the program. Formative evaluation processes usually require more time than do summative evaluation procedures. Other differences are represented in Table 9.1 (Payne, 1994; Worthen & Sanders, 1987).

In early childhood settings, both formative and summative evaluation approaches are appropriate. For example, if a teacher in a new pre-k program funded by the state desires to gather ongoing feedback from parents regarding their satisfaction with, and usefulness of, the parent education/involvement component of his new class, then that teacher can ask for both qualitative and quantitative feedback from parents at strategic times during the school year. He may wish to do a needs assessment at the

Table 9.1   Differences between summative and formative evaluation

Criterion	Formative Forms of Evaluation	Summative Forms of Evaluation
Purpose	To improve program components	To certify program utility and continuance
Audience	Program administrators and staff	Potential consumer or funding agency
Who should do it	Internal evaluator	External evaluator
Main characteristic	Timely	Convincing
Measures	Often informal	Valid/reliable
Frequency of data collection	Frequent	Limited, usually in conclusion
Sample size	Often small but varies	Usually large
Questions asked	What is working? What needs to be improved? How can it be improved?	What results occur? With whom? Under what condition? With what training? At what cost?
Design constraints	What information is needed? When?	What claims do you wish to make?

Source: Adapted from Worthen, B. R., & Sanders, J. R. (1987) *Educational evaluation: Alternative approaches and practical guidelines.* New York: Longman.

beginning of the year and then collect formative evaluation data at the midpoint of the year and then again at the end of the year. He may also use other strategies, such as putting up a suggestion box at a convenient location for parents so that they can maintain an ongoing dialogue with the teacher throughout the school year. He also can make himself accessible for telephone calls, appointments with parents, and other informal communication strategies so that he is able to maintain ongoing feedback from the parents. These ongoing strategies are examples of formative evaluation; the decision at the end of the year in terms of continuing the parent involvement component of the early childhood classroom will be based on the gathering, analyzing, and making decisions regarding both the formative data and a final, summative evaluation that parents will complete at the end of the year.

◇◇ Needs, Authentic, and Portfolio Assessment

Needs Assessment Strategies

The first step for most teachers and other school professionals in determining programmatic and individual family needs within the early childhood education classroom is to measure specific needs. With U.S. schools using so many transitions and with new early childhood education programs and classrooms forming each fall, the real need is for teachers to learn as much as they can about the child and parent populations for the current academic year. Thus, needs assessments are typically completed in the fall, sometimes during the enrollment and orientation phase of the school year. During this time, when parents are accustomed to filling out school forms, teachers can integrate a parent and family needs assessment into the beginning-of-the-year routine.

Needs assessments can be standardized instruments, or they can be designed by the teacher for the particular parent population currently being served (Berger, 1981). We clearly favor the latter approach. As stated earlier, part of developing appropriate assessment procedures is taking into account the particular characteristics of the population being assessed. Just as we advocate using developmentally appropriate child assessment techniques (Bredekamp & Rosegrant, 1992; NAEYC & NAECS/SDE, 1991), we also advocate designing needs assessment tools for parents that are sensitive to such demographic characteristics as age range, racial makeup, educational level, lifestyle profiles, marital and family status, socioeconomic status, and other traits that make these parents unique.

The purpose of needs assessment is to determine specific programmatic needs for a population. In this case, the target population includes the parents and families of the children enrolled in an early childhood education program. Needs assessments should include the following:

- Demographic information that includes the names, ages, addresses, telephone numbers, and other identifying data for that specific family and its members (mother, father, sisters, brothers, and other significant others in the immediate family; see Figure 9.1)

- Description of the family's lifestyle in terms of work patterns, dual- or single-earner status, preferences for meeting times and programs for interfacing with school professionals

- Specific types of programmatic needs (e.g., parenting skills, nutrition, study habits and skills, discipline, allowances and budgeting, communication between parents and children, sibling rivalry, intergenerational family needs, divorce and remarriage, stepparenting)

- Identification of personal needs of family members so that teachers can address specific issues related to the child in the class

- Selection of options that are best for this family in terms of communicating on a regular basis with the teacher, principal, director, or other school professionals; this can be done by offering a menu of options, such as newsletters, telephone calls at work and/or home, breakfasts, evening meetings, pot luck dinners, open houses, field trips, and other avenues for communicating directly with the teacher throughout the school year.

Open-ended questions that encourage parents and other family members to express their expectations related to parent involvement, teacher-parent conferences, student outcomes, and other issues that are relevant to them are recommended. This qualitative section is quite important because it allows each family to express its own needs in a personalized way and gives

Part II. Sibling Information

    a. List the names and ages of your child's brothers and sisters:

              Name   Age   School or Child Care Attended

_____

_____

_____

_____

_____

    b. Describe your child's relationships with his/her siblings, especially those brothers and sisters with whom he/she seems to have an especially close or difficult relationship:

_____

_____

_____

    c. What, if any, information would you like the teacher to be aware of related to these siblings?

_____

_____

_____

_____

Part III. Parent and Family Program Preferences

Place an X by those items that reflect your preferences in terms of scheduling activities and events for parent and family involvement during this academic year:

_____ I would like to receive regular newsletters from the teacher about my child's classroom and activities.

_____ I would enjoy attending breakfasts that provide me with more information about my child's classroom performance, parent information, and opportunities to learn more about my child's school.

_____ Evening meetings are usually easier for me to attend, if I am given at least a week's notice.

_____ I appreciate receiving telephone calls from my child's teacher regarding special events, concerns about my child, or other school-related information.

_____ I am interested in having a parent-teacher conference several times during the school year so that I can discuss issues about my child, observe his/her work in the classroom, and learn about assessment and evaluation information gathered on my child in the classroom setting.

_____ I enjoy attending meetings at school that assist me with my role as a parent. Topics I would enjoy learning more about include:

      _____ Technology in the home

      _____ Child discipline and setting limits

Figure 9.2 *continued*

_____ Nutrition and making good choices about food

_____ Sibling relationships

_____ Family communication strategies

_____ Identifying special needs of my child

_____ Divorce and remarriage

_____ Stepparents and blended families

_____ Learning good study habits and skills

_____ Conflict resolution

_____ Budgeting, allowance, and managing money

_____ Inclusion and understanding disabilities

_____ Intergenerational family issues and relationships

_____ Strengthening a sense of family history and identity

Other topics of interest to me: _____

_____

_____

_____

_____ I would be interested in volunteering in my child's classroom on a regular or occasional basis.

_____ I would enjoy going on field trips and providing assistance with special events in the classroom.

_____ I would be interested in serving as a parent committee chair or facilitator.

_____ I would be interested in assisting with making telephone calls or writing newsletters to inform other parents/families about classroom events.

_____ I would be interested in assisting with securing guest speakers and developing programs for parents and families to attend at the school during the school year.

_____ I would be interested in communicating with my child's classroom via the internet or e-mail system.

Part IV. General Information

a. Explain any issues or concerns you have about your child in terms of his/her performance and adjustment to the classroom setting._____

_____

_____

_____

_____

b. In terms of your own family and parenting situation, identify and explain any issues or concerns that you would like addressed during this school year: _____

_____

_____

_____

c. Other comments: _____

_____

_____

_____

Figure 9.2   *continued*

more adaptable, appropriate assessment methods (Puckett & Black, 1994). The Goals 2000 national educational initiative focuses on teaching children to think, problem-solve, become more self-reliant, and interface in a much more complex, global world. As teaching and learning strategies change, the need to assess children's work in the classroom also needs to change.

One response to this need is authentic assessment. According to Puckett and Black (1994), the most desirable skills and characteristics of early learners for the 21st century include the following:

- Ability to communicate orally, in writing, and technologically
- Ability to cooperate, collaborate, and negotiate
- Ability to think critically and to solve complex problems efficiently
- Ability to view the human experience and the constantly changing world from a global perspective (p. 4)

These goals reflect complex human behavior, qualitative interaction between people, and sensitivity to individual and ethnic differences.

Although paper-and-pencil tests and standardized instruments that employ objective questions and answers are appropriate for some factual learning, the type of assessment indicated for the above-stated learning goals reflect a need for more qualitative measures of performance. In addition, the push for less stringent and fixed testing techniques for young children brings the early childhood field to a need for more progressive, developmentally appropriate assessment approaches (NAEYC & NAECS/SDE, 1991). According to the Southern Early Childhood Association (SECA), the following are criteria for good assessment:

1. Assessment must be *valid*. It must provide information related to the goals and objectives of each program.

The new era of assessment is represented by such methods as authentic assessment.

2. Assessment should *not include* standardized tests, which are group administered, pencil and paper, multiple choice, and claim to measure achievement (for young children).
3. Assessment must deal with the *whole child*. Programs must have goals and assessment processes which relate to children's physical, social, emotional, and mental development.
4. Assessment must involve *repeated observations*. Many observations help teachers find patterns of behavior and avoid quick decisions which may be based on unusual behavior by children.
5. Assessment must be *continuous* over time. Each child should be compared to his or her own individual course of development over time rather than to average behavior for a group.
6. Assessment must use a *variety of methods*. Gathering a wide variety of information from different sources enables informed and professional decisions.
7. Assessment information must be used to change the curriculum to meet the individual needs of the children in the program.[1]

---

[1]From *Developmentally Appropriate Assessment: A Position Paper* by the Southern Early childhood Association, 1992, Little Rock, AR: Author. Copyright 1992 by the Southern Early Childhood Association. Reprinted by permission.

Authentic Assessment with Parents and Families

Collaboration between parents and teachers is essential for learning to be most effective for the child. The Task Force on Early Childhood Education of the National Association of State Boards of Education (NASBE, 1988) describes school partnerships with parents as *multilateral*, in which parents and professionals exchange information in a reciprocal process (Puckett & Black, 1994). Partnerships with parents should encourage them to feel comfortable in their child's classroom, strengthen the parents' and their child's self-concepts, engage parents in important discussions and decisions that affect the classroom and their child, stimulate exchange of ideas between parents and teachers, and recognize and enhance the important parent-child relationship. Teachers can assess their own attitudes and feelings about involving parents in their classrooms by using such assessment instruments as Berger's (1991, p. 228–229), in which teachers assess their own current parent-involvement strategies and feelings about collaborating with parents.

From the guidelines stated above, we are able to adapt authentic assessment strategies for parent and family involvement in the school setting. Puckett and Black (1994) outline the essential characteristics of authentic assessment as follows:

1. Authentic assessment celebrates development and learning
2. Authentic assessment emphasizes emerging development
3. Authentic assessment capitalizes upon the strengths of the learner
4. Authentic curriculums are, first and foremost, developmentally appropriate
5. Authentic assessment is based on real-life events
6. Authentic assessment is performance based
7. Authentic assessment is related to instruction
8. Instruction informed by research on early learning and child growth and development can be valid and can inform continuing education
9. Authentic assessment focuses on purposeful learning
10. Authentic assessment is ongoing in all contexts
11. Authentic assessment provides a broad and general picture of student learning and capabilities
12. Authentic assessment is collaborative among parents, teachers, students, and other professional persons as needed (p. 22)

Although these guidelines were designed to meet the assessment needs of young children, they are appropriate for assessing adults and programs designed for parent populations. The essence of authentic assessment is matching the assessment strategy to the context and quality of the learning experience. Thus, authentic assessment is transferable to the assessment of parents and families involved in school settings.

Authentic assessment is defined in various ways, but the following elements seem to be consistent in most definitions. Authentic assessment:

- Is **performance-based**
- Focuses on defined learning objectives

- Is closely connected to teaching and learning
- Provides a broad picture of student or parent performance, learning, and abilities
- Is based on real-life events
- Uses a variety of methods for documenting individual work
- Uses work sampling and other concrete, tangible means of documentation of actual work completed
- Is sensitive to individual developmental, cultural, and gender needs and issues
- Provides a greater congruence between the individual learner and the assessment process (Berger, 1991; Maykut & Morehouse, 1994; Puckett & Black, 1994; Worthen & Sanders, 1987).

Specific areas of parent education and family involvement that lend themselves particularly to the use of authentic assessment include the following:

- Physical development, exercise, nutrition, and general well-being of the family
- Family expressions of language and literacy, including oral histories
- Socioemotional dynamics of the family
- Family history and developing a sense of roots
- Artistic expression and the family
- Assessment of school-based activities, such as breakfasts, evening events, field trips, classroom parent centers, parent walls (described below), and almost any other parent-related activity that links the school with the parent and/or family

Teachers who wish to engage the parents and families of the children in their classrooms can be very creative in the use of authentic assessment with parent education and family involvement programs. Authentic assessment can be applied to any population of learners. Key questions the teacher must ask at the beginning of the school year include the following:

- What knowledge (facts, ideas, concepts) will the parents in my classroom gain this year?
- For each family, what is its beginning point in each of the identified programmatic areas for family involvement?
- What unique goals does each family in my classroom have?
- How will each family need my assistance to reach their goals?
- What cultural or ethnic considerations are involved in planning for these families?
- What financial or socioeconomic considerations are involved in planning for these parents and families?
- What barriers or obstacles may exist for each family in my classroom?

Puckett and Black (1994), on the basis of an integrated review of the literature, identified learning categories as target behaviors within each domain of evaluation. The domains are as follows:

- *Knowledge,* described as facts, concepts, ideas, vocabulary, stories, and curricular areas
- *Skills and processes,* to include physical, social, verbal, thinking, reasoning, problem solving, representational strategies, communicating, decision making, and so on
- *Feelings,* to include competence, belonging, security, self-respect, self-confidence, and feelings about others, school, teachers, and specific program initiatives for parents
- *Dispositions,* to include curiosity, friendliness, creativity, initiative, cooperation, social responsibility, and inquiry and using new knowledge and skills (p.170)

Formal and Informal Assessment.   For each of the above domains, the teacher has a wide repertoire of assessment strategies from which to choose. In some cases, formal tests and assessments may be the best choice and represent the most authentic way to conduct an assessment. In the case of parents, using standardized parent satisfaction instruments, parent decision-making instruments, or other standardized instruments designed to gather baseline data on parenting skills and attitudes may be very helpful. These instruments may be administered at the beginning of the school year, and the data can then be organized, analyzed, and used in decision making for parent education and family involvement themes and activities for the school year (see "Recommended Assessment and Evaluation Resources for Teachers and Parents" at end of this chapter for standardized instruments suitable for use with parent groups in school settings).

Informal assessment techniques provide greater latitude for parent expression and demonstration of skills, attitudes, and efforts. According to Puckett and Black (1994), informal strategies include performance, process, products, and portfolios. Thus, standardized, quantitative instruments are referred to as formal means, whereas informal means are more varied and subjective. Informal means must have strict criteria for use, however, and to be effective, rigorous guidelines and criteria must be written out and followed. Critics of informal assessment strategies say it is not possible to identify specific rates of validity and reliability as is possible with formal strategies, but the goals of informal assessment are more subjective and phenomenological.

Using the needs assessment form (shown in Figure 9.2), the teacher can begin the new academic year with an abundance of information that will guide decision making about parent involvement and family processes for each child. Thus, the early childhood teacher can tie authentic assessment to the

Family involvement themes can be documented and displayed through photographs in the classroom.

actual planning and teaching process for the academic year. Because steps in this process are so interrelated, it is possible for the teacher to plan themes, units, and learning activities for the children that match similar themes, plans, and activities geared to the parent population, thus enhancing the connection between learning in the classroom with learning in the home.

Needs assessment and program planning for parents are not separate processes, but rather are closely intertwined. For example, if the needs assessment information indicates that a majority of parents are seeking information about health, child discipline, financial management, and technology in the home, then the teacher can design a parent program to match these identified needs. Topics, formats for learning, timing or scheduling of events, and assessment processes can be planned at the first of the year. Each event or initiative will take on its own profile and character, and authentic assessment will be reflected in the choices the teacher makes in deciding how to evaluate the parent involvement process. There will be no right or wrong answers (except for highly technical or factual information). Instead, the teacher will assist each family in documenting its own progress throughout the school year by using a variety of assessment techniques.

Examples of Authentic Assessment with Parents and Families.
Examples of authentic assessment techniques appropriate for use with parent and family groups include the following:

- *Standardized instruments* that assess parent attitudes, skills, compatibility, philosophy, discipline techniques, and so forth (often used as part of the needs assessment and for pre- and posttesting to determine program gains and effectiveness).
- *Checklists, rating scales, observational strategies* such as running records and anecdotal records, *personal interviews, time sampling,* and *event sampling,* all of which provide the teacher or parent with multiple types of information about the child, parent-child interactions, parent behaviors, and family dynamics.
- *Individual family albums or portfolios* that include photographs of the child in the classroom, pictures from the home, photographs of parents engaged with the child at home, and pictures of this family involved in events at the school.
- *Family journals* maintained jointly by parent and child. This journal requires a commitment from both the parent and the child. Each will make entries into the journal on a regular basis, such as every week, and the themes of the journal will match topics or events the child and/or parent is involved with in the school setting, as well as self-selected family themes.
- A *family tree* that traces the child's history back three generations (longer, if feasible). This family tree can be a year-long project and can be the theme for a family night at the end of the school year in which families bring their own family trees to share with other families in the classroom. The family tree can be enhanced with photographs of great-grandparents, grandparents, uncles, aunts, and immediate family members, including the child in the class. Parents who are very involved in genealogy can provide ongoing support for parents who are beginners in the art of tracing and documenting family history.
- *Videotaping,* on a regular basis, of family events in the classroom or the school. For example, a theme can be chosen for each month of the school year; each family will videotape at least one segment for each theme. These videos can then be shared at a family night at the school.

Family involvement themes. Family involvement themes can include making a favorite family dish and sharing the recipe with other families, renovating some part of the home, documenting a family trip or adventure, and role-playing child-parent issues and videotaping the role play.

The use of photography and videotaping is a constructive way to document family activities—for example, videotaping the family engaged in a special event such as a family reunion, planting the garden, bathing the dog, wallpapering in the home, washing the car, spontaneous plays or pantomimes, or attending a professional ballgame or athletic event. Other examples are videotaping members of the extended family, such as cousins, uncles, aunts, and grandparents. Audiotapes of children and parents reading stories together are also appropriate. The same storybook could be passed around from family to family in the classroom, and each family could have an audiotape available to share.

Finally, a classroom pet could be "adopted" by each family for a period of time (perhaps a week). During this designated time, the family must document its involvement with this pet. Pictures and other artifacts from this experience can be placed in a special place in the classroom or become part of the parent wall, described below.

The parent wall. In terms of the school classroom itself, the teacher can also use authentic assessment strategies. For example, he or she can designate a **parent wall** in the school. This wall becomes the responsibility of the parents, and a parent committee can be appointed to plan and care for it. The parent wall should reflect samples of work, photographs of actual parent and family involvement in the classroom for the year, as well as current pictures that reflect the day-to-day lives of the children and families in the class. The parent wall should be large enough to accommodate numerous items and pictures. Themes can be developed for the school year, and parents can donate items for each theme. This is an example of authentic assessment because it documents the real-life experiences of young children and their parents and families as they unfold.

The parent wall is an idea adapted from the Reggio Emilia programs of Northern Italy and is well-received in programs in the United States that have chosen to use this concept of documentation of parent involvement (Edwards, Gandini, & Forman, 1993). The parent wall can include pictures

Parents enjoy school events and sharing their own interests on the playground.

from each child's home and family activities, pictures from family events in the classroom, and pictures from field trips or excursions that involve the children and their parents and/or other family members. The parent wall is a useful tool that allows for much creativity. Parents delight in sharing their pictures or artifacts, and a sense of ownership and pride results from the parent wall. The parent wall provides an avenue for families to get to know each other, thus creating a stronger home-school connection for the teacher, children, and the parents.

Classroom photograph albums.   Classroom photograph albums are another example of authentic assessment in the early childhood classroom. All families and the teacher must make a commitment to this project. A large photograph album is purchased at the beginning of the school year. Parents may appoint or elect a parent committee to be in charge of organizing the album. The album evolves as the school year progresses, with each month having a particular theme selected by the parents and the teacher. Pictures of classroom events, as well as pictures from home settings, can be included. This album becomes part of the history of that class and that teacher. Albums can be stored in secure but accessible areas so that children develop a sense of history about other children who have been in this classroom in the past. Along with the album, a large group picture can also be posted in a visible place in the classroom. As each new class enters this classroom, a large group picture can be posted and labeled. If possible, a group picture of the parents and the children, along with the teaching staff,

Children can create a special parent wall for their classroom.

can also be posted. Over the years, the classroom takes on a sense of permanence and history, and the children and families who have been a part of that classroom become an important part of future classes' history. This idea too originated with the Reggio Emilia programs of Northern Italy.

◇◇ Portfolio Assessment Strategies

Numerous schools, districts, and even states around the nation are now experimenting with the use of portfolios. In the business world, *portfolio* means the collection of stocks, bonds, and other investments a person owns or controls at a particular time—very much a picture of that individual in the eyes of other investors (Farr & Tone, 1994). Portfolio assessment is an example of authentic assessment that is becoming more popular in early childhood settings. Briefly, we provide a definition and an overview for the rationale for the use of portfolio assessment, give suggestions for developing portfolios, provide a context for their use, give an example of a parent portfolio, and discuss ways to determine their use and effectiveness.

Definitions and Rationale

In educational settings, the term *portfolio* is used to designate a collection employed to evaluate or assess something related to an individual. Portfolios are used by teachers to document their own professional experience, for personnel evaluation purposes, and to market their skills to a prospective employer. Classroom portfolios are collections of writing and other materials that reflect the learning process and outcomes of students, parents, and other learners (Farr & Tone, 1994). The portfolio itself can take many forms, such as an expandable folder, a box, a shopping bag, or just space on a shelf. In a recent graduate class on creative expression in early childhood education, a student presented a large pizza box as an example of a portfolio container that she used in her early childhood classroom. It had been decorated by the student, and a variety of items had been placed in it throughout the school year (D. Stegelin, personal communication, 1997).

The portfolio container and its design can be a source of creative expression for the learner—in this case, the parent. Accessibility to the portfolios is essential. From the outset, creating and designing a unique portfolio is part of the portfolio assessment process. Portfolio holders should be large enough to hold a variety of materials such as art products, audio- and videotapes, drawings, photographs, and other items but be small enough to be readily stored; be sturdy enough to withstand frequent handling; and be personalized by each family and contribute to a shared understanding of that family's identity and values. Portfolio containers that have been used effectively include (a) plastic boxes for storing clothes or other household items, (b) large square boxes, (c) sturdy grocery bags, (d) corrugated boxes from office settings, (e) expandable file folders, (f) large mailing envelopes,

(g) large, flat pizza boxes (unused), and (h) shopping bags with sturdy bottoms (Puckett & Black, 1994). Portfolios must be "owned" by their users; thus, it is important to encourage parents to select their own portfolio containers and then to personalize them.

Portfolios are not new in the assessment arena, but they are being used more extensively now and for many more purposes. They are not designed to replace traditional assessment strategies; rather, they are another tool that provides more information in our goal of securing comprehensive assessment of outcomes (Farr & Tone, 1994). Portfolios make sense in many learning environments, including those for parents and families. If they are thoughtfully planned, organized, and constructed, portfolios provide valuable insight into the learning process and outcomes. For example, a random selection of 10 parent or family portfolios in an early childhood classroom will provide administrators, teachers, other parents, and school board members with a realistic measure of what has been happening in this classroom in terms of parent and family involvement. Portfolios encourage self-assessment and creative ways to document learning, integrate the total elements of a parent or family involvement program, and provide an important form of documentation. Portfolios are excellent examples of authentic assessment because the means of documenting and verifying parent and family involvement are just as open and adaptable as the projects, themes, parent events, activities, and outcomes of the parent education program itself.

Rationale for Using Portfolios in Parent Involvement Programs

- Portfolios for parent and/or family involvement reflect the content and character of the planned parent program for that particular early childhood classroom.
- Parents learn from the portfolio, and it serves as instruction itself.
- Portfolios promote the integration of language, writing, photography, visual arts, and other means of expression.
- Portfolios encourage the parent to "own" their learning process throughout the academic year.
- Portfolios provide a source for teacher-child-parent discussion and exchange of ideas.
- Portfolios keep the focus of instruction in the parent involvement program on the themes that are reflected in the portfolio itself.
- Portfolios allow for creative documentation of the parent, family, and school-family dynamics throughout the year.
- Portfolios encourage family involvement and interaction; they strengthen the sense of self and a positive identity within that family.
- Portfolios promote positive teacher-child-family interactions.
- Portfolios are a creative avenue for the parent and/or family to document their own participation in their child's classroom events and activities.

- Portfolios provide the early childhood teacher with documentation of his or her parent or family involvement efforts.

- Portfolios can assume many forms, and they allow for the creative expression of ideas among parents, children, and teachers.

Contexts and Uses of Portfolios with Parents and Families

Family portfolios can be maintained in virtually every early childhood classroom because of their adaptability. For parents who are not familiar with portfolios, the classroom teacher can provide a model. At the beginning of the school year, the teacher should schedule a meeting with all interested parents for the purpose of explaining the parent involvement program for the year. During this meeting, data collected from the needs assessment form (see Figure 9.2) can be shared with parents. The teacher can identify those topics or themes receiving the most votes by parents, and then the parents can work with the teacher to establish a timeline and calendar of events, topics, and special activities that will involve the parents. Parents should assume a partnership perspective with the classroom teacher and be prepared to elect officers, appoint parents to special committees and roles, and facilitate the decision-making process for the parent involvement program for that year.

One topic that will need to be discussed is the documentation process of the parent involvement component of the early childhood classroom. This is the ideal time for the classroom teacher to explain the portfolio process, and having sample portfolios will facilitate this process. The teacher's initial introduction of portfolios to parents should cover the following topics:

- What a family portfolio is and what it consists of
- The purpose of family portfolios
- Who will select the items to place in the family portfolios
- What each family portfolio will look like and what the options are for decorating and creating them
- When parents will work on their portfolios
- Where in the classroom or school setting the portfolios will be stored
- How students will assist with the family portfolios
- Who else will see the portfolios and for what reasons
- How the classroom teacher will use the family portfolios
- What outcomes the classroom teacher is looking for in the family portfolios
- How parents can use the family portfolios for self-assessment purposes

Having sample portfolios available for parents to examine will facilitate their understanding of the *portfolio* concept. Here are other tips for preparing parents to work on their family portfolios: (a) Have a sample available,

(b) have any forms ready that you wish for parents to include, (c) set up a timeline for crucial elements of the family portfolio and how they will be used for conferencing throughout the school year, (d) encourage parents to involve their children in the planning and construction of the family portfolio, and (e) have parents make covers or design special features that will make their family portfolios unique.

Farr and Tone (1994) describe a basic plan that is recommended for initiating a portfolio process. This basic plan, adapted for parents and families, is shown in Table 9.2.

Other specific items that can be placed in the family portfolio are self-selected family reading and writing activities; pictures drawn and captioned by members of the family; lists of stories, books, television programs, and movies the family has shared; letters or notes from family friends or relatives that need answering; journals and self-reflections; fictional stories and imaginative writings; personal narratives; descriptions and/or pictures of intriguing people, places, things, events; poems and other expressive writings; records of what the student and/or family members have read and written; audio- and videotapes of the student reading or of shared family literacy experiences; and student-teacher conference notes, parent-teacher conference notes (Farr & Tone, 1994, pp. 50, 51). Organizing the family portfolio can include using such strategies as a table of contents (see Figure 9.3), checklists, anecdotal records, and other means of keeping the family records in a manageable yet meaningful format.

Family portfolios serve several purposes. First, they provide a mechanism for members of a family to work together toward common goals. Second, they provide a rich history of shared experiences among family members. Third, they serve as a communication tool for the classroom teacher to interact with the child, parents, and family unit. Finally, they are a form of **informal evaluation** and provide the teacher, administrators, and school board members with convincing evidence of the value of parent involvement programs and efforts in school settings. Because portfolio assessment is so versatile and open ended, family portfolios are especially meaningful and appropriate. They allow the classroom teacher, the parents, and the child to embark on a shared adventure that strengthens the home-school connection, enhances the child's self-esteem and the family's sense of family history and identity, and allows for individual creative expression.

Determining Portfolio Effectiveness

How will the classroom teacher know whether his or her family portfolio effort has been successful? Assessing whether this year-long process has been meaningful and worthwhile may be done in several ways. During the school year, the teacher can gather informal, formative data on the family portfolio experience. For example, he or she can give an open-ended, qualitative questionnaire to parents during the break between fall and spring. This instrument can simply ask focused questions such as What has been

Table 9.2 Basic plan for starting a family portfolio

ACTIVITY	SCHEDULE	PARENT ROLE	TEACHER'S ROLE
Parents keep a journal on family activities for the year	Weekly entry	Decide on format Rotate family members Decide on themes and topics	Review journals Provide monthly feedback Give written feedback
Develop a photograph section	Add photos to portfolio on a monthly basis	Arrange for camera Rotate picture-taking responsibilities Encourage children's participation	Suggest photo options/ideas Give feedback monthly
Collect writing samples (notes, drafts, final drafts)	Add one sample per family member per month	Decide on themes/topics Arrange for time and materials Encourage children's participation	Review writing samples Give feedback Suggest topics for writing samples
Develop a media section	Set a goal for number of entries and time schedule for making entries	Facilitate family decision making about media entries (audio and video taping entries)	Suggest common themes/topics Facilitate locating of media equipment for recordings Provide feedback
Develop a family tree section in the family portfolio	Set a timeline for obtaining family history information	Identify sources of information about family history: genealogy, older relatives, sources of family history from family Bibles, records, and so forth	Facilitate family identification and use of genealogy information Provide classroom materials, equipment, and table space Provide feedback
Conferencing with teacher	Establish a calendar that allows for individual family conferences two times per year	Determine preferred times for conference	Develop a master plan for family conferences

most meaningful for you in the family portfolio project? What are two strengths of this parent involvement project? What are two concerns or issues you have about the family portfolio project? and What changes would you recommend in the family portfolio process?

On an informal basis, the classroom teacher can gather feedback from parents during the fall semester regarding their attitudes about the family portfolio project. The classroom teacher can keep a list of suggestions and

---

Ms. Smith's Second Grade Class
Mars Hill Elementary School
Anywhere, USA
Academic Year: 1998–1999

Title: FAMILY PORTFOLIO: TIM ANDREWS' FAMILY

Table of Contents

SECTION I: Goals, Activities, and Timelines for Academic Year 1998–1999
- Family goals for this year, signed by family members and Ms. Smith
- Timeline of planned events throughout the calendar year
- Copy of needs assessment for parents (confidential)
- Planning materials for this family portfolio
- Family journal/log for the academic year

SECTION II: Family history of the Andrews family
- Family tree of three generations
- Interviews with five older relatives (audiotapes and narratives)
- Photographs of family reunion, elder relatives, and the Andrews family this year
- History of migration from Germany to United States in 1861
- Anecdotes and artifacts from older relatives

SECTION III: Andrews family activities and events in Ms. Smith's Classroom (1998–1999)
- Copies of handouts and written materials from Parent Orientation and Family Days at Mars Hill Elementary School
- Photos of Andrews family members involved at school (Parent Work Day; Halloween Costume Contest; Christmas party; Spring Fling; End-of-Year Festival)

Figure 9.3   Sample family portfolio

verbal feedback he or she has received during the first semester. Responding to parents' suggestions will please the parents involved in this project. For example, one suggestion from the fall semester might be to make the classroom available several evenings each month for parents to come to the school and add items to their family portfolios, perhaps indicating a need for more flexibility and access to the school for portfolio work. Another suggestion might be to have a videocamera available for families who do not own one but who wish to include videotapes from home in their family portfolios. Keeping track of this informal feedback and then making responsive adjustments will increase the family's level of satisfaction with the project as a whole.

At the end of the school year, the classroom teacher can devise and distribute a checklist for summative evaluation purposes. This checklist should include questions that are relevant to the family portfolio experience

- Videotape of Mr. Andrews giving a special talk to Tim's class on being a veterinarian
- Other items selected throughout the year

SECTION IV: Samples of Tim Andrews's work in second grade at Mars Hill Elementary School
- Three samples of artwork, selected by Tim
- Three samples of writing, selected by Tim
- Three samples of writing, selected by Ms. Smith
- Four samples of math/numbers work, selected jointly by Tim and Ms. Smith
- Five miscellaneous work samples, selected by Tim throughout the year
- Copies of narratives of parent conferences with Ms. Smith, twice a year
- Photos of Tim in the classroom, selected by Tim (at least 10)
- Videotape of Tim in the class play at Christmas
- Other samples to be added as the year progresses and selected by Tim and Ms. Smith (to include selected test scores, self-assessment and goal statements, teacher's notes and comments, and other evaluation information)

SECTION V: New friends at school
- Photos of the Andrews family with new friends at Mars Hill Elementary School
- Photos of the Andrews family's contributions to the Parent Wall
- Videotape of the Andrews family and their experience with the Jones family on their trip to Stone Mountain
- Photos of the field trip to the Andrews family home for the Cook-Out; include as many other families as possible
- Photos of the End-of-the-Year Festival

Note: The Andrews family selected a large three-ring binder for their family portfolio. They scheduled use of the classroom camcorder for videotaping family events at home, as well as the school's audiotape recorder.

Figure 9.3   *continued*

and that relate to specific themes or projects undertaken by this group of parents. The checklist is a quantitative instrument that allows the teacher to count, average, and make future decisions based on numbers. Along with the checklist, the teacher should include an open-ended, qualitative section that allows parents to give written feedback about their family portfolio experiences and their attitudes and feelings as they conclude the school year. From these forms of formative and summative evaluation, the classroom teacher will be able to assess the quality of this experience for the families, make decisions about continuing the family portfolio project in the coming year, and then decide what changes would be good to make. The classroom teacher can also document the family portfolio experience by taking snapshots of families engaged in the portfolio construction process throughout the year, recording verbal comments made by parents and children, and using other forms of documentation that will be influential with school administrators and others who make budgetary and facility-related decisions for the school.

◇◇ Program Evaluation Strategies for Early Childhood Teachers

Definitions and Purposes of Program Evaluation

Program evaluation has different meanings for different professionals, depending on their professional training and experience, as well as their individual program evaluation needs. According to Payne (1994), there probably will never be total agreement on the nature of the activities and sequence of steps in the evaluation process (p. 12). Evaluation can be informal (based on private and impressionistic information) or formal (based on systematic observations and use of data; Worthen & Sanders, 1987). Teachers use informal evaluation techniques every day as they make decisions about which textbook to use, what destination to go to for a field trip, which color of paper to use on a special bulletin board, and so forth. This section focuses on how teachers in early childhood settings can plan, implement, and improve their programs through systematic evaluation.

Each school or center has a history of how it evaluates its programs, and the final process of evaluation is dependent on several factors: time, resources, experience and knowledge of the professionals in the school setting, questions to be asked, type of program to be evaluated, and availability of resources available for evaluation purposes (Payne, 1994; Scriven, 1993; Worthen & Sanders, 1987). Instead of seeking an absolute way to do program evaluation, the early childhood professional should be creative and confident that he or she can do a good job of designing program evaluation that meets the needs of the particular program of concern.

The purposes of program evaluation are multiple. First, it provides the teacher with feedback about the effectiveness of his or her program efforts. In this case, we are concerned about the effectiveness of parent and family involvement programs. Particularly for teachers who are beginning, revising, or attempting to improve their parent and family involvement components of their early childhood programs, program evaluation is a crucial process. Second, administrators and program sponsors usually are interested in knowing the results of program evaluation. Effective programs can be replicated by other teachers, whereas ineffective program strategies can be modified or eliminated. Third, funding or granting agencies need to know about program outcomes for continuation purposes. That is why program evaluation is very important for early childhood programs sponsored entirely by a funding agency or that have program components funded separately. Finally, parents and families themselves benefit from knowing the effectiveness of these programs. Particularly for parents involved for the first time in their child's academic classroom setting, program evaluation

Administrators and program sponsors are interested in knowing the results of program evaluation.

outcomes and benefits can play an important role in reinforcing that their time has been spent well.

According to Worthen and Sanders (1987), **formal evaluation** has played many roles in educational settings, including providing a basis for decision making and policy formation, assessing student achievement, evaluating curricula, accrediting schools, monitoring expenditure of public funds, and improving educational materials and programs. The overall goal of educational evaluation, however, is to determine the worth or merit of whatever is being evaluated (Worthen & Sanders, 1987, p. 5).

The evaluation process usually consists of several steps that are common. These steps usually include the following and are adapted from Payne (1994, p. 13):

1. Statement of program goals and evaluation objectives
2. Determination of specific objectives
3. Planning of suitable evaluation design
4. Selection of data-gathering methods and techniques
5. Collection of data and information for evaluation purposes
6. Processing, summarizing, and analyzing of data
7. Reporting of results to appropriate individuals
8. Determination of program effectiveness and financial feasibility

Potential **stakeholders** in the evaluation process include several possible constituents. Scriven (1991) lists the following as potential stakeholders:

Policy makers and decision makers: Persons responsible for deciding whether a program is to be instituted, continued, discontinued, expanded, or curtailed

Program sponsors: Organizations that initiate and fund the program to be evaluated

Evaluation sponsors: Organizations that initiate and fund the evaluation

Target participants: Persons, households, or other units that participate in the program or receive the intervention services under evaluation

Program management: Group responsible for overseeing and coordinating the intervention group

Program staff: Personnel responsible for actual delivery of the intervention (e.g., teachers)

Evaluators: Groups or individuals responsible for the design and/or conduct of the evaluation

Program competitors: Organizations or groups that compete for available resources

Contextual stakeholders: Organizations, groups, individuals, and other entities in the immediate environment of a program (e.g., local government officials, individuals situated on or near the program site)

Evaluation community: Other evaluators, either organized or not, who read and evaluate evaluations for their technical quality (adapted from Payne, 1994, pp. 40, 41)

Within school settings, effective program evaluation can also serve as a political tool (Payne, 1994; Worthen & Sanders, 1987). Teachers who believe in the value of their early childhood programs are frequently called on to justify or substantiate their programs or to otherwise convince administrators, funding sources, and other decision makers that the programs are of value to children and families. Thus, it strengthens a teacher's overall professional skills to be able to determine the value of his or her teaching and program efforts and to document the value of quality early childhood programs.

Program evaluation should be seen as an ongoing process, as opposed to separate and individual, discrete efforts. It is also an important mind-set for the teacher to develop: Quality early childhood programs result from ongoing and continuous documentation and improvement. If teachers can adopt a positive attitude toward the evaluation process, then they are more likely to be successful and confident in conducting evaluations with their own programs. Evaluation is a complex process because it requires a series of steps and activities that take place over a period of time.

Terminology Used in Evaluation

Several terms are used in the evaluation process. These terms are found in textbooks on testing and evaluation and on instruments designed for evaluation purposes. The evaluation terms and definitions listed in Figure 9.4 were derived from Scriven (1991) and were adapted for educational programs suitable for young children. They are standard terms that teachers should be familiar with in order to understand evaluation processes and instruments.

Objective and Subjective Program Evaluation

Since the mid-1960s, new approaches to program evaluation have surfaced. Program evaluation strategies can be very traditional, or they can assume the character of one of the alternative evaluation strategies. Evaluation can be either objective or subjective. On the one hand, *objective evaluation* is more traditional and involves data collection, analysis, and results that are reproducible and, usually, quantifiable. *Subjective evaluation*, on the other hand, bases its validity on the tester's experience and perception. Subjective evaluation is also known as *phenomenologist epistemology* or **phenomenology** (Worthen & Sanders, 1987). The validity of a subjectivist evaluation depends on the relevance of the evaluator's background and qualifications and the keenness of his or her perceptions. In this sense, the evaluation procedures are "internalized," existing largely within the evaluator in ways that are not explicitly understood or reproducible by others (Worthen & Sanders, 1987, p. 46).

In educational settings, objective evaluation has come under fire for not being adaptable or sensitive to settings that require more than quantifiable documentation, such as early childhood settings that place a value on children's and parents' feeling, perceptions, needs, and attitudes. Critics of subjective evaluation note, however, that it is confusing when individual sensory perceptions are to be taken as the basis for understanding. How can one evaluate conflicting interpretations (Worthen & Sanders, 1987)? This ongoing debate over the advantages of **objective versus subjective evaluation** actually contributes to a rigorous and healthy climate for changing strategies in evaluation.

Deciding to evaluate a program or not is a major decision and involves many factors. For a thorough review of the decision-making process about when to conduct an evaluation, please see Worthen & Sanders, 1987, p. 172. Among the considerations discussed by Worthen & Sanders are legal requirements for evaluation, the need to determine impact or importance of an initiative, adequate resources to conduct an evaluation, the need to make significant decisions, the capacity to conduct a legitimate evaluation, and the real need for the evaluation data versus other sources of information.

Anonymity.   The preservation of the anonymity of respondents in an evaluation procedure, which sometimes requires great ingenuity to accomplish.

Attitudes.   The compound of cognitive and affective variables describing a person's mental set toward another person, thing, or state.

Authentic measures.   A test that is nearer to measuring the real ability or achievement level (or cognitive structure) than traditional tests, especially multiple-choice tests. Authentic measures are said to have more complexity, breadth, depth, or number of dimensions of performance.

Baseline.   Refers to data or measures. Facts about the condition or performance of subjects prior to treatment or intervention of some kind.

Behavioral objectives.   Specific goals of, for example, a program, stated in terms that will enable their attainment to be checked by observation or test/measurement.

Case study method.   A method at the opposite end of the spectrum from survey research, the micro end, rather than the macro end. Complements large-scale quantitative research or evaluation by providing detailed descriptions of one or more subjects.

Checklist.   A mnemonic device used to gather systematic information or data about a group, learning environment, or other subject of observation. Consists of categories of descriptors that break down more complex behaviors so that observation and documentation can be done quickly and accurately.

Competency-based.   An approach to teaching or training or evaluating that focuses on identifying the competencies needed by the trainee and on teaching/evaluating to mastery level on these, rather than on teaching allegedly relevant academic areas (Scriven, 1991, p. 84).

Confidentiality.   Providing anonymity to subjects who are participating in evaluation procedures.

Criteria.   Indicators of success or merit that are included in the evaluation process.

Effect.   An outcome or type of outcome.

Evaluation.   Determination of the value or merit of something.

Formative evaluation.   Evaluation conducted during the development and implementation of an educational process or program.

Goal-based evaluation.   Any type of evaluation based on and knowledge of the goals and objectives of the program, person, or product (Scriven, 1991, p. 178).

Interactive evaluation.   Evaluation in which the individuals being evaluated have the opportunity to react to the content of a draft of an evaluation report.

Reliability.   The consistency of measures or readings obtained in any evaluation procedure.

Validity.   A test is valid if it measures what it purports to measure. The phrase "validity of a test" (or an evaluation) really refers to the validity of a claim about its use in a certain context (Scriven, 1991).

Generalizability.   The extent to which the findings can be generalized to other populations or similar contexts. In contrast with research, which has as one of its main purposes to be highly generalizable, evaluation data often focus on the specific situation at hand. Whenever possible, however, the issue of generalizability should be included in devising meaningful evaluation strategies.

Figure 9.4   Common terms used in educational evaluation

Naturalistic, Participant-Oriented Program Evaluation

> The best way to find things out is not to ask questions at all. If you fire off a question, it is like firing off a gun—bang it goes, and everything takes flight and runs for shelter. But if you sit still and pretend not to be looking, all the little facts will come and peck round your feet, situations will venture forth from thickets, and intentions will creep out and sun themselves on a stone; and if you are very patient, you will see and understand a great deal more than a man with a gun does. (Huxley, 1982, cited in Worthen & Sanders, 1987, p. 138)

Worthen and Sanders (1987) describe categories of evaluation strategies commonly used in educational settings: objectives-oriented approaches (described earlier in this chapter); management-oriented approaches; consumer-oriented approaches; expertise-oriented approaches; adversary-oriented approaches; and naturalistic, participant-oriented approaches. We now describe two of these approaches that are suitable particularly for early childhood classrooms: naturalistic, participant-oriented evaluation and consumer-oriented approaches.

The **naturalistic, participant-oriented evaluation** approach is appropriate for early childhood teachers. This approach, begun in 1967 when several evaluation theorists began to react to what they considered to be the dominance of mechanistic and insensitive approaches to evaluation in education, focuses on firsthand experience with educational settings and activities. During the 1970s and 1980s, the naturalistic approach began to flourish, and its growth parallels the proliferation of early childhood programs in the United States. The purpose of the naturalistic approach to evaluation is aimed at observing and identifying all (or as many as possible) concerns, issues, and consequences integral to educational enterprise (Worthen & Sanders, 1987, p. 128). An important aspect of this approach is the belief that program participants themselves should be involved in the endeavor being evaluated. In naturalistic evaluation, the evaluator attempts to represent the different values and needs of all individuals and groups served by the program or curriculum, weighting and balancing this plurality of judgments and criteria in a largely intuitive fashion. Thus, what is weighed to be "best" depends very much on the values and perspectives of whichever groups or individuals are doing the judging. One advantage of this approach is that the evaluator truly values the opinions, perceptions, and values of the program participants, and because of their direct involvement in the evaluation process, program participants end up being well informed about the program itself. For early childhood teachers who want to learn more about naturalistic, participant-oriented program evaluation, we recommend literature written by Stake (1967) and Guba and Lincoln (1981).

The Responsive Evaluation Model

For purposes of illustration, we have selected the **responsive evaluation model** for use in early childhood education classrooms, an example of a naturalistic, participant-oriented evaluation approach. The responsive evaluation model allows the teacher great flexibility in terms of use of the steps, timing of the evaluation process, and selection of the participants. Responsive evaluation's central focus is addressing the concerns and issues of a "stakeholder" audience. Stake (1967) developed this model and states its importance in being *responsive* to realities in the program and to the reactions, concerns, and issues of participants, rather than in being *preordinate* with evaluation plans, relying on preconceptions and formal plans and objectives of the program.

The purpose, framework, and focus of the responsive evaluation approach emerge from interactions with teachers, children, parents, and other constituents in the early childhood learning environment. Responsive evaluators must interact continuously with members of various stakeholding groups to ascertain what information they desire and the way they prefer to receive such information. Stake described the responsive evaluator's role in this way:

> To do a responsive evaluation, the evaluator of course does many things. He makes a plan of observations and negotiations. He arranges for various persons to observe the program. With their help he prepares for brief narratives, portrayals, product displays, graphs, etc. He finds out what is of value to his audience. He gathers expressions of worth from various individuals whose points of view differ. Of course, he checks the quality of his records. He gets program personnel to react to the accuracy of his portrayals. He gets authority figures to react to the importance of various findings. He gets audience members to react to the relevance of his findings. He does much of this informally, iterating and keeping a record of action and reaction. He chooses media accessible to his audiences to increase the likelihood and fidelity of communication. He might prepare a final written report; he might not—depending on what he and his clients have agreed on. (Stake, 1975, p. 11, cited in Worthen & Sanders, 1987, p. 135)

Listed here are the steps to the responsive evaluation model described by Stake. Note that these steps can be placed in a clocklike fashion and can be completed in any desired order. One benefit of this model is its flexibility and adaptability to different settings, populations, and evaluator backgrounds. Imagine these 12 steps as free-floating entities that can be interchanged or addressed in any desired order:

1. Talk with clients, program staff, audiences
2. Identify program scope
3. Overview program activities
4. Discover purposes, concerns
5. Conceptualize issues and problems
6. Identify data needs, re. issues
7. Select observers, judges, instruments, if any
8. Observe designated antecedents, transactions, and outcomes
9. Thematize; prepare portrayals, case studies

10. Validate, confirm, attempt to disconfirm
11. Winnow, formal for audience use
12. Assemble formal reports, if any

Although the evaluator might begin the evaluation at the 12 o'clock and proceed clockwise, Stake emphasizes that any event can follow any other event and that at any point the evaluator may want to move counterclockwise or crossclockwise; many steps will occur several times during an evaluation. The "clock" serves to remind us that flexibility is an important part of using this naturalistic, participant-oriented approach (Worthen & Sanders, 1987).

Consumer-Oriented Evaluation Approach

The **consumer-oriented evaluation** approach is mainly a summative evaluation strategy. The developers of educational products, materials, and equipment, however, have used such tools as checklists and lists of criteria for evaluation purposes while the products and other items were being developed. This provides more of a formative use of evaluation. The 1960s saw an influx of new materials, equipment, and products in the educational arena. Prior to that time, textbooks were the main products of the educational field (Worthen & Sanders, 1987). Scriven made major contributions to this approach by recognizing the need for, and the value of, summative evaluation approaches for decision making. Scriven developed criteria for use in evaluating any educational product (e.g., program, material, product, piece of equipment):

- Evidence of achievement of significant or major educational objectives
- Evidence of achievement of important non-educational objectives
- Follow-up results
- Secondary and unintended effects, such as effects on the teacher, the teacher's colleagues, other students, administrators, parents, the school, the taxpayer, and other incidental positive or negative effects
- Range of utility (that is, for whom will it be useful)
- Moral considerations (unjust uses of punishment or controversial content)
- Costs (Scriven, 1967, cited in Worthen & Sanders, 1987, p. 88)

Other checklists and product analysis tools emerged, developed by such individuals as Komoski (1987), who is considered a leader in this effort. A variety of product evaluation checklists have been developed and used during the past several years by individual evaluators and agencies too. A key questions is, What does one need to know about a product before deciding whether to adapt or install it? Other questions posed within each checklist include the following:

Process Information

1. What is the nature and frequency of interactions among students/ teachers/administrators/relevant others? Have these interactions been evaluated?

2. Is the teaching strategy to be employed described so that its appropriateness can be determined? Has the strategy been evaluated?

3. Is the instructional schedule required by the program or product described so that its feasibility can be determined? Has the schedule been evaluated?

4. Are the equipment and facilities required by the program or product described so that their feasibility can be determined? Have they been evaluated?

5. Are the budget and human resource requirements of the program or product listed so that their feasibility can be determined? Have the following requirements been included?

6. Is evaluation an integral part of the (a) development and (b) implementation of the program or product?

Content Information

1. Is the existence or lack of basic program or product elements, such as the following, noted?

   Clearly stated objectives?

   Sufficient directions?

   Other materials required?

   Prerequisite knowledge/attitudes required?

   Fit with disciplinary knowledge base and existing curriculum and sequence of a school?

2. Have these elements been evaluated?

3. Has the content of the program or product been evaluated by recognized content specialists?

4. Is there sufficient information about the program or product rationale and philosophy to permit a decision about whether it is within the realm of school responsibility or consist with a district's philosophy?

5. Do the objectives of the program or product have cogent rationales? Are they compatible with the school philosophy and the values of the community? (Worthen & Sanders, 1987, p. 94)

The consumer-oriented approach to evaluation is not without drawbacks. It can increase the cost of educational products, and the time and money invested in product testing will usually be passed on to the consumer. However, the consumer-oriented approach does provide a manageable tool for

educators to use in evaluating early childhood programs, program components, educational materials or products developed within the early childhood program, and so forth. For example, an early childhood teacher could
use the consumer-oriented evaluation approach to evaluate such educational products as family portfolios, student portfolios, parent walls, and
special curriculum-related materials and products used in the early childhood classroom. In this case, the teacher would seek the input of parents,
children, administrators, and outside experts in order to gather comprehensive information about the usefulness and appropriateness of this particular educational product or initiative.

◊◊ Recommended Assessment and Evaluation Resources for Teachers and Parents

Portfolio Assessment

Calfee, R. C., & Perfumo, R. C. (1993, April). Student portfolios: Opportunities for a revolution in assessment. *Journal of Reading, 36*(7), 532–537.

> A survey reports rapid growth in the use of portfolios and raises con-
> cerns about its effective use.

Farr, R. (1991). Portfolios; Assessment in language arts. *ERIC Digest* (ERIC
document ED3346093). Bloomington, IN: ERIC Clearinghouse on Reading
and Communication Skills.

> This is a summary of the rationale for using portfolio assessment, stress-
> ing how portfolios can serve multiple purposes, address language arts
> goals, and serve as *authentic* assessments.

Johns, J. L., & Leirsburg, P. V. (1992, Fall). How professionals view portfolio assessment. *Reading Research and Instruction, 32*(1), 1–10.

> In comparing current results of an ongoing study to previous studies,
> researchers found that educators' familiarity with portfolios is increasing
> and that fewer practical problems in using them are being reported. Still,
> users express concerns with planning, managing, and "organizing" them.

Miller, M. L. (1992, June). The ins and outs of portfolios. *Communiqué,
20*(6), 3, 4.

> This perspective in a publication of the National Association of School
> Psychologists describes portfolio assessment as a viable multidimen-
> sional evaluation.

Steward, R. A., et al. (1993, March). Portfolios: Agents of change (Have you
read?). *Reading Teacher, 46*(6), 522–524.

> This review of three textbooks on portfolios in reading and writing class-
> rooms published in 1991 and 1992 recommends portfolios, but with
> some caveats.

Valencia, S. (1990). A portfolio approach to classroom reading assessment: The whys, whats, and hows. *Reading Teacher, 43*(4), 338–440.

This short article argues that theory, research, and instructional experiences recommend a portfolio approach to reading assessment.

Wiggins, G. (1989, April). Teaching to the (authentic) test. *Educational Leadership, 46*(7), 41–47.

A leading authority recommends portfolios as one form of authentic assessment, offering a descriptive example.

Performance Assessment

Brandt, R. (1992, May). On performance assessment: A conversation with Grant Wiggins. *Educational Leadership, 49*(8), 35–37.

Wiggins expresses concerns about assessment reforms failing because high stakes will be attached to them too soon and judgments will be unreliable. He urges attention to task validity, score reliability, portfolio sampling, and solving problems related to generalizability.

Coley, R. J. (Ed.). (1990, August). Testing. *ETS Policy Notes, 2*(3).

This issue includes one article that discuses the role of testing in educational reform and one that describes some work done in Connecticut in the area of student performance assessment and in two other innovative assessment programs.

Feuer, M. J., & Fulton, K. J. (1993, February). The many faces of performance assessment. *Phi Delta Kappan, 74*(6), 478.

Performance assessment is defined as seven common forms that include both analysis of student writing in general and portfolios.

Gardner, H. (1991). *The unschooled mind: How children think and how schools should teach.* New York: Basic Books.

An expert on understanding the development of the human mind makes an eloquent plea for educational reformation that will help students move beyond rote learning to achieve genuine understanding. Gardner makes use of what is known about human development and cognitive science, turning it into well-grounded advice that is both practical and very readable.

Hansen, J. B. (1992). *A purpose-driven assessment program.* Paper presented at the annual meeting of the American Educational Research Association.

This paper describes the assessment program of the Colorado Springs (Colorado) Public Schools. It includes norm-referenced, criterion-referenced, and performance-based assessment, which includes "direct writing" and portfolio assessment. (ERIC document ED344928)

Linn, R. L., Baker, E. L., & Dunbar, S. (1991, November). Complex, performance-based assessment: Expectations and validation criteria. *Educational Research, 20*(8), 15–21.

This article makes a case for developing assessment criteria that are sensitive to the expectations for new assessments. It includes a list of 51 relevant references.

Moss, P. A., et al. (1992, Fall). Portfolios, accountability, and an interview approach to validity. *Educational Measurement: Issues and Practice, 11*(3), 12–21.

This article provides answers to questions related to the reporting of portfolio assessment results to audiences interested in school accountability, recommending that it is time to explore alternative assessments. The questions include, How can the results of classroom-based portfolio assessment be communicated outside the classroom? How might a portfolio-based assessment system be designed and implemented? How can we evaluate the merits of portfolio-based assessments?

O'Neil, J. (1992, May). Putting performance assessment to the test. *Educational Leadership, 49*(8), 14–19.

This article reports that officials in Vermont, California, Kentucky, Maryland, and other states are betting that performance assessments may prove as powerful a classroom influence as short-answer testing used to be.

Resnick, L. B., & Resnick, D. P. (1989, October). *Tests as standards of achievement in schools.* Paper presented at the Invitational Conference of the Educational Testing Service.

The question whether tests can be both curriculum-neutral and effective means of monitoring and motivating educational practice is discussed. Educational reform is linked directly with assessment reform. (ERIC document ED335421)

Werner, P. H. (1992, February). Integrated assessment system. *Journal of Reading, 35*(5), 416–418.

This is a descriptive review of the Integrated Assessment System published by the Psychological Corporation.

Wolfe, D. P., et al. (1992, May). Good measure: Assessment as a tool for educational reform. *Educational Leadership, 49*(8), 8–13.

This article argues that portfolios are essential as tools of educational reform that will lead to individual and internal accountability in schools.

Worthen, B., Borg, W. R., & White, K. R. (1993). *Measurement and evaluation in the schools.* New York: Longman.

This comprehensive examination of educational measurement covers all traditional concerns, creating and selecting assessment for the classroom, and designing school- and districtwide assessment programs.

Newsletters Published on Portfolios

Portfolio Assessment Clearinghouse. San Dieguito Union High School District, 710 Encinitas Boulevard, Encinitas, CA 92024.

Portfolio News. Published by the Northwest Evaluation Association, P.O. Box 2122, Lake Oswego, OR 97035

Authentic Assessment with Families and Parents

Berger, E. H. (1991). *Parents as partners in education: The school and home working together.* New York: Merrill/Macmillan.

> This book contains the following two instruments:
>
> *Teacher's Attitude About Collaborating with Parents.*
>
> A very straightforward instrument developed to assess the teacher's own attitudes about working with parents and families (p. 124).
>
> *How Do You Collaborate with Parents Now?*
>
> A questionnaire designed to assess the current methods of collaboration used by the classroom teacher (p. 125).

Roberts, T. W. (1994). *A systems perspective of parenting: The individual, the family, and the social network.* Pacific Grove, CA: Brooks/Cole.

General Assessment for Early Childhood Classrooms

Bredekamp, S., & Rosegrant, T. (Eds.). (1992). *Reaching potentials: Appropriate curriculum and assessment of young children* (Vol. 1). Washington, DC: National Association for the Education of Young Children.

Kamii, C. (1990). *Achievement testing in the early grades: The games grown-ups play.* Washington, DC: National Association for the Education of Young Children.

Leavitt, R. B., & Eheart, B. K. (1991). Assessment in early childhood programs. *Young Children, 46*(5), 4–9.

Marsden, D. B., Meisels, S. J., & Jablon, J. R. (1993). *The Work Sampling System: Preschool through grade three.* Ann Arbor: University of Michigan, Center for Human Growth and Development.

Meisels, S. J. (1987). Uses and abuses of developmental screening and school readiness testing. *Young Children, 42*(2), 4–6, 68–73.

National Association for the Education of Young Children (NAEYC) & National Association of Early Childhood Specialists in State Departments of Education (NAECS/SDE). (1991). Guidelines for appropriate curriculum content and assessment in programs serving children ages three through eight. *Young Children, 46*(3), 21–38.

Formal Rapid Assessment Instruments

For early childhood teachers interested in more quantitative and formal assessment of the parents and families in their learning settings, the following instruments may be used with the assistance of a school or community professional counselor or psychologist. Information from these instruments should remain confidential and are designed for programs that have structured and defined parent involvement program components.

> Parent-Child Relationship Survey
>
> Environmental Assessment Index
>
> Family Adaptability and Cohesion Evaluation Scale
>
> Family Assessment Device
>
> Family-of-Origin Scale
>
> Family Times and Routines Index
>
> Family Traditions Scales
>
> Kansas Family Life Satisfaction Scale
>
> Kansas Parent Satisfaction Scale
>
> Family Functioning Scale

These instruments are included in:

Fischer, J., & Corcoran, K. (1994). *Measures for clinical practice* (2nd ed., Vol. 1). New York: Free Press.

Summary Statements ◇

- A new era of assessment and evaluation in early childhood education now encourages the use of qualitative methods such as portfolios.

- Evaluation and assessment should allow for creative and individual designs to determine the value and quality of parent and family involvement.

- No one model for educational evaluation is best; use of eclectic and systems evaluation models are encouraged.

- Accountability issues never have been greater in early childhood school settings; thus, the need for ongoing and appropriate methods of assessment and evaluation are crucial.

- *Authentic assessment* is a standard term now used to describe efforts to assess a program, outcome, or process in a way that is sensitive to and matches the character and type of learning process used.

- National educational and advocacy organizations for young children and school-age children recommend the use of developmentally appropriate assessment and evaluation strategies for young children and their families.

- Early childhood teachers may feel uncomfortable with assessment and evaluation, and teachers should assess their own attitudes and aptitudes in this area.

- Assessment refers to informal and divergent ways of determining individual and parent needs, of documenting work processes and products, and of measuring program merit.

- Evaluation refers to quantitative and formalized ways of measuring program effectiveness and quality; measuring child, parent, and family outcomes; and determining whether programs should be continued.

- Summative evaluation refers to evaluation conducted at the conclusion of a program initiative, whereas formative evaluation refers to measures taken during developmental and ongoing phases of the program initiative.

- The objectives-oriented evaluation approach, conceptualized by Tyler and Tuba, has been used extensively in educational settings; it is a traditional model.

- Needs assessments are administered at the beginning of the academic year or educational initiative to determine individual program needs and to establish baseline data.

- Authentic assessment involves the use of creative approaches, emphasizes and celebrates development and learning based on real-life events, is performance-based, relates to instruction, is collaborative, and provides a broad and general picture of student learning and capabilities.

- Formal assessment refers to the use of standardized instruments, whereas informal assessment provides greater latitude for parent expression and demonstration of skills, attitudes, and efforts.

- Needs assessment and program planning for parents and families are not separate processes, but rather are closely intertwined.

- Family involvement can be shaped around relevant and meaningful themes that are decided jointly between teachers and parents.

- Documentation of parent involvement events and activities should build on the characteristics of the building and classroom, as well as the collective skills and interests of the parents involved.

- A parent wall is a family involvement strategy adapted from Reggio Emilia programs of Northern Italy.

- Family portfolios are collections of writings, photographs, and other documentation materials that reflect the shared learning experiences of children, parents, and siblings.

- Portfolio assessment encourages self-directed learning, documentation of work, and shared decision making. Portfolios can assume many formats, shapes, and sizes.

- Each school setting has its own history of program evaluation, and each teacher should develop a meaningful program evaluation process that builds on past successful experiences and encourages new, creative evaluation approaches.

- Program evaluation serves many purposes in educational settings and serves as a basis for decision making, policy formation, student achievement assessment, evaluation of curricula, accreditation processes, monitoring of fiscal expenditures, and improvement of educational materials and programs.

- Naturalistic, participant-oriented program evaluation is a more contemporary approach aimed at observing and identifying concerns, issues, and consequences integral to educational experiences.

- The responsive education model is appropriate for use in early childhood classrooms; it is characterized by fluid steps, involvement of all stakeholders, and informal observation and recording of information and data.

- Consumer-oriented evaluation is an appropriate model for some early childhood programs in which program products, materials, or concrete outcomes are evaluated. It is a very discrete approach involving the use of checklists and other quantitative ways of determining the value and merit of educational products.

- Assessment and evaluation instruments and tools should be selected from a wide array of available resources designed by the teacher to measure the unique aspects of his or her program and used creatively to reflect the teacher's philosophy of program development and implementation.

Activities ◊

1. As a preassessment tool, write about your own perceptions of assessment and evaluation. Think back to your early years of schooling and recall how your attitudes toward tests were formed. (Note: This exercise can be used as a pre- and posttest.) Write about your new perceptions of assessment and evaluation at the end of this chapter.

2. Join other students in teams of two or three and develop an outline for a family portfolio. Then, each team divides tasks and responsibilities and creates a skeleton family portfolio. Display your portfolio at a Portfolio Day in class and view each other's work.

3. Develop a resource list of assessment and evaluation instruments and resources. Categorize these items under specific topics, such as parent education, family involvement, child development, problem solving, family history and preservation, technology, human diversity, and selected curriculum areas.

4. Invite a panel of five or six parents of early childhood education (ECE) students (birth to age 8) to class to discuss their feelings, attitudes, perceptions, and concerns about parent involvement programs in school settings.

5. Make a plan for a bulletin board that explains and depicts authentic assessment. Identify the target audience for the bulletin board: parents, policymakers, other teachers, administrators, other college students, and so on.

6. Complete Berger's attitude instrument on collaborating with parents. Share the results with other students (from E. H. Berger [1991]. *Parents as partners in education: The school and home working together* [3rd ed., p. 125]).

7. As a college class, develop a shared list of interview questions and then interview from three to five parents about their attitudes toward participating in parent and family involvement programs in school settings. Share the results of the interviews; collate the data and distribute to other class members.

8. Select an early childhood classroom teacher in a school or child care setting. With the ECE teacher, develop an overall draft assessment and evaluation strategy for 1 academic year. Write up and turn in the results as an assignment.

References ◊

Berger, E. H. (1981). *Parents as partners in education: The school and home working together.* St. Louis: C. V. Mosby.

Berger, E. H. (1991). *Parents as partners in education: The school and home working together* (3rd ed.). New York: Merrill/Macmillan.

Bredekamp, S. & Rosegrant, T. (Eds.). (1992). *Reaching potentials: Appropriate curriculum and assessment of young children* (Vol. 1). Washington, DC: National Association for the Education of Young Children.

Brophy, K., Grotelueschen, A., & Gooler, D. (1974). *A blueprint for program evaluation* (Occasional Paper No. 1). Urbana-Champaign: University of Illinois, College of Education, Office for Professional Services.

Edwards, C., Gandini, L., & Forman, G. (1993). *The hundred languages of children.* Norwood, NJ: Ablex.

Farr, R., & Tone, B. (1994). *Portfolio performance assessment.* Fort Worth, TX: Harcourt Brace.

Guba, E. G., & Lincoln, Y. S. (1981). *Effective evaluation.* San Francisco: Jossey-Bass.

Komoski, P. K. (1987). Beyond innovation: The systemic integration of technology into the curriculum. *Educational Technology, 27*(9), 21–25.

Maykut, P., & Morehouse, R. (1994). *Beginning qualitative research.* London: Falmer Press.

National Association for the Education of Young Children (NAEYC) & National Association of Early Childhood Specialists in State Departments of Education (NAECS/SDE). (1991). Guidelines for appropriate curriculum content and assessment in programs serving children ages three through eight. *Young Children, 46*(3), 21–38.

National Association of State Boards of Education (NASBE). (1988). *Right from the start: The report of the NASBE Task Force on Early Childhood Education.* Alexandria, VA: Author.

Payne, D. A. (1994). *Designing educational project and program evaluations.* Boston: Kluwer.

Puckett, M. B., & Black, J. K. (1994). *Authentic assessment of the young child.* Upper Saddle River, NJ: Merrill/Prentice Hall.

Scriven, M. (1991). *Evaluation thesaurus* (4th ed.). London: Sage.

Scriven, M. (1993). *Hard-won lessons in program evaluation* (New Directions in Program Evaluation, No. 58). San Francisco: Jossey-Bass.

Southern Early Childhood Association. (1992). *Developmentally appropriate assessment: A position paper.* Little Rock, AR: Author.

Stake, R. E. (1967). The countenance of educational evaluation. *Teachers College Record, 68*, 523–540.

Taba, H. (1962). *Curriculum development.* New York: Harcourt, Brace, & World.

Webster's new world dictionary (Concise ed.). (1960). New York: World.

Worthen, B. R., & Sanders, J. R. (1987). *Educational evaluation: Alternative approaches and practical guidelines.* New York: Longman.

10 Parent and Child Advocacy

The Role of the School and the Early Childhood Professional

The worlds of early childhood education and the . . . schools are intertwined in several ways. For instance, one important part of the mission of early childhood programs is to prepare children for success in school. In the minds of parents, the "proof of the pudding" for a successful early childhood program lies in the reception of its "graduates" by the public school. This expectation is shared by policymakers choosing to invest public dollars in early childhood services.

Schultz, 1992, p. 137

Key Terms

Americans with Disabilities Act
   (ADA)
barriers to advocacy
child advocacy
child development associate
child poverty rates
collaboration
DAP
deficit model
early intervention
family advocacy
family policy
First Sixty Months
four C's
Great Society
Head Start
NAEYC

NASBE
National Governors Association
parent activist group
parent interest group
P.L. 99-457
P.L. 101-476
P.L. 102-119
policy process
project approach
PTO/PTA
public choice theory
Reggio Emilia approach
Right from the Start
special education
vertical collaboration
zeitgeist

Schools provide more services for children and parents today than ever before. One of the more recent roles of the school is that of a forum for child and family advocacy, a reflection of the consumer-orientation of parents today. In terms of advocacy, the rationale for the natural linkages between school and family is strong. Perhaps the most widely recommended "solution" to the problems that confront American society is more and better schooling (Dye, 1992, p. 162). Social science research also suggests that when children perceive that the school is an extension of or substitute for their families, academic performance is enhanced. In addition, parents choices among schools and school options not only improve academic achievement but also increase parents' satisfaction and teacher morale (Dye, 1992).

Providing an opportunity for parents to voice their concerns and issues in a constructive and organized manner is an important advocacy role for schools that serve young children. From a policy perspective, the issues that affect parents, families, and children have never been more significant or visible. The evolution of child and family policy to the forefront of both state and federal legislative agendas is unprecedented (Kagan, 1989, 1992; Stegelin, 1992; Weikart, 1989). Significant pieces of legislation that affect the well-being of children with special needs and their families have been discussed already in this book (see Chapter 5, P.L. 99-457, and the IDEA legislation). In addition, the emergence of the Reggio Emilia approach to

Schools provide more services today for parents than ever before.

early childhood education is providing convincing evidence of the power of parent involvement and the significant contributions parents can make to the curriculum and quality of their children's daily school lives.

Justifying the school's role in supporting advocacy efforts is not difficult, as considerable documentation establishes a clear relationship between successful experiences during the early childhood years and subsequent adult development (Lazar, Darlington, Murray, Royce, & Snipper, 1982; Schweinhart & Weikart, 1986, 1992). Add to this research documentation the U.S. demographic data reflecting increased maternal employment; higher divorce rates, **child poverty rates,** and at-risk status; increased incidence of HIV/AIDS and drug-related cases; and the changing welfare scenario, and the result is a growing need for parents and children to be supported and empowered through effective advocacy.

This chapter addresses the role of the school and the early childhood professional in collaborating with parents and families to ensure that the voice of the child and her parents and family will be heard by decision makers who develop, implement, and evaluate child and family policy, particularly as it relates to the care and education of young children. Included in Chapter 10 are the following topics:

- Definitions of child and family advocacy
- Brief history of the evolution of family policy
- Advocacy strategies in early childhood settings
- Examples of recent advocacy initiatives
- Role of the school in child and family advocacy
- Collaboration and its role in child and family advocacy

> Never before have so many different individuals, child populations, interest groups and agencies been involved in the early childhood movement. . . . . There is a wide window of opportunity for parents, teachers, school officials, and state education officials to impact directly the policy process on behalf of young children. (Stegelin, 1992, p. x)

◊◊ Child and Family Advocacy: Definitions and History

> For as long as I can remember, Americans have found it very difficult to talk about family policy as a political issue. I think that is largely because we are a country that has (as one of its foremost values) the importance of individualism, the importance of individual families, and the idea that the government ought not to reach into individual or family life any more than is absolutely necessary. Furthermore, I think that whenever we talk about family policy as a political issue, we can't help bringing to bear our own experiences and our own understandings. Sometimes, that can be very painful, and it is always very personal. (Clinton, 1992, p. 21)

Definitions

Advocacy, according to *Merriam-Webster's Collegiate Dictionary* (1993), is "the act of advocating or supporting a cause or proposal" (p. 18). The term *advocacy* is used in this text to refer to organized efforts and initiatives that have as their goal or cause the improvement of services and programs for young children, their parents, and/or their families. **Child advocacy** refers to focused initiatives to improve services for children in general or a target group of children with defined needs. **Family advocacy** refers to advocacy initiatives designed to better the lives of all families or families with specific or defined needs. *Advocacy* is also used in a broad manner to include both formal and informal efforts to seek needed services, enhancements, visibility, and innovations related to meeting the needs of young children and their families. Advocacy and policy are surely related, as focused, well-organized advocacy initiatives can result in policy changes.

Formal advocacy efforts are sometimes associated with official policy-making efforts. James Buchanan, the Nobel-Prize-winning economist and leading scholar in modern **public choice theory,** argues that individuals come together in the political process for their own mutual benefit. Public choice theory assumes that all political actors—parents, teachers, voters, taxpayers, interest groups, and other constituents—seek to maximize their personal benefits in politics, as well as in the marketplace (Dye, 1992).

Within the school setting, the roles of individuals related to child and family advocacy can range from very informal efforts at the local, grassroots level to moderately formalized efforts at the regional level to more formal and organized advocacy efforts that may lead directly to new legislation, change, or revision in existing law or other formal outcomes. Most parents and teachers of young children are engaged in less formal advocacy efforts, such as voting on educational options within a local school district, serving as assistants at the voting booths during elections, or actively engaging in a campaign effort for a local candidate who embraces a new idea or notion that will result in a desired educational outcome.

Some parents and teachers, however, are engaged actively in formalized advocacy efforts that lead directly to new legislation or policy changes within school settings. These individuals may hold offices in decision-making groups that effect change within the educational community, serve as representatives for a local or state jurisdiction, or actually vote directly on legislative initiatives. Thus, the range of involvement in advocacy efforts varies greatly in most school settings.

Barriers to Advocacy Efforts

According to Lombardi (1986), individuals such as early childhood teachers and parents of young children are frequently hesitant to become involved in advocacy or policy-related efforts on behalf of children and families. Common **barriers to advocacy** include the following:

- Feelings of powerlessness to change anything
- Lack of knowledge regarding government regulations
- Fear of the political process
- Lack of confidence in their own expertise
- Lack of time (p. 65)

As an example of the difficulty and challenge of making educational change in early childhood education, Schultz (1992) assessed the complexity of integrating developmentally appropriate practice (**DAP**) in early childhood school settings and identified six inhibitors to its quick and universal implementation:

1. The size and complexity of the educational system
2. The complexity of decision making
3. The scope of changes required in implementing DAP
4. The current policy focus on accountability
5. The shifting, never-ending demands placed on the educational system, making it difficult for schools to focus on any one agenda
6. The competing ideas and "packages of curriculum" promoted for early childhood education

Parents may sometimes feel powerless to make change in a school setting.

In short, the advocacy process for teachers and parents within a school setting can be viewed as a series of political processes and activities that involve problem identification, formulation, legitimation, implementation, and evaluation (Dye, 1992). Advocacy, as used in this text, refers to more informal political processes on behalf of children and their families. But as the steps described above suggest, advocacy efforts can become, with time and organizational commitments, very real and effective political activities and processes.

Parents who function within school systems today are more informed and consumer-oriented than their predecessors. They, with the support of informed and supportive teachers, can make a difference for children and families because they are in a position of being able to identify salient issues as a consumer and then to organize, collaborate, and communicate with decision makers so that services and programs for young children continuously improve.

> When schools were an integral part of stable communities, teachers quite naturally reinforced parental and community values. At school, children easily formed bonds with adults and experienced a sense of continuity and stability, conditions that were highly conducive to learning. (Comer, 1990, p. 23)

History

Pre-World War II Era. Child and family policy has evolved primarily through the outcomes of wars and national crises. During these times, families have had to rely on extraordinary means to meet the demands of child care and family support (Stegelin, 1992). The earliest efforts to advocate for children and families can be found in the initiatives to establish child care services for families in the 1800s. Child care began in the 1800s as a charitable function for women who worked outside the home only out of economic necessity, usually widows or wives of incapacitated husbands (Farnum, 1987). One of the first real national crises that resulted in expanded child needs was the Civil War. According to Farnum (1987), in the aftermath of the Civil War, churches and communities in some eastern cities developed children's charities that cared for children while their mothers worked. These early initiatives at establishing child care were more like orphanages than today's developmentally appropriate child care settings but are significant because they were the first vestiges of systematic child care in the United States.

The Depression brought about a few child care centers that provided meals, play, and parent education. It was World War II, however, that brought government into the child care business in a major way. Large centers for child care were developed in areas where many women were employed in munitions plants, shipyards, and other war-related industries. The growth of the child development movement in the United States during the 1920s also raised the awareness of the well-being of the young child. University laboratory schools were established across the country and were used primarily as a means of studying young children (Irwin & Bushnell, 1980) and observing and recording their typical and atypical growth and development. Although it would take 50 years, until the 1970s, before child advocacy and active pro-child legislation would come into fruition, the establishment of this network of laboratory schools serves as an important benchmark in the history of child development and child advocacy.

Post-World War II Era. The era after World War II served as a transitional period. American families were changing rapidly, and child care was emerging as a growing need for these families. The persistent efforts of such states as California were responsible for the maintenance of the momentum toward national child care concern and public policy.

In the 1960s, the research focus on children grew dramatically. Coupled with the child-focused initiatives of President Lyndon Johnson's **Great Society,** this research focus began to address such issues as the disadvantaged and at-risk child. The 1960s saw a renaissance of interest in early childhood education as a means of addressing issues related to child and family poverty (Schweinhart & Weikart, 1986). Also, a clear link between the positive outcomes of early childhood programs for children from low-income families and longitudinal research findings was established. The **early intervention** movement began to emerge, couched primarily within a **deficit model.** At that point, early childhood intervention represented the main early childhood initiative. As a result, federal and state funds began to be used for programs for young children before they entered public school settings. Kindergarten programs expanded, and the Head Start program was born. Thus, the 1960s marked a significant passage for early childhood policy. The field began to be defined as more than child care, and in its place came the concept of *early childhood education* as being a comprehensive, developmental focus on young children, ages birth to 8 years, with special attention to youngsters with special needs (Stegelin, 1992).

The 1970s was a decade of expansion of programs and initiatives for young children and their families. Teacher training programs proliferated in the areas of child development and early childhood education. The federally sponsored **Child Development Associate** program was born in an effort to make available competency-based training programs for individuals who desired to work with younger children. Research methods became more refined and collaborative. Such fields as education, sociology, psychology, medicine, and related areas began to conduct interdisciplinary research on children and families. Parent education became an important and noted part of educational settings for young children. Children began to be viewed as complex, evolving individuals who have very special developmental needs in four distinct areas: social, cognitive, emotional, and psychomotor.

The New Era. The 1980s marked an escalation in policy efforts for young children. For example, the **National Governors Association** focused on chil-

The 1960s brought about the Great Society and new programs for young children, such as Head Start.

dren's issues and hosted a national conference and final report entitled *First Sixty Months* (National Governors Association & Center for Policy Research, 1987). Then Governor Richard Riley of South Carolina urged governors to continue playing expanding roles in the development of legislation to support early childhood education programs (Riley, 1986). Over half the states adopted new legislation that expanded programs for young children (Schweinhart & Weikart, 1986), and New York City's prekindergarten program was established for more than 100,000 4-year-olds (McCormick, 1986). **Head Start** continued to expand at the federal level, and a general awareness of "early childhood education" developed in both federal and state policy arenas. By the end of the 1980s, 3 out of every 10 U.S. children under the age of 5 were enrolled in child care homes, child care centers, or nursery schools (Schweinhart, 1992). The 100th Congress introduced more than 100 child- and family-related bills, many of them with bipartisan sponsorship (Kagan, 1989). In 1988, the National Association of State Boards of Education (**NASBE**) released a comprehensive Task Force Report entitled *Right from the Start,* which advocated a clear and defined role and responsibility of the public schools in the development of futuristic early childhood education programs for young children and their families. During the 1980s, state departments of education also established new divisions of early childhood education that were designed to strengthen both the research and practice components of the public school's involvement with young children.

During the 1990s, policy on behalf of children and families came full-circle. Once an uncomfortable issue, **family policy** came into its own during this decade as political candidates embraced platforms that openly addressed such issues as family medical leave, maternity and paternity leave, child care vouchers, services for special needs children, and advocacy rights of parents and families. Presidential candidates' campaigns featured young children and their parents' needs and concerns related to accessible, affordable, and appropriate child care, as well as government-sponsored school programs for younger children, both typical and atypical in their development.

Toffler, in *The Third Wave* (1981), stated, "A powerful tide is surging across much of the world today creating a new, often bizarre, environment in which to work, play, marry, raise children or retire" (p. 1). Innovative school-business partnerships continued to develop during the 1990s as corporate America awakened to the crucial needs of working parents and young children in a variety of ways. School-business partnerships focused on providing more child care options for employees, as well as on forming formal working relationships between corporations and specific schools for the purposes of financial assistance and innovative program development. Corporations came to be more concerned about the well-being of young children and the skill levels of American school children in the areas of literacy and mathematics. Quality early childhood education programs came to be seen as a wise investment in the future workforce and as a guarantee that the Baby Boomer generation would be supported adequately by a well-prepared and well-educated younger generation of workers.

Changing Definition of the Child

The evolution of policy for young children mirrors a changing definition of the child in U.S. culture. As the 1990s began to unfold in the United States, the ways Americans viewed the child reflected deeply rooted changes in the fabric of society (Stegelin, 1992). The deficit model associated with the early intervention movement begun in the 1960s gave way to a more comprehensive and holistic view of the child as part of a functioning, vital family constellation. As a result of seven decades of building a policy agenda in support of the young child and her or his family, the term *early childhood education* has come to have a collective meaning that includes child care, early intervention, at-risk, preschool, kindergarten, and a host of family support and parent education programs.

It is politically correct to act on behalf of young children, their parents, and their families. The new millennium lies close at hand, and the need to provide a rationale and argument for quality programs for children and families has evolved into a need to develop new and innovative state and federal policies that combine existing resources so that collaborative programs for children and parents are an integral part of our educational system. Kagan (1989) described this evolution of early childhood policy as a much more sophisticated, integrated, comprehensive, and family-oriented level of program and policy operation than the United States had experienced prior to the 1980s.

◊◊ **Effective Advocacy Strategies for Parents and Teachers**

From the preceding discussion, it is apparent that advocacy efforts and policy initiatives, even those developed informally by parents in school settings, can be creative, imaginative, purposeful, and effective. This section focuses on several types or strategies of advocacy for children and families within school (school or child care arrangements) settings.

Dye (1992) describes several noted models of politics in his book *Understanding Public Policy.* Dye's understanding of the policy process is clear, and he suggests the following guidelines to determine whether a strategy or process is being effective for its given purpose:

• The strategy should order and simplify reality.
• The strategy should identify what is significant.
• The strategy should be congruent with reality.
• The strategy should facilitate meaningful communication.
• The strategy should direct inquiry and research.
• The strategy should suggest explanations and solutions.

Advocacy efforts on behalf of young children and their families that occur within school settings can take many forms. These informal but organized efforts may, for example, take a simple but effective direction, described as **policy process.** According to Dye (1992), the general outline for this approach is the following:

Identifying a Problem	Demands are expressed for government action
Formulating Policy Proposals	Agenda is set for public discussion
	Development of program proposals to resolve problem
Legitimating Policies	Selecting a proposal
	Building political support for it
	Enacting it as law
Implementing Policies	Organizing bureaucracies
	Providing payments or services
	Levying taxes
Evaluating Policies	Studying programs
	Reporting "outputs" of government programs
	Evaluating "impacts" of programs on target and nontarget groups in society
	Suggesting changes and adjustments

Advocacy efforts on behalf of young children can take many forms.

Following is a discussion of advocacy strategies that have been effective in early childhood settings. These strategies are less formal than organized political action groups, but they may evolve from grassroots advocacy initiatives to more systematically organized political processes.

Parent Interest Groups

A **parent interest group** may formulate its own policy proposals, perhaps in association with key decision makers within the school setting or the surrounding community. These key individuals might include a school administrator, superintendent, local political representative, respected community leader, Congressional Representative, and other appropriate individuals. Interest group staff often bring valuable technical knowledge to the formation of a policy process. An interest group forms when a sufficient number of individuals, usually parents and teachers, desire to address a specific issue or concern. Examples of interest groups that might form within the school setting for young children are:

Attention deficit disorder	Sex education
Down syndrome	Child management and discipline

Learning disabled	Drug awareness and prevention
After-school care	Technology in the school and home
Nutrition and health issues	Curriculum integration
School transportation	Testing and assessment
HIV/AIDS	Developmentally appropriate learning settings
Mixed-age classrooms	Inclusion in the classroom

Interest groups can vary widely in terms of size, frequency of meeting, diversity of parent makeup, resources available, and amount of school personnel support. Interest groups can serve multiple purposes:

- Provide an informal forum for parents, teachers, and other individuals to discuss a focused issue or concern
- Serve as a springboard for a formal advocacy or policy initiative
- Serve as a means of bringing diverse families together
- Can become a community source of information and can serve in a collaborative role with other community agencies
- Provide current information through the sharing of books, journals, magazines, videos, and other educational means in an inexpensive, timely way
- Provide a forum for constructive dialogue between parents and teachers or other school representatives
- Can become part of the systematic parent education and family involvement component of the school setting

Parent-Organized Advocacy or Activist Groups

Parents can be tremendously effective in forming their own power-based groups, especially if (a) a central and committed core group of parents serve as leaders, (b) the level of commitment to the project is high, (c) parents understand the give-and-take of the policy process, (d) parents understand the time that will be required, and (e) parents are able to solicit and recruit effective individuals to help them with their cause.

For example, Anderson (1992) describes her efforts as a parent involved with a **parent activist group** advocating for a developmentally appropriate curriculum and classroom for kindergarten children in their Baltimore school district. Issues effectively addressed by this parent activist group included overcrowding of classrooms, lack of teacher aides, inadequate child-teacher ratios, and lack of administrative personnel and support to implement developmentally appropriate classrooms. The steps to forming an effective parent activist group are as follows:

1. Becoming organized with adequate parent representation
2. Writing a proposal for change or to address specific issues

Parents can serve as very effective activists in the school setting.

3. Focusing the parent group's efforts and developing a strategy
4. Writing letters of support to key decision makers
5. Conducting follow-up and monitoring of desired change
6. Evaluating and reinforcing positive changes made by key decision makers and practitioners

Anderson's (1992) poignant and realistic story of this Baltimore kindergarten parent group gives insight into the power of parents when they are organized and committed to change. Their story documents firsthand the struggle they experienced as they changed traditional kindergarten classrooms to more developmentally appropriate classrooms for their daughters and sons. Perhaps most salient in Anderson's account is the commitment to time, struggle, negotiation, and perseverance that is required for successful parent advocacy groups. Lessons learned from this experience are vividly described by Anderson:

1. Form a strong core group of three to five very committed people who share responsibility for leadership. They need to talk with each other a lot and to give each other personal support when things look bleak.
2. Learn to call people "in the know" and ask their advice. Make contacts with "friendly" people in power. Start with one or two names and go from there. Pave the way for each request or demand.

3. Be willing to stick your necks out and demand that something be done even when you're told it's impossible. Although this doesn't always work, parents become recognized as a force to be contended with.

4. It is absolutely key to have teachers with energy, commitment, and the ability to adapt and learn. No amount of parent effort can make up for unwilling or unskilled teachers.

5. Have a coordinator who is in a position to mediate change and communication related to the school's curriculum, learning environment, teacher training, and other salient issues.

Reggio Emilia-Inspired Project Groups

The early childhood programs of Reggio Emilia, Italy, are influencing American preschool settings in an increasingly systematic manner. The view of the young child is perhaps the most crucial concept that has affected American efforts to understand and adapt this highly-regarded early childhood approach. Central to the view of the child is the critical role of the parent in the life of the child and the school.

> Parents are considered to be an essential component of the program, and many among them are part of the advisory committee running each school. The parents' participation is expected and supported and takes many forms: day-to-day interaction, work in the schools, discussions of educational and psychological issues, special events, excursions, and celebrations. Parents are an active part of their children's learning experience and, at the same time, help ensure the welfare of all children in the school. (Gandini, 1997, p. 17)

Reggio Emilia's philosophy of schooling as a system of relationships (Malaguzzi, 1993) is put into practice in such a way that high-quality and enduring relationships are an integral part of children's lives. These relationships are reinforced and encouraged through the physical environments of the early childhood center, the documentation of children's growth and progress, the systematic involvement of parents in the curriculum planning and implementation, the close ties between the (Reggio Emilia) schools and the surrounding community, and the highly personalized exchanges between teachers and parents (New, 1997).

Parents' involvement via Reggio Emilia preschools is redefining parent involvement in many American preschools. "I am the teacher; you are the parent; I'll explain education to you" is no longer valid for many preschool teachers in the United States (Geiger, 1997, p. 143). Indeed, the parent is seen as an important partner in the learning process. Parents' involvement in Reggio Emilia schools includes participation in the daily routine, involvement in teacher-parent conferences throughout the year, planning for special events and projects, and facilitating fund-raising events, picnics, and other schoolwide activities. Parents become partners with their children and the teachers both in the classroom and on the playground.

Parents can become involved in long-term projects, typified by the project approach of Reggio Emilia.

Examples of this high level of parent involvement can be seen in special projects that are representative of the **project approach.** The project approach, an integral part of the **Reggio Emilia approach,** involves children, teachers, parents, community representatives, and other supportive individuals in the planning, implementing, and evaluating of longer term learning projects. The project approach is influencing early childhood curriculum in the United States and is a key way that parents are becoming more involved in their children's learning experiences.

Projects may last several days, several weeks, or even many months. The project approach encourages children to plan an activity, project, or special event around a special interest of a small group of students. Documentation of projects is extensive throughout the Reggio Emilia schools, and examples can be found on the playground, as well as in the classroom. Through the project approach, parents become advocates for their children's learning by helping plan the curriculum; securing materials and needed resources; spending time actually building or developing the project; assisting the teacher with documentation through photographs, portfolios, or other means; and giving valuable feedback to the teacher and children about the experience.

School-Based PTA or PTO Groups

On a national level, a system of parent groups has been established, called Parent-Teacher Associations (PTAs) or Parent Teacher Organizations (PTOs), at schools. The level of organization of these groups varies widely from school district to school district. The advantage of these types of parent advocacy groups is that they have potential political power because of the large numbers of parents who are members. Many states hold local, regional, and state conventions of PTA or PTO groups, and in some states these parent groups are courted by national educational associations or teacher lobbying groups. Usually, parents join these groups at the beginning of the school year, officers are elected, and an agenda for fund-raising and special school events is established. These groups are also effective in strengthening the relationships between parents and teachers, and teacher appreciation and teacher recognition days are an important part of these parent group agendas. For parents seeking an already-established group with potential political power, the existing **PTA/PTO** may be a good choice. Parents who are advocates for curriculum changes, transportation improvements, enhanced after-school programs, developmentally appropriate primary classrooms, and reduced teacher-child ratios may wish to assume a leadership role in one of these school-based groups and provide needed direction for these causes.

◊◊ Examples of Successful Advocacy Initiatives

The history of child and family policy has been described briefly, and it reflects an ongoing process of change and growth. Conflict between child-centered and instructional approaches, for example, has a history extending back to the first public school kindergarten (Goffin, 1992). Gregory, in 1908, stated:

> In passing from the kindergarten to the primary school, there is a break. Do what you will to soften the change, to modify the break, it still remains a break (Goffin & Stegelin, 1992). Three general methods of dealing with the difficulty have been employed: (1) To provide a connecting class to take the child out of his kindergarten habits and introduce him to those of the primary school; in the words of some teachers, "to make him over." (2) To modify the kindergarten and make it more nearly resemble the primary schools. (3) To modify the primary school to make it more nearly resemble the kindergarten. (p. 22)

When we consider the above description of the needs of kindergarten children in 1908, we readily recognize the more contemporary efforts to establish transitional first grades, to make first- through third-grade classrooms more developmentally appropriate, and to make kindergarten classrooms more like primary classrooms. History seems to repeat itself in this case.

Advocacy on behalf of children and families is an important part of American educational and social history. Issues that have received the most attention from child advocates include child care accessibility and quality, developmentally appropriate learning environments, services for special needs and at-risk children, child poverty, child health concerns, and child violence. Recent examples of successful advocacy efforts on behalf of young children can be seen in the following:

National Association for the Education of Young Children (**NAEYC**). (1984). *Accreditation criteria and procedures of the National Academy of Early Childhood Programs*. Washington, DC: Author.

These guidelines have provided a framework for the systematic improvement of child care and early childhood learning environments and the provision of developmentally appropriate care and education in the United States.

National Association of State Boards of Education (NASBE). (1988). *Right from the start: Report of the NASBE task force on early childhood education.*

This report resulting from a task force study of the needs of young children in school settings has helped standardize developmentally appropriate philosophy and programs for young children in public school settings. Advocates included parents, teachers, and administrators of schools serving preschool children, as well as national leaders of educational and advocacy organizations.

P.L. 99-457, the Education of the Handicapped Act Amendments of 1986.

This public law provides for the services of young children with special needs, beginning at age 3, by the respective school district. Parents of special needs children, as well as early intervention researchers, practitioners, and policymakers, were responsible for a large part of the successful lobbying that resulted in this legislation in 1986.

P.L. 101-476, the Individuals with Disabilities Education Act (IDEA).

Regulations governing the individuals with disabilities act (IDEA) require that children with disabilities be placed in the least restrictive environment (LRE) in which the individual child will learn.

P.L. 102-119, or Part H of the IDEA legislation of 1991.

This public law requires that early intervention services be provided in regular settings with typically developing children, as appropriate for each child. The term *natural environments* is used to refer to regular settings for typically developing age peers.

Americans with Disabilities Act (ADA) of 1990.

This act sets into place a broad range of services for individuals with disabilities. It requires businesses and publicly sponsored agencies to adapt to and provide services for individuals with special equipment and developmental needs. Included in this act are specifications for accessibility to public buildings and rest rooms, design of doorways and curbs, and other dimensions of the physical environment.

Bredekamp, S., & Rosegrant, T. (Eds.). (1992). *Reaching potentials: Appropriate curriculum and assessment for young children* (Vol. 1). Washington, DC: National Association for the Education of Young Children.

> This book is a compilation of guidelines by experts in the fields of early childhood and early childhood special education that facilitates decision making about assessment strategies for young children in various learning settings. Child advocates including parents, teachers, teacher preparation professionals, educational leaders, and testing/assessment experts all contributed to the advocacy effort that led to this important publication that now influences decision making of individuals responsible for screening and assessing preschool children in educational settings.

◊◊ Role of the School in Child and Family Advocacy

> Today's schools are expected to do many things: resolve racial conflict and build an integrated society; inspire patriotism and good citizenship; provide values, aspirations, and a sense of identity to disadvantaged children;. . . . reduce conflict in society by teaching children to get along with others and to adjust to group living; . . . fight disease and poor health through physical education, health training, and even medical treatment; . . . end malnutrition and hunger through school lunch and milk programs; fight drug abuse and educate children about sex; . . . In other words, nearly all the nation's problems are reflected in demands placed on the nation's schools. (Dye, 1992, p. 162)

Family-school involvement is a two-way street (Edwards & Young, 1992), and school professionals are having to rethink what they want for children and what they expect from families and communities. Where should schools draw the line? Are schools the new and primary place where the interwoven needs of children are to be met (Edwards & Young, 1992)? Schools must do more than encourage parent and family involvement within the classroom that is frequently isolated from the broader context of the family itself. Schools must do more than become referral sources for other community agencies and service providers. Schools, in fact, are becoming the hub of multiple-service brokerage for children and their families.

Several efforts currently under way are redefining the relationships of school, family, and community. School professionals are forging new alliances and partnerships with community organizations and agencies. Schools are expanding their definitions of "family" to include single parents, working parents, foster parents, grandparents, and others who have significant responsibilities for children. They are challenging the separateness of systems designed to support children and their families (Edwards & Young, 1992).

Once again, we call on the ecosystem model (Bronfenbrenner, 1979) to help in understanding the need for interrelationships for children and their families. School professionals are becoming more creative at developing styles and strategies that acknowledge this important interrelationship of the social context and the individual. Moving to broader notions of community alliances means moving beyond incremental thinking or assessing the needs of parents, teachers, schools, and communities. Edwards and Young (1992) make the following recommendations regarding the role of the school in establishing an environment conducive to child and family advocacy:

- Home/school strategies should be founded on the strengths of the families and their understandings of their own children.

- Efforts should be organized around preventive strategies. Therefore, school personnel must understand the children and families they serve— social, personal, economic, and psychological stressors.

- Schools need to explore multiple models for reaching out to families and providing avenues to them for organizing and advocating for their needs.

- The school should view itself as an integral part of an ecosystem that supports the family, and the school should be able to refer families readily to needed resources within the community.

- Understanding the complexity of families and the new strategies needed for teachers and schools to reach out to them should become an integral part of teacher preparation programs (p. 100).

Borrowing from the Reggio Emilia early childhood programs of Northern Italy, we can draw important parallels about the role of the school in advocating for young children and their families. New (1997) implores U.S. educators to view the child and the rights of the child in a much more committed and impassioned way. The marginal status of American children is reflected in the paradox of the United States having both the highest standard of living and the highest rate of child poverty among all industrialized nations (New, 1997, p. 232).

> Thus, the gift of Reggio Emilia's illustrious example comes in the form of a challenge to American educators—a challenge not only to improve our practices and to align them more closely with our beliefs, but also to learn how to draw public attention to our work and to the children for whom we are working. It behooves us, if we truly wish to take advantage of what Reggio Emilia has to offer, to turn to the mirror our Italian friends hold up so that we might better know ourselves, discover children's capabilities, and acknowledge our responsibilities. Surely these are the most critical "next steps" that we can take on behalf of young children in our society. Reggio Emilia can point the way. But we must decide if we wish to follow. (New, 1997, p. 233)

Today, the debate over the role of the school in early childhood education is ready to move beyond the question of whether to the question of how. Necessary conditions for quality early childhood programs in school settings must include the following:

- Children in small groups

- *Child Care and the Schools.* This program was designed to assist families by providing child care services on-site at the schools, rather than to coordinate other existing child care services.

- *Head Start and the Schools.* Several federal initiatives linked Head Start and the schools, including Project Developmental Continuity, designed to ensure continuity of experience of children as they completed Head Start and continued on through the primary years.

- *Special Education and the Schools.* The field of **special education** may be one of the strongest examples of collaboration in early childhood education. Inherent in special education is the belief that children need coordinated services, least restrictive environments, family and community involvement and support, and the inclusion of the parents in the planning process (Kagan, 1991).

- *Interagency Coordinating Councils.* These councils were mandated through P.L. 99-457, which legislated that schools would provide services for special needs children from age 3 onward.

- ***Vertical Collaborations*** *of the 1990s.* These are collaborative efforts, born in the 1990s and the new era of collaboration that is initiated directly by schools, families, and teachers, as opposed to the federal government, that encourage the use of local, state, and federal agencies and programs to construct unique service programs.

The political and economic climate of the 1990s is affecting the nature of educational collaborations. Kagan (1991) describes this phenomenon as a new **zeitgeist,** or way of viewing and conceptualizing the meaning of collaboration. Grassroots efforts are now more responsible for the development of collaborative efforts. As states assume more responsibilities through Block Grants, there will be ample opportunity for school professionals and parents to develop their own unique collaborations.

Traits of Successful Collaborative Efforts

- The context is fertile, especially the political and social climate
- The goals are clear
- Structure matches mission
- The mandate is facilitative, not restrictive
- People are really invested
- Resources are available
- Process and policies are clear

In short, the school serves as a fertile ground for collaborative efforts among parents, teachers, administrators, community and agency representatives, policymakers, and other interested constituents. The school, because of its location and commitment to serve the public's young children, can become the hub of the community's successful collaborative efforts.

Suggestions for Collaborating with Parents

Parents' feelings may be a forgotten component when working with young children in school settings, particularly if the parents are dealing with special needs children. The early childhood teacher will be more successful in communicating and collaborating with parents if they keep the following guidelines in mind (adapted from Gargiulo & Graves, 1991):

- Explain terminology that is relevant.
- Acknowledge parents' needs and feelings.
- Listen to parents and validate their ideas.
- Adapt communication and planning to the specific situation.
- Keep parents informed and include them in planning.
- Be accountable on an ongoing basis.
- Recognize the part of cultural diversity in parent relations.
- Involve parents in all aspects of the process.
- Delegate parents to assume important roles.
- Keep a journal or record of collaboration efforts.
- Follow the general guidelines for interagency collaboration when working with parents and families.
- Document collaboration efforts and initiatives.

Collaboration in the school setting requires patience, planning, and a positive attitude. As teachers become involved in working with parents on advocacy issues and concerns, knowing how to collaborate successfully is essential.

Summary Statements ◇

- Schools are called on to provide more services to children and families than ever before; one of these services is the support of child and family advocacy.

- Family and child policy has a more than 100-year history in the United States, but not until the 1980s did family policy gain the level of recognition and political power that it enjoys today.

- Advocacy is the act of pleading a cause and defending, endorsing, or promoting particular ideas, principles, or individuals.

- Public choice theory was conceptualized by economist James Buchanan and argues that individuals come together in the political process for their own mutual benefit.

- Common barriers to citizen involvement in advocacy include feelings of powerlessness to change, lack of knowledge about governmental process, fear of the political process, lack of confidence in their own expertise, and lack of time.

- The integration of developmentally appropriate practice into school settings in preschool through primary grades is an example of successful advocacy efforts in early childhood education.

- Parents today are more consumer-oriented, well-educated, and activist-minded in their interactions with teachers and other school personnel.

- Child and family policy in the earlier years arose from national crises, such as war. An example is the establishment of child care centers for mothers who worked during the war movement.

- The era after World War II was a transitional period for child and family policy. After World War II, the momentum of efforts toward improved child and family policy rapidly escalated.

- Lyndon Johnson's Great Society and the early intervention movement targeted at at-risk children combined to make the 1960s a significant decade for child and family policy.

- The Child Development Associate program, developed in the 1970s, was evidence of a growing commitment to formal training of teachers who taught young children.

- The 1980s marked an escalation in policy efforts for young children, including initiatives by the National Association of State Boards of Education, the National Association for the Education of Young Children, and the National Governors Association.

- During the 1990s, child and family policy in the United States came full-circle as political candidates placed issues related to child care, early education, and family work issues high on their campaign priority list.

- Preschool children are viewed in a more holistic, integrated way than children in the 1960s. Integrated services for chil-

dren and families are seen as a real need for most families.

- Parents are involved directly in advocacy efforts and are sophisticated in their knowledge-level about the policy process; parents are also consumer-oriented.

- Parent interest groups, parent activist groups, PTOs/PTAs, and Reggio Emilia-inspired parent project groups are examples of current parent advocacy efforts in school settings.

- Early advocacy efforts on behalf of young children include the kindergarten movement in the early 1900s that attempted to keep the kindergarten curriculum play-based.

- Significant advocacy initiatives that have influenced child and family policy and programs include P.L. 99-457, P.L. 101-476, the Americans with Disabilities Act, developmentally appropriate practice and assessment guidelines by the NAEYC, and *Right from the Start*, published by the NASBE.

- Schools have become brokers of services for young children and their families and the major source of information coordination and advocacy initiatives.

- School and community partnerships are becoming common ways of strengthening programs and opportunities for young children and their families within the school settings; businesses recognize the importance of investing in the young child as a future productive worker and citizen.

- Collaboration in services for young children and their families is essential and considerably more sophisticated than in the past, according to Kagan. Collaboration requires time, patience, commitment to excellence, and a child-centered focus.

- Vertical collaborations are more commonplace in the 1990s as federal programs dismantle and more power is given to the states. Vertical collaboration requires cooperation and teamwork between local, state, and federal agencies and service providers.

- Because collaboration is an essential component of successful child and family advocacy and policy development, the early childhood professional needs to learn and practice the steps to collaboration and be aware of the barriers and limitations of collaboration.

Activities ◊

1. Select a child and family policy topic of interest, do an extensive review of the literature, and then write a summary paper to share with the class. Examples of appropriate topics: (a) the history of child care regulation, (b) maternity leave policies, (c) corporate child care, (d) school involvement in early intervention, (e) child care programs for teenage mothers, (f) the Family Leave Act, (g) child poverty, and (h) the Americans With Disabilities Act. Students should interview individuals with knowledge and expertise, as well as study the research and policy literature.

2. Invite a local or state politician to class. Develop an itinerary of questions to ask this person about the current status of child and family policy as compared with 20, 15, and 10 years ago. Discuss with this person her or his own beliefs about the role of the school in advocating for children and families.

3. Select and interview a political figure, child advocate, or community leader about what she or he sees as the most salient child and family issues today. Summarize the content of this interview and present it in class. You may videotape or audiotape the political representative.

4. Invite a panel of parents of preschool children to class. Develop a set of ques-

tions and issues to discuss with these parents. Ask each of the panelists to identify the most important child and family issues, about their role in child advocacy, where they believe child and family advocacy should occur, and what role the school should play in encouraging and facilitating the discussion of issues relevant to parents.

5. Take a field trip to the state capitol and schedule a meeting with a political representative in her or his official office. Ask to see pieces of legislation that are currently being considered that affect the lives of children and families.

6. View a video by the Children's Defense Fund. Discuss how this video benefits children and families, in what settings would it be appropriate to show, and how the Children's Defense Fund serves as a silent legislator in the decision-making process.

7. Invite an administrator and several key staff of a state- or federally funded program for young children and families to your class. Ask these individuals to respond to a set of questions developed by the class that can include such items as the following: (a) What is the funding source for this program? (b) What are the specific goals and desired outcomes for children and families? (c) What evi-

dence is there that collaboration is occurring in this program? (d) How is accountability addressed? Program and staff evaluation? (e) What child or family populations are targeted? (f) What is most challenging and rewarding about administering or implementing this program? and (g) How would they change this program to make it stronger?

8. Select a key piece of legislation of interest to you. Track this legislation from the point of inception to the point of legislation. Develop a calendar of significant events and a schedule that denotes when benchmark decisions were made regarding this legislation. Identify the barriers or opponents to this legislation, the strongest and most effective advocates, the key political figures involved in the process, and how you believe this legislation is currently affecting children and families.

9. During the Week of the Young Child, sponsored annually in the spring by the National Association for the Education of Young Children, ask to participate with a local elementary school to promote the idea of child and family advocacy. You, along with other students, can hang posters of children and families, set up a booth to interview parents and teachers about issues of concern, and cosponsor a key speaker at the school to address a prominent child issue in the local area.

10. Select an early childhood classroom and serve as a "partner" to strengthen the advocacy efforts within that classroom. Identify an early childhood teacher who will work with you to implement parent-teacher-child events, meet with parents about important issues, and develop an understanding of how the school serves as a source of advocacy support for children and families. Document your advocacy partnership experience through a portfolio.

Resources for Parents and Teachers on Advocacy and Public Policy ◊ ◊

Suggested Reading for Parents

Ashton-Warner, S. (1963). *Teacher*. New York: Simon & Schuster.

Bredekamp, S. (Ed.). (1987). *Developmentally appropriate practice in early childhood programs serving children from birth through age 8* (exp. ed.). Washington, DC: National Association for the Education of Young Children.

Elkind, D. (1987). *Miseducation: Preschoolers at risk*. New York: Knopf.

Goffin, S. G., & Stegelin, D. A. (1992). *Changing kindergartens: Four success stories*. Washington, DC: National Association for the Education of Young Children.

Kamii, C. (Ed.).(1989). *Achievement testing in the early grades: The games grownups play*. Washington, DC: National Association for the Education of Young Children.

Meisels, S. J. (1985). *Developmental screening in early childhood: A guide* (rev. ed.). Washington, DC: National Association for the Education of Young Children.

National Association of State Boards of Education (NASBE). (1988). *Right from the start*. Alexandria, VA: Author.

National Association for Elementary School Principals. (1990). *Early childhood education and the elementary school principal: Standards for quality programs for young children*. Alexandria, VA: Author.

Schultz, T. (1992). Developmentally appropriate practice and the challenge of public school reform. In D. Stegelin (Ed.), *Early childhood education: Policy issues for the 1990s*. Norwood, NJ: Ablex.

Stegelin, D. A. (1992). *Early childhood education: Policy issues for the 1990s*. Norwood, NJ: Ablex.

General Advocacy Issues and Strategies: Suggested Readings for Teachers and Administrators

Almy, M. (1985). New challenges for teacher education: Facing political and economic realities. *Young Children, 40*(6), 10–11.

Bennis, W., & Nanus, B. (1985). *Leaders: The strategies for taking charge*. New York: Harper & Row.

Bird, L. B. (1989). *Becoming a whole language school: The Fair Oaks story*. Katonah, NY: Richard C. Owen.

Davis, M. (1989). Preparing teachers for developmentally appropriate classrooms. *Dimensions, 17*(3), 4–7.

DeClark, G. (1985). From skepticism to conviction. In C. K. Kamii, *Young children reinvent arithmetic: Implications of Piaget's theory* (pp. 195–202). New York: Teachers College Press.

Duckworth, E. (1987). *The having of wonderful ideas and other essays*. New York: Teachers College Press.

Freeman, E. B. (1990). Issues in kindergarten policy and practice. *Young Children, 55*(4), 29–34.

Fullan, M. (1982). *The meaning of educational change*. New York: Teachers College Press.

Goffin, S. G. (1991). Supporting change in a school district's early childhood programs: A story of growth. *Early Child Development and Care, 70*, 5–16.

Goffin, S. G. (1992). Creating change with public schools: Reflections of an early childhood teacher educator. In D. Stegelin (Ed.), *Early childhood education: Policy issues for the 1990s*. Norwood, NJ: Ablex.

Hitz, R., & Wright, D. (1988). Kindergarten issues: A practitioner's survey. *Principal, 67*, 28–30.

Hord, S. M., Rutherford, W. L., Huling-Austin, L., & Hall, G. E. (1987). *Taking charge of change*. Alexandria, VA: Association for Supervision and Curriculum Development.

Humphrey, S. (1989). Becoming a better kindergarten teacher: The case of myself. *Young Children, 45*(1), 17–22.

Kagan, S. (1989). Early care and education: Tackling the touch issues. *Phi Delta Kappan, 70*, 433–439.

Katz, L. G., & Chard, S. C. (1988). *Engaging children's minds: The project approach*. Norwood, NJ: Ablex.

Lieberman, A. (1990). Navigating the four C's: Building a bridge over troubled waters. *Phi Delta Kappan, 71*(7), 531–533.

McDonald, J. P. (1989). When outsiders try to change schools from the inside. *Phi Delta Kappan, 7*(3), 206–212.

Murphy, C. U. (1991). Lesson from a journey into change. *Educational Leadership, 48*(8), 63–67.

National Association for the Education of Young Children (NAEYC). (1990). NAEYC position statement on school readiness. *Young Children, 46*(1), 21–23.

National Association of Elementary School Principals. (1990). *Early childhood education and the elementary school principal*. Alexandria, VA: Author.

National Association of State Boards of Education (NASBE). (1988). *Right from the start*. Alexandria, VA: Author.

Sarason, S. B. (1987). Policy, implementation, and the problem of change. In S. L. Kagan & E. F. Zigler (Eds.), *Early schooling: The national debate* (pp. 226–126). New Haven, CT: Yale University Press.

Schlechty, P. C. (1990). *Schools for the 21st century*. San Francisco: Jossey-Bass.

Schultz, T. (1992). Developmentally appropriate practice and the challenge of public school reform. In D. Stegelin (Ed.), *Early childhood education: Policy issues for the 1990s*. Norwood, NJ: Ablex.

Walsh, D., Baturka, N., Colter, N., & Sith, M. E. (1991). Changing one's mind—Maintaining one's identity: A first-grade teacher's story. *Teachers College Record, 93*, 73–86.

Advocacy Related to Early Childhood Education

Bredekamp, S., & Sheppard, L. (1989). How best to protect children from inappropriate school expectations, practices, and policies. *Young Children, 43*(3), 14–24.

Elkind, D. (1987). Early childhood education on its own terms. In S. L. Kagan & E. F. Zigler (Eds.), *Early schooling: The national debate* (pp. 98-115). New Haven, CT: Yale University Press.

Goffin, S. G., & Lombardi, J. (1988). *Speaking out: Early childhood advocacy*. Washington, DC: National Association for the Education of Young Children.

Mitchell, A., & Modigliani, K. (1989). Public policy report: Young children in the public schools? The "only ifs" reconsidered. *Young Children, 44*(6), 56–61.

National Association for Elementary School Principals. (1990). *Early childhood and the elementary school principal: Standards for quality programs for young children*. Alexandria, VA: Author.

National Association of State Boards of Education (NASBE). (1988). *Right from the start*. The report of the NASBE Task Force on Early Childhood Education. Alexandria, VA: Author.

Educational Organizations That Support Advocacy for Young Children

National Association for the Education of Young Children, 1834 Connecticut Ave., N.W., Washington, DC 20009-5786

National Head Start Association, 1220 King St., Alexandria, VA, 22314

National Association for Elementary School Principals, Alexandria, VA

Innovations in Early Education: The International Reggio Exchange, Wayne State University, Merrill-Palmer Institute, 71-A E. Ferry Ave., Detroit, MI 48202

National Association of State Boards of Education (NASBE), 1012 Cameron St., Alexandria, VA. 22314

Division for Early Childhood of the Council for Exceptional Children (DEC/CEC), 1920 Association Dr., Reston, VA 22091

Office of Special Education Services (OSERS), U.S. Department of Education, 400 Maryland Ave., S.W., Washington, DC 20202

National Childhood Technical Assistance System (NEC*TAS), 500 Nations Bank Plaza, 137 East Franklin St., Chapel Hill, NC 27514

References ◇◇

Anderson, L. (1992). Parent power: The developmental classroom project. In S. G. Goffin & D. A. Stegelin (Eds.), *Changing kindergartens: Four success stories*. Washington, DC: National Association for the Education of Young Children.

Bronfenbrenner, U. (1979). *The ecology of human development*. Cambridge, MA: Harvard University Press.

Clinton, W. (1992). State policy related to disadvantaged and at-risk preschoolers. In D. A.

Stegelin (Ed.), *Early childhood education: Policy issues for the 1990s*. Norwood, NJ: Ablex.

Comer, J. P. (1990). Home, school, and academic learning. In J. I. Goodlad & P. Keating (Eds.), *Access to knowledge: An agenda for our nation's schools*. New York: College Entrance Examination Board.

Dye, T. R. (1992). *Understanding public policy*. Upper Saddle River, NJ: Prentice Hall.

Edwards, P. A., & Young, L. A. (1992, May). Beyond parents: Family, community, and school involvement. *Phi Delta Kappan*, 72–80.

Farnum, L. (1987). Child care and early education: A partnership with elementary education. *Thrust, 6*, 19–20.

Gandini, L. (1997). Foundations of the Reggio Emilia approach. In J. Hendrick (Ed.), *First steps toward teaching the Reggio way*. Upper Saddle River, NJ: Merrill/Prentice Hall.

Gargiulo, R. M., & Graves, S. B. (1991, Spring). Parental feelings. *Childhood Education*, 176–178.

Geiger, B. (1997). Implementing Reggio in an independent school: What works? In J. Hendrick (Ed.), *First steps toward teaching the Reggio way*. Upper Saddle River, NJ: Merrill/Prentice Hall.

Goffin, S. G. (1992). Creating change with the public schools: Reflections of an early childhood teacher educator. In D. A. Stegelin (Ed.), *Early childhood education: Policy issues for the 1990s*. Norwood, NJ: Ablex.

Goffin, S. G., & Stegelin, D. A. (Eds.). (1992). *Changing kindergartens: Four success stories*. Washington, DC: National Association for the Education of Young Children.

Gregory, B. C. (1908). The necessity of continuity between the kindergarten and the elementary school: The present status, illogical and unFrobellian. In S. Goffin & D. A. Stegelin (Eds.), *Changing kindergartens: Four success stories*. Washington, DC: National Association for the Education of Young Children.

Irwin, D., & Bushnell, M. (1980). *Observational strategies for child study*. New York: Holt, Rinehart & Winston.

Kagan, S. L. (1989). Early care and education: Tackling the tough issues. *Phi Delta Kappan, 70*(6), 433–439.

Kagan, S. L. (1991). *United we stand: Collaboration for child care and early education services*. New York: Teachers College Press.

Kagan, S. L. (1992). Birthing collaborations in early care and education: A polemic of pain and promise. In D. A. Stegelin (Ed.), *Early childhood education: Policy issues for the 1990s*. Norwood, NJ: Ablex.

Lazar, I., Darlington, R., Murray, H., Royce, J., & Snipper, A. (1982). Lasting effects of early education. *Monographs of the Society for Research in Child Development* (1–2 Serial No. 194).

Lombardi, J. (1986). Training for public policy and advocacy. *Young Children, 42*, 65–69.

Malaguzzi, L.(1993). For an education based on relationships. *Young Children, 49*(1), 9–12.

McCormick, K. (1986). If early education isn't on your agenda now, it could be—and soon. *American School Board Journal, 41*, 69–71.

Mitchell, A. (1989). Old baggage, new visions: Shaping policy for early childhood programs. *Phi Delta Kappan, 70*(9), 664–672.

Molnar, J. (1991). What good prekindergarten programs look like. *Streamlined Seminar, 9*(5), 1–7.

National Association of State Boards of Education (NASBE). (1988). *Right from the start: Report of the NASBE task force on early childhood education*. Alexandria, VA: Author.

National Governors Association & Center for Policy Research. (1987). *The first sixty months: A handbook of promising prevention programs for children 0–5 years of age*. Washington, DC: National Governors Association.

Riley, R. (1986). Can we reduce the risk of failure? *Phi Delta Kappan, 68*, 214–219.

Schultz, T. (1992). Developmentally appropriate practice and the challenge of public school reform. In D. A. Stegelin (Ed.), *Early childhood education: Policy issues for the 1990s*. Norwood, NJ: Ablex.

Schweinhart, L. J. (1992). How much do good early childhood programs cost? *Early Education and Development, 3*(2), 115–127.

Schweinhart, L. J., & Weikart, D. P. (1986). Consequences of three preschool curriculum models through age 15. *Early Childhood Research Quarterly, 1*, 15–35.

Schweinhart, L. J., & Weikart, D. P. (1992). The High/Scope Perry preschool study, similar studies, and their implications for public policy in the U.S. In D. A. Stegelin (Ed.), *Early childhood education: Policy issues for the 1990s*. Norwood, NJ: Ablex.

Stegelin, D. A. (Ed.). (1992). *Early childhood education: Policy issues for the 1990s*. Norwood, NJ: Ablex.

Toffler, A. (1981). *The third wave*. New York: Bantam Books.

Weikart, D. P. (1989). Hard choices in early childhood care and education: A view to the future. *Young Children, 45,* 25–30.

Merriam-Webster's New Collegiate Dictionary (10th ed.). (1993). Springfield, MA: Merriam-Webster.

Index

About the Authors

Kay Wright Springate, Ed.D., is Professor of Child and Family Studies in the Department of Human Environmental Sciences at Eastern Kentucky University. During the past 23 years of work in the early childhood field, she has been a preschool and kindergarten teacher, a consultant with the Kentucky Department of Education, Director of the Child Development Center at Eastern, and a teacher educator. She was instrumental in the founding of Ecumenical Preschool and served on its board for several years. Most recently, she has been involved in the implementation of the Interdisciplinary Early Childhood Education Certificate for teachers preparing to work with children from birth to primary school in Kentucky. She has served as President of the Kentucky Association for Children Under Six and has served in a variety of service capacities through professional organizations. She has also coordinated several state training grants and written numerous publications for the Kentucky Department of Education. She has conducted many workshops at the state, local, and national level and has authored publications in the field of early childhood. Her professional interests include emergent curriculum, literacy and families, and exploring the ongoing needs of families through the lifespan.

Dolores A. Stegelin, Ph.D., is Associate Professor and Program Coordinator of Early Childhood Education at North Georgia College and State University. Her professional experience includes more than 20 years in teacher education programs in California, Oklahoma, Ohio, and Georgia. She has studied at Reggio Emilia, Italy, and she is currently coordinating efforts to study and implement Reggio Emilia in early childhood settings in Georgia. She has edited a policy book entitled *Early Childhood Education: Policy Issues for the 1990s* and coedited a book on kindergarten change and developmental practice entitled *Changing Kindergartens: Four Success Stories*. Her research interests include health issues for young children, mixed-age learning settings, and early childhood family policy. She serves on the public policy committee for the Georgia Association on Young Children and provides leadership for resource development for this organization.